AF707424

STOP THE CLOCK

HOW THE AI LAW FIRM MOVES FROM BILLABLE HOURS TO VALUE-BASED PRICING

Shaun Jardine

BENNION KEARNY

First published 2026 by Bennion Kearny

Woodside, Oakamoor, ST10 3AE

www.BennionKearny.com

ISBN: 978-1-915855-50-3

Shaun Jardine has asserted his right under the Copyright, Designs and Patents Act 1988, to be identified as the author of this book.

Copyright Shaun Jardine 2026. All Rights Reserved.

No part of this publication may be reproduced, stored in a retrieval system, or transmitted in any form or by any means, electronic, mechanical, photocopying, recording or otherwise, without the prior permission of the publisher.

A CIP catalogue record for this book is available from the British Library.

This book is sold subject to the condition that it shall not, by way of trade or otherwise, be lent, re-sold, hired out or otherwise circulated without the publisher's prior consent in any form of binding or cover other than that in which it is published and without a similar condition including this condition being imposed on the subsequent purchaser.

Bennion Kearny has endeavoured to provide trademark information about all the companies and products mentioned in this book by the appropriate use of capitals. However, Bennion Kearny cannot guarantee the accuracy of this information.

Bennion Kearny Limited. 6 Woodside, Churnet View Road, Oakamoor, ST10 3AE, United Kingdom.

Cover design by Hannah Powell.

This book is dedicated to my wife of over 40 years, Debbie, whom I met at a law lecture on the very first day of University in September 1980. I can't remember what the subject of the first lecture was, but I still remember what she was wearing!

Debbie had far more sense than me to become a lawyer.

ABOUT THE AUTHOR

Shaun Jardine is the UK's leading champion of value-based pricing in the legal sector, and the author of the game-changing books *Ditch the Billable Hour!* and *Ditch & Switch!* – two books that have helped law firms rethink the way they price, sell and deliver legal services.

A former practising lawyer, equity partner and law firm CEO, Shaun has lived the realities of legal practice from the inside. He knows the pressure of targets, the comfort of the billable hour, the fear of changing a long-established model and the commercial opportunity waiting for firms brave enough to do things differently.

Shaun now leads the consultancy Big Yellow Penguin, where he works with law firms and professional services businesses on pricing innovation, value-based pricing and strategic change. His mission is simple: to liberate firms from billable hour tyranny and help them build more profitable, client-focused and sustainable businesses.

He is the creator of the 8 P Point Plan, a practical change methodology for implementing value-based pricing, and the creator of Declan AI, the only penguin value-based pricing assistant in the known world. Yes, really.

Known for his engaging, practical and occasionally penguin-assisted presentation style, Shaun speaks regularly at legal conferences in the UK and internationally.

He is a trainer, coach and consultant who combines hard-earned law firm experience with a deep understanding of pricing, client value and change management.

Stop The Clock continues Shaun's campaign to help lawyers stop selling time, start pricing value and build firms fit for the future.

ACKNOWLEDGEMENTS

No book like this is ever written alone.

Although my name appears on the cover, *Stop The Clock* has been shaped by conversations, challenges, stories, encouragement, disagreements, questions and generous contributions from people across the legal world.

I owe a huge thank-you to all the Wise people who gave their time, thoughts, warnings, stories, and practical experience while I was researching this book. They did not have to do it. They had proper jobs, busy diaries, clients, businesses, deadlines, inboxes and lives. Yet they still found time to speak to me, answer my questions, challenge my thinking, and in some cases, patiently put up with my incessant follow-up questions when I wanted to understand something properly.

Law firms do not need one neat answer repeated loudly. They need different voices, different warnings, different experiences and different ways of looking at the same problem. So, thank you to the wise.

Andrew Allen
Mark Barrett
Joanna Gaudoin
Rob Hanna
Kerry Jack
Wendy Jephson
Noo Jones
Mitch Kowalski
Chantal McNaught
Felix Riley
Quentin Solt
Aku Sorainen
Sam Stamp
Heather Suttie
Karolina Šilingienė
Ben Weinberger
Abby Winkworth

Thank you to Mitch for writing the Foreword.

A special thank you to Greg Kyte for kindly allowing me to reproduce his cartoons in this book. Greg has a wonderful ability to capture serious points with humour, clarity and just the right amount of mischief. As the old saying goes, a picture really does paint a thousand words – and his cartoons help make some of the book's key messages land far better than another paragraph from me ever could.

Thank you to those mentioned in the book, many of whom I have not ever met, who have written articles, books, podcasts, posts on LinkedIn or passing comments that made me stop, think and occasionally mutter, "That needs to go in the book." Their insights have helped me test, sharpen and improve my thinking. Any good ideas in these pages probably came from them. Any daft ones are mine.

A special thank you to James Lumsden-Cook of Bennion Kearny for taking yet another punt on a value-based pricing tome for lawyers – proof, if nothing else, that publishers can be brave too.

I also want to thank my friends, contacts and collaborators from around the world who have supported my work on value-based pricing. The legal profession may sometimes feel slow to change, but I have been lucky enough to meet many people who are curious, generous and willing to think differently.

Thank you to the conference organisers who have trusted me with a platform, a microphone and, occasionally, a penguin. Every invitation to speak has helped me develop these ideas. Every event has given me the chance to listen, learn and see how lawyers in different firms, countries and markets are grappling with the same questions.

Thank you to the delegates who came along to listen. Whether you agreed with me, challenged me, laughed at the right places, or looked faintly horrified when I suggested ditching the billable hour, you helped me refine the message. Speakers need audiences. But more than that, they need thoughtful audiences. I have been fortunate to have many.

Thank you to the law firms that have retained me, trusted me and invited me inside their businesses. It takes courage to examine pricing properly. It takes even more courage to admit that the old model may not be serving the firm, the lawyers or the clients as well as it should. I have learned a huge amount from every firm I have worked with.

Thank you also to the lawyers, partners, finance teams, business development teams, knowledge lawyers, innovation teams and support staff who have attended my training sessions, and masterclasses, and purchased the books. Your questions, concerns, objections and examples have made this work better. They have reminded me that value-based pricing is not a theory, it is a practical change project involving real people, real clients and real pressures.

A special thank you goes to those who have read drafts, commented on ideas, pointed me towards articles, shared examples and generally kept the conversation going. Books improve when people are prepared to be honest. I am grateful to everyone who was.

And finally, thank you to my family.

Writing a book takes time. Writing a book while running a business, travelling, speaking, training and occasionally dressing up as a penguin takes even more time. My family, especially my wife Debbie, have supported me, encouraged me and put up with the usual author nonsense: the distracted conversations, the sudden ideas, the "I just need to finish this bit" moments, and the piles of paper that seem to follow me around.

This book is about moving from hours to outcomes. But in truth, the best outcomes in life are rarely achieved alone.

So, to everyone who has helped, challenged, encouraged, booked, attended, listened, argued, laughed, retained, trained, read, supported or simply said, "Keep going" – thank you.

CONTENTS

FOREWORD TO THE FOREWORD! i

FOREWORD ii

SO WHY ANOTHER BOOK? 1

P#1. PARADIGM: THE BUSINESS MODEL MUST CHANGE 13

P#2. PIONEERS: FINDING THE PEOPLE WHO WILL HELP BUILD THE FUTURE 67

P#3. PLAN: DESIGN THE AI-ENABLED VALUE MODEL 81

P#4. PROMOTE: EXPLAIN THE NEW STORY INTERNALLY AND EXTERNALLY 125

P#5. PERMIT: GIVE LAWYERS PERMISSION TO THINK AND PRICE DIFFERENTLY 143

P#6. PRIZES: CREATE QUICK WINS THAT PROVE THE MODEL 157

P#7. PERSEVERE: EMBED THE NEW OPERATING MODEL 163

P#8. PASSION: CREATE THE NEW CULTURE 179

CONCLUSION 187

PART 2 189

WORDS WITH THE WISE 189

APPENDIX 1: INTRODUCTION TO THE JUDGMENT AND BUSINESS ACUMEN AND PRICING CANVAS EXAMPLES 267

APPENDIX 2: MANAGING PARTNER CHECKLIST 303

APPENDIX 3: PEOPLE TO FOLLOW 309

ENDNOTES 313

FOREWORD TO THE FOREWORD!

I am delighted that Mitch Kowalski has generously agreed to write the Foreword to this book.

Mitch's own book, *Avoiding Extinction: Reimagining Legal Services for the 21st Century*, was the book that first properly introduced me to the concept of value-based pricing. It made me stop, think, and realise that the billable hour was not some immovable law of nature. It was a choice. And if it was a choice, then law firms could choose something better.

Mitch was making the VBP argument before AI made it unavoidable. He was saying, back in 2012, that law firms must stop monetising inefficiency. That argument has aged rather well. In an AI world, it becomes even sharper. If technology reduces the time taken, then time-based pricing starts to look even more exposed.

Mitch's fictional future firm was built around outcomes, process, technology and client value. Very much *Stop The Clock* territory.

Since then, I have recommended Mitch's book to thousands of lawyers, managing partners, finance directors and anyone else who will listen. I will continue to do so.

If you have not bought a copy, buy one. Read it.

Then ask yourself the uncomfortable question: if Mitch was warning the legal profession about this more than a decade ago, what excuse do we have for still standing still?

FOREWORD

One of the most curious things about the billable hour is that almost nobody likes it.

I have yet to meet a lawyer who genuinely enjoys recording time – or who consistently records time with absolute accuracy. Nor have I met a client who enjoys reviewing page upon page of time entries describing conferences, emails, drafting, reviewing, revising and reporting. Nor have I met many lawyers who believe e-billing dramatically improved the experience.

So, if almost nobody likes the system, perhaps the better question is not how we preserve it, but rather, why do we continue to organize so much of our profession around it?

For much of my professional life, I have been asking variations of that question.

When I wrote *Avoiding Extinction* in 2012, I suggested that the legal profession needed to rethink its entire business model. Later, in *The Great Legal Reformation*, I argued that what many regarded as isolated developments were really part of a much broader transformation taking place across the global legal services market. Different books and different examples, but fundamentally the same conversation.

I first met Shaun Jardine almost a decade ago. What struck me almost immediately was that, although we approached these issues from different experiences, we kept finding ourselves asking many of the same questions.

Why do lawyers continue to measure value through time spent?

What happens when technology changes the economics of legal work?

Every pricing model is a product of the economic realities of its time. The billable hour emerged in an era when access to legal knowledge was relatively scarce, legal work was inherently labour-intensive, and time was a reasonable proxy for value. Those realities are changing rapidly, and artificial intelligence is accelerating that change.

So the question is no longer whether the billable hour is right or wrong.

The question is whether the economic conditions that gave rise to it still exist.

Stop The Clock is Shaun's latest contribution to that ongoing conversation. Neither of us claims to have all the answers. In fact, I'm increasingly convinced that asking better questions is more important than defending old answers.

A central idea running through Shaun's book is that artificial intelligence has not created weaknesses in the billable hour as a pricing model.

It has exposed them.

AI forces us to distinguish between production and judgment. As production becomes faster, cheaper and increasingly automated, judgment becomes the scarcer – and therefore more valuable product – but it is much harder to reduce to an hourly rate.

Readers shouldn't expect to agree with every point Shaun makes. Nor should they. Shaun and I certainly don't. That isn't a weakness. It is precisely why conversations like this are worth having.

Read this book not because it tells you what to think.

Read it because it asks questions that every lawyer should now be asking themselves.

When you've finished reading, ask yourself one final question:

If you were creating a legal services business from scratch, with everything we now know about clients, technology and value, would you really build it around the clock?

Mitchell Kowalski, Sherman, Texas. Independence Day, 2026

SO WHY ANOTHER BOOK?

I thought that would be it. One book. Done.

When I wrote *Ditch The Billable Hour!* in 2023, the billable hour was already under pressure. Clients wanted certainty, transparency and value. They did not want six-minute units, open-ended budgets and invoices that arrived after the damage had been done. *Ditch The Billable Hour!* made the case for value-based pricing and explained how law firms could move away from time as the default measure of value. On pain of death, I have agreed with my publisher, James, *not to regurgitate* that book here… it's worth reading if you come to the conclusion that you have to price legal services by value. You will! So, buy a copy.

In 2025, I wrote *Ditch & Switch!* because I grew tired of lawyers telling me their practice areas were too specialised, too complex, or too different to offer pricing choices. So, I created 50 legal scenarios that show how lawyers can offer options, service levels, and pricing choices in real-world work.

So why a third book?

It's simply because AI has made the pricing issue impossible to ignore.

In April 2026, I received an email from a large law firm that had already invested heavily in AI. They wanted help answering questions about how to price AI-enabled work, how to protect margins, how to demonstrate savings to clients, and how to explain the value and cost behind the firm's use of AI.

One partner put it perfectly:

"We need to work out how to price and sell a model that demonstrates real savings to clients, while still recognising the value and cost behind our use of AI."

That sentence is the problem this book is about. This is why the book is called *Stop The Clock*. Because that is the commercial choice AI has forced onto the table.

Because if AI helps a firm do work faster, clients will ask the obvious question: why should they pay the same? The answer cannot simply be, "Because we used to charge this much."

AI may reduce the time taken to complete parts of legal work, but it does not eliminate the need for legal judgment, supervision, accountability, risk assessment, client communication, professional liability or commercial acumen. Those are the things law firms must learn to price.

The large firm had spent money on AI before answering the pricing question.

Then, a few weeks later, I saw the other end of the market.

At a legal tech conference in Bristol, the managing partner of a smaller firm described herself as representing the "rabbit in the headlights brigade". Her firm had held a partners' meeting to discuss AI. Partners asked whether AI could do certain things, and the Head of IT had to point out that some of those things could already be done by Microsoft Word or by the firm's existing case management system. That got a laugh, but it is not really funny.

At one end of the profession, large firms are spending serious money on AI and then asking how to price, sell and profit from it. At the other end, smaller firms are spending little or nothing and do not fully understand what their existing systems can already do.

Both are heading towards the same iceberg. This book is about that iceberg.

It is not a book about prompts, tools or technology for the sake of technology. It is about the business model. It is about pricing. It is about value. It is about why law firms must stop assuming that time is the safest unit of value when AI is making time a weaker measure by the day.

AI is not free magic. It has cost, risk, governance, supervision and accountability attached to it. But it also creates the opportunity to deliver better, faster and more certain outcomes for clients.

The firms that understand that will price outcomes, not hours.

WHO THIS BOOK IS FOR

This book is for the rabbit-in-the-headlights brigade and for the bewildered Big Law practitioner who may feel that some of the issues highlighted in the book apply to their firm.

And before anyone gets offended, I am not calling you stupid, far from it. You are not lazy. You are not anti-technology. You are not sitting there wishing AI would go away so everyone can return to carbon paper, dictation tapes and fax machines. You are simply trying to work out what on earth is happening.

- What matters?
- What is hype?
- What is risk?
- What is opportunity?
- What should your firm actually do next?

And you are trying to work all of that out while still running a business, serving clients, managing people, training junior lawyers, perhaps doing some legal work yourself and, with any luck, having some form of life outside the office.

I get it, it is a lot. I have been in that role.

If you are in a large firm with a Chief Technology Officer, an innovation team, data specialists, project managers and people who can explain APIs without causing everyone else in the room to stare at their shoes, you may already understand much of the technology. Your challenge may be different, and your job may be to persuade the management team, the partners, the owners and the finance people that AI is not just a shiny tool issue. It is not something that can be parked in the innovation cupboard and brought out for demonstrations.

- It is a pricing issue
- It is a margin issue
- It is a client value issue
- It is a risk issue
- And, ultimately, it is a business model issue

You may get the tech. But do your owners get the commercial consequences?

That is where value-based pricing comes in. If AI changes how legal work is done, how should your firm price the outcome?

That is the question this book tries to answer.

INTRODUCING THE 8 P POINT PLAN

The 8 P Point Plan you are about to read about is inspired by the work of Professor John Kotter of Harvard Business School, one of the world's leading authorities on change management. All I did when creating the 8 P Point Plan was take a Kotter heading and label it with a word beginning with P, as it was easier for me to remember the eight steps! It's Kotter's methodology. It is sound.

Kotter, together with Holger Rathgeber, wrote *Our Iceberg Is Melting*, a fable about a colony of penguins who have to change the way they live or face disaster. I first read it when preparing for a major change management project in 2014, and it has stayed with me ever since.

In my opinion, *Our Iceberg Is Melting* is the perfect change management book for lawyers. It takes about an hour and a quarter to read, the print is large, there are coloured pictures, and one of the penguins even carries a briefcase. What more could a lawyer want?

The story introduces a number of penguins, including Fred, the curious penguin who spots the problem; Alice, the get-stuff-done penguin who helps make change happen; and No No, the Naysayer penguin who resists almost everything.

You will have Freds, Alices and No Nos in your firm. Everyone does.

Our Iceberg Is Melting is also the reason behind the name of my business and, yes, the penguin obsession. Yellow penguins exist; they are a genetic abnormality and if you and I ever meet in real life, you will see I am 6'4" tall. Hence the name, the Big Yellow Penguin. The penguin is a metaphor for change. It is not because I am some strange man who dresses up as a penguin at legal conferences. (Apart from the occasions when I have dressed up as a penguin at legal conferences.)

ABOUT THE BOOK

This book is not designed to be read like a dry management textbook. You can, of course, start at page one and keep going until the end. That would be very sensible.

It is not really a book about specific AI tools. It is not a book about prompts. It is a book about pricing, value and commercial survival. You can also use it as a working guide for changing how your firm thinks about pricing, value, AI and the billable hour. Think of it as a map. Or, better still, think of it as a Haynes Manual for legal pricing.

(If you are of a certain age, you will know exactly what I mean. A Haynes Manual was the book that told you how to service your car, take things apart, put them back together again and, with luck, not have too many bits left over at the end.)

That is the spirit of this book. It is not theory for theory's sake; it is a practical guide to help you lift the bonnet, understand what is really going on, and start making changes without blowing up the engine.

At the heart of the book is the **8 P Point Plan**. Each #P helps you move from concern, confusion or polite avoidance into practical action. Use what works for your firm. Adapt it. Improve it. Make it useful.

I use some words interchangeably: client and customer, firm and business, partner and owner, CEO and project leader. The labels matter less than the job that needs to be done.

If value-based pricing is going to be implemented, you need to capture and collate your learnings and practices. You cannot leave pricing knowledge trapped in people's heads, buried in old emails or reinvented every time a new matter arrives.

You need a place to record decisions, examples, pricing approaches, client responses, lessons learned, and internal guidance.

I call that the Big Book of Usefulness – the BBU. In your firm, it might be a manual, playbook, policy bank, knowledge hub or part of your practice management system. I do not mind what you call it, but you will need one. Value-based pricing only becomes repeatable when you capture what works, share it, improve it and use it again.

THE 8 P POINT PLAN

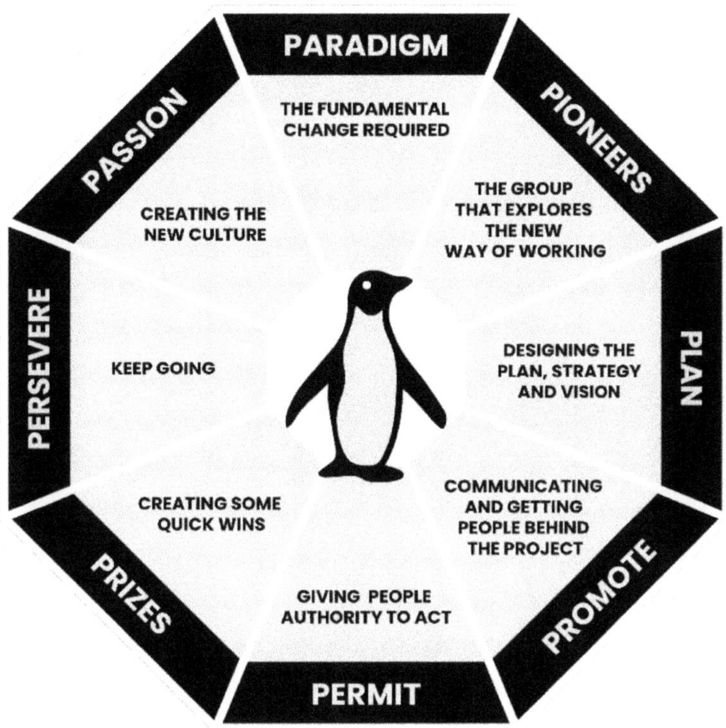

P#1 PARADIGM

Understand why the business model must change

This is the wake-up call. AI is not just a technology issue; it is a pricing, margin, client value and business model issue.

P#2 PIONEERS

Find the people who will help make change happen

You cannot do this alone. You need curious, practical, influential people who are willing to test, challenge, learn and lead.

P#3 PLAN

Build the knowledge, tools, vision and plan

This is the engine room of the book. It covers what firms need to know, what tools they need, what they are trying to become and how they can start moving.

It perhaps won't surprise you to learn that the majority of this book focuses on P#3 Plan. This section is by far the largest and is broken down into four subsections: Knowledge, Tools, Vision, and Plan.

P#4 PROMOTE

Give people the words and confidence to explain the change

If lawyers cannot explain value-based pricing to clients, colleagues and themselves, the change will not stick.

P#5 PERMIT

Remove the barriers that stop people acting differently

Lawyers need permission, authority, templates, guidance and support. Otherwise, they will drift back to the old ways.

P#6 PRIZES

Create quick wins and celebrate progress

Change needs evidence, and small wins build belief. Progress should be noticed, shared and repeated.

P#7 PERSEVERE

Keep going when the novelty wears off

This is where firms either embed the change, or quietly slide back into hours, targets and old habits.

P#8 PASSION

Create the new culture

The aim is not a pricing project. The aim is a firm that thinks differently about value, clients, technology, people and profit.

LOOK OUT FOR THESE FEATURES

BRACE YOURSELF

Short, provocative statements designed to make you stop and think. You may not agree with all of them. Thinking is the point.

BRACE YOURSELF…
incoming provocative statement

QUOTES

Here is a self-explanatory quote!

> 'My son Shaun's book 'Ditch The Billable Hour!' was an excellent read. He gave me two signed copies for Christmas.'
>
> **Gwen Jardine**

Dotted around each chapter, I have included quotes from a variety of individuals. Hopefully, one or two will strike a chord with you (ignore my mum), and you can use them in any presentations/business cases you have to make in the future.

PENGUIN LOGIC

Practical tips, observations and reminders from me. Usually short. Occasionally blunt. Hopefully useful.

8 PPP PENGUIN LOGIC

SHINGLES

SHINGLES LOGIC

Warnings from Shingles & Co… Shingles represents old habits, old assumptions and old business model thinking. Why Shingles? Because shingles is painful, unpleasant and most commonly associated with older people, which felt about right for a fictional firm clinging to old habits, old assumptions and old ways of working.

When you see the dinosaur image, take the hint. Dinosaurs belong in the past, and so does Shingles thinking. Shingles & Co. is not intended to represent any particular firm, although you would be amazed how many lawyers read *Ditch The Billable Hour!* and quietly asked whether Shingles was based on their own organisation. It was not. Probably.

WORDS WITH THE WISE

When you see the image of a person at a lectern, you are going to hear from some wise people who have thought deeply about AI, pricing, leadership, legal services and change. They bring other voices to the same iceberg.

WORDS WITH THE WISE

6 MINUTES OF YOUR TIME

Articles, videos, podcasts and resources worth a look. Some will help you make the business case. Some will challenge you. Some may simply make you smile. Some of the recommendations are more than 6 minutes long.

6 MINUTES OF YOUR TIME

POSSIBILITY THINKING

POSSIBILITY THINKING QUESTION

I am a great believer in the power of the crowd. Get the right people in a room, ask them a good question and give them permission to think properly, and they will usually produce better answers than one person trying to be clever on their own.

The process is simple. Take a problem and turn it into a possibility question.

Instead of saying, "I do not have enough time to do X," ask, "How could I possibly make more time to do X?" or "Who might help me with X?"

That small shift is important. You are no longer admiring the problem. You are looking for answers. Then set a timer for four minutes and write down as many possible answers as you can. Do not judge them. Do not edit them. Do not hold a committee meeting in your own head. Some answers will be obvious. Some will be ridiculous. That's okay. Ridiculous often sits next door to useful.

Once the list is complete, highlight what might work, reject the nonsense and turn the best ideas into actions.

Lawyers are trained to spot problems, risks and flaws. Very useful when reviewing a contract. Less useful when trying to solve old business problems in new ways. Your people may already have the answers. They may simply not have been asked the right question yet.

At the end of each section, the Crib Sheets include lists of Possibility Questions and CEO questions to help you start those conversations.

CRIB SHEETS

CRIB SHEET

Further reading, watching, listening, questions and miscellany to help you go deeper, prepare meetings, brief colleagues, and continue the journey.

In a proper grown-up academic book, this section would probably be called "References" and contain lots of Harvard-style citations, Latin phrases, ibid, supra, infra and other words designed to make everyone feel slightly underdressed. This is not that kind of book. I put links in boxes where they might be relevant. I do put some footnotes to articles I am quoting. Also, at the back of the Crib Sheets, you will find some items in a Miscellany section.

Treat the materials in the Crib Sheets as a guided rummage through the things that have helped shape my thinking. Click the links. Scan the QR codes. Plug in your headphones. Go for a walk. Listen in the car. Watch with a notebook. Send the useful bits to your Pioneer Penguins. Argue with the bits you disagree with. Use the best ideas in your own business case, partner meeting, training session or awkward conversation with a Naysayer Penguin.

Some of the links may change over time. Some may disappear. Some may lead you somewhere unexpected. But I hope many of them will help. Enjoy.

PRICING CANVAS

You will also find pricing canvas examples in Appendix 1.

Do not treat these as decorative appendices or something to flick through with a cup of tea and a vague sense of approval. They are working tools.

The point of the canvas is to help you separate the parts of legal work that AI may assist with from the parts that still require lawyer judgment, business acumen, supervision, risk assessment and professional responsibility. That distinction is important because it is where the pricing conversation now lives. If AI can help produce the chronology, summary, first draft or comparison table, fine. But the client is still paying for the lawyer who knows what matters, what is risky, what is commercially sensible and what outcome the client actually needs.

The canvas is designed to help firms have that conversation properly, internally and with clients. The examples are for you to show others that it can be done.

You will understand more when you get to that section. Trust me… I am a lawyer!

AI USE

Given the subject of this book, it would be more than a little odd if I pretended that AI had not been involved in writing it.

So yes, I have used AI tools, including ChatGPT-5.5, during the writing process, but not to do my thinking for me, outsource my judgement or remove the human being – or indeed the penguin – from the process.

What AI has helped me do is organise ideas, test structure, challenge woolly thinking, create examples and make some of the writing clearer. It has acted as a useful sparring partner.

I have also drawn on many books, articles, reports, conversations and generous contributions from wise people across the legal world. Many of those are referenced in the text and in the Crib Sheets. A good example is the aforementioned pricing canvas examples in Appendix 1. Once I had worked out the template and its logic, AI helped generate the twenty or so worked examples. That is a sensible use of the tool. The thinking, framework and purpose came first; the machine then helped with the donkey work.

You may also notice, as you read, that I repeat myself in places. That is not AI getting stuck in a loop. That is me. Believe it or not, this book went through 21 drafts, so I know some points appear more than once. I have left some of that repetition in deliberately because *some points matter and need to be made more than once*, from more than one angle, in more than one way. It is also likely that you will give the book to a colleague and say, "Read chapter X." Well, if that is the only chapter they read, they will need some of the basic points made again.

This is not a book about a minor operational tweak. It is not about changing a template, buying a new piece of software or asking lawyers to fill in a slightly different spreadsheet. It is about changing how law firms think about value, price, clients, technology, profit and the future of legal work.

A book about outcomes, not hours, should make sensible use of the tools available. But it should also have a human being firmly in charge of the point being made. Or, in this case, a penguin.

Right. That is the introductions and housekeeping sorted. Let's get started.

P#1. PARADIGM: THE BUSINESS MODEL MUST CHANGE

P#1. PARADIGM – THE FUNDAMENTAL CHANGE REQUIRED

- Why the change is necessary.
- What the benefits and risks are.
- Why change should be part of the strategy.
- Why people should get onboard.

WELCOME TO P#1 – PARADIGM

P#1 Paradigm is a leadership wake-up call. AI is not an IT project, it is a business model challenge. The firms that thrive will not be those that merely buy AI tools, but those that redesign their model around client value, judgment and outcomes. That is the paradigm shift: outcomes, not hours.

A WEALTH WARNING

Clayton Christensen was a Harvard Business School professor and the author of *The Innovator's Dilemma*, one of the most influential business books of the last 30 years. Lots of people commenting about AI in the legal sector talk about his work. His central point was simple, brutal and very relevant to law firms: good companies often fail not because they are badly run, but because they are well run. The profitable ones. The ones with impressive offices, sensible boards, decent clients, healthy PEP and a room full of people saying, "We've always done it this way, and it has served us rather well."

And that is the trap.

Christensen's point was that good businesses often collapse because they keep doing the very things that made them successful. They listen to their best clients, they protect their best margins, they improve the existing model. They ignore the scruffy little newcomer because, at first, it looks cheap, basic and not quite good enough.

Then the scruffy little newcomer gets better.

And better.

And then one day the incumbent looks up and says, "Hang on, where did our market go?"

That is the innovator's dilemma.

For law firms, the billable hour version is painfully obvious.

The firm says: "We are very profitable. Our clients are not asking for value-based pricing. Our partners will never accept it. AI cannot do the complex stuff we do. We will wait and see."

Lovely.

That is not a strategy. That is a rabbit in the headlights with a spreadsheet.

The dilemma is that the old model still works just well enough to make change feel optional. Until it isn't.

Do not confuse current success with future safety! The thing that looks small, clunky and slightly ridiculous today may be the thing that rewrites the rules tomorrow.

> The problem with the billable hour is, it's hard to tell a room full of multi-millionaires their business model is wrong.
>
> **Ron Baker**

WORDS WITH THE WISE

Quentin Solt

The law will increasingly be sold as a utility.

That is where I think this is going.

But the real threat may not come wearing a lawyer's suit. It may arrive inside the tools clients already use. It may arrive with tokens, usage limits and an insurance wrapper.

Think about your old mobile phone contract. You bought minutes. Texts. Data. You had a bundle. If you used more, you paid for more. I can see legal going the same way. HR and legal support bundled into a utility contract. A basic allowance. More units if you go over. A practical answer when you need it. Not a partner opening a file and starting the clock.

If legal capability becomes a utility, and if the client can get good enough legal assistance inside the business, with insurance, at predictable cost, then the law firm has a problem.

Not a pricing problem.

A relevance problem.

AI HAS SWITCHED THE LIGHTS ON

For years, the legal market has been built on a comfortable belief system. Clients had problems they could not solve on their own. Lawyers had the knowledge, experience and machinery to solve them. Therefore, if a client wanted a legal outcome, they had to come to a lawyer. That was the deal.

The client had the problem. The lawyer had the capacity. The billable hour sat neatly in the middle.

I used to say in presentations that a client had four options.

1. They could buy from you
2. Buy from your competitor
3. Do it themselves
4. Or do nothing

I would then point out that if they had called you, they had probably disregarded the last two options. That is no longer true. There is now a fifth option. Use AI and that may be coming from someone who is not a lawyer at all!

That changes everything, because clients are no longer simply comparing your firm with another firm. They are also comparing your firm with what they can now do themselves, what their in-house team can do with AI, and what a technology-enabled alternative provider may be able to deliver at speed and scale.

But for law firms still addicted to the billable hour, there is a rather awkward problem… speed does not automatically mean profit.

In fact, under the wrong business model, speed can be financially painful. If a job used to take many hours and AI helps the lawyer finish it in one, the client may think that is marvellous, the lawyer may think it is marvellous, and the software vendor will certainly think it is marvellous.

The finance director, however, may be less enthusiastic when eight billable hours have quietly disappeared.

That is the trap. AI may make the work quicker, but if the firm is still built around selling time, it has not solved the problem. It has accelerated it.

The partner who championed the AI investment may then have to explain why the technology budget has increased while recorded time and revenue have gone down.

That is the Efficiency Trap. A concept which is explained in greater detail by Colin Levy in Part One of his online publications *AI & Client Value.*

6 MINUTES OF YOUR TIME

(Will take a bit more to be honest)

Read *AI & Client Value* by Colin Levy[1]

AI has not created the weakness in the billable hour. It has simply switched the lights on.

For years, many law firms have made money from a model that rewards busyness rather than progress.

The more people involved, the more time gets recorded. The more time gets recorded, the bigger the bill. The longer the matter takes, the better the financial result for the firm. Put bluntly, the slower the horse, the more attractive the invoice.

That may have worked for law firms, but it was never a model designed around the client.

Clients do not wake up wanting to buy six-minute units. They do not lie awake at night hoping a lawyer will spend more time on their file. They want the problem fixed, the risk reduced, the deal done, the dispute avoided, the family protected, the business defended, the pain removed or the opportunity captured.

That was one of the central points I made in *Ditch The Billable Hour!* Clients care about how quickly and effectively you help them reach the right result. They are not interested in how much time you can record on the journey.

AI now makes that paradigm shift urgent.

In his 2024 article, *Does AI Signal the End of the Billable Hour?* [2], Ken Crutchfield asks a very good question. What will generative AI do to the billable hour?

He sets out four possible answers.

1. Rates will go up
2. Rates will go down
3. Work will shift to alternative fee arrangements
4. Some work will move in-house

And his answer?

All of the above.

When I first read that, it made me laugh out loud. But I think it is exactly the answer law firms need to sit with. AI will not produce one neat pricing consequence. It will not affect every client, every matter, every practice area or every firm in the same way.

For high-value, bespoke work – the "bet the company" litigation, the high-stakes dispute, the complex judgment call – rates may go up because the client is still buying the outcome, the judgment, the risk management and the responsibility. If AI helps the firm get there more efficiently, the value of the outcome has not disappeared. In some cases, it may have increased.

But for commoditised work, repetitive work and tasks that can be done faster, cheaper and more predictably, the pressure will go the other way. Rates will come down. Alternative providers will compete. Clients will ask harder questions. More work will move to fixed fees, subscriptions and other alternative fee arrangements. And where the work is repeatable, systemised and does not require much outside expertise, clients may simply take it in-house.

So no, AI does not mean one thing for pricing. It means many things at once. That is why firms must stop thinking only about hourly rates and start monitoring whether their pricing structures – flat fees, subscriptions, success fees or hourly rates – are actually meeting the firm's commercial goals and the client's needs. Crutchfield is not saying the billable hour disappears overnight. He is saying something more thought-provoking, and more uncomfortable. The old model is going to be pulled in several directions at the same time.

A client using a contract review tool can produce a contract review. A lawyer using the same tool can also produce a contract review. On routine work, the output may look very similar, and if the output is interchangeable, then the output is not where the real value lives.

If the "work product" can be produced by lots of people, or by AI, and looks broadly the same, then the value cannot simply be in the hours spent producing it. So, what were those hours really buying? If the answer is judgment, risk reduction, certainty and commercial progress, then the price should follow the outcome, not the hours. But many firms have not priced those things properly because they have been too busy pricing time.

> **WORDS WITH THE WISE**
>
> **Ben Weinberger**
>
> If the firm is billing by the hour, and AI reduces the time needed to do the work, then the billable hour model becomes a problem. The firm may become more efficient, but it may also reduce the amount it can charge.
>
> Clients are spending money to lose money.
>
> Again.

The real question is not whether the firm has AI. The real question is whether the firm knows what to do with it, how to govern it, how to explain it, how to price it and how to turn it into better client outcomes.

If corporate clients begin adopting their own AI billing rules (and they are), AI-specific pricing expectations and internal delivery models, firms that remain wedded to the hourly model will face an uncomfortable choice. They can disclose that AI has reduced the time taken and accept lower revenue, or they can stay silent and hope the client does not ask too many questions.

Neither option is sustainable.

The answer is not to pretend AI is irrelevant, and it is not to hand all of the efficiency gain to the client by default. The answer is to change the pricing conversation so that it is no longer about time saved, but about value created, risk managed, judgment applied and outcomes delivered.

AI is not causing the problem. It is showing us the problem.

> We expend effort. We create value. It's easy to get confused about which one we're going to ultimately be compensated for.
>
> **Seth Godin**

BRACE YOURSELF…
incoming provocative statement

Law firms don't know how to charge clients for the shiny, shiny AI products they have purchased.

WORDS WITH THE WISE

Quentin Solt

AI is becoming "good enough".

That phrase matters. And "good enough" is not a fixed point. It is moving up the food chain. What is good enough for low-value, high-volume transactions today becomes good enough for more complex work tomorrow. The threshold keeps rising.

I sit on boards. I hear people saying it already: "We did this one by AI." Not because they hate lawyers. Not because they are trying to be clever. Because they know their own business. They know the pitfalls. They know the scale of the deal. And for that piece of work, they do not need a lawyer in the middle.

THE TOOL IS NOT THE STRATEGY

8 PPP PENGUIN LOGIC

AI is not the strategy. AI is a capability. The strategy is deciding how the firm will use that capability to create, explain and price better client outcomes.

One of the most difficult questions facing law firms is no longer whether AI exists, whether it matters, or whether it will affect legal work, because those arguments are largely over. The harder and more practical question is now this: which AI tools should we use, for what purpose, in what order, and with what commercial consequences?

That is not an easy question to answer when the market is moving at such speed. And I am delighted that – in this book – I don't try and answer this question. According to Legal Tech Hub, as of 31st March 2026 there were 1,014 solutions in the LTH Directory incorporating generative AI, with new providers appearing at a remarkable rate. In other words, law firms are not choosing between a handful of carefully understood options; they are being confronted by a huge, fast-growing, noisy and confusing marketplace full of products, promises, pilots, demos and enthusiastic sales decks.

60 MINUTES OF YOUR TIME

The State of AI Keynote 2026[3]

Watch Nikki Shaver, founder of LegalTech Hub, deliver a landmark keynote on the state of AI in legal: what's real, what's hype, and what law firms must do right now to survive.

This creates a real problem for law firm leaders.

They are being asked to make investment decisions about products that may be expensive, difficult to compare and hard to implement, while also worrying that some of those products may reduce the very billable time on which the firm's current revenue model depends. That is the uncomfortable commercial tension sitting underneath many AI conversations. The tool may make the work faster, but if the firm still prices by time; faster can mean less revenue.

At the same time, clients are becoming more sophisticated, more demanding and more willing to move work. Some are already sending cases to smaller firms because they are less costly, while others may increasingly favour firms that can demonstrate sensible, safe and efficient use of GenAI products. So, the risk is not simply that AI reduces the time recorded on existing work; the risk is also that firms *lose work altogether* because clients conclude that another provider can deliver the same or better outcome more efficiently.

This is why the "which tool should we buy?" question is too narrow.

The better question is "where can AI improve the business first?"

SHINGLES LOGIC

Tools Before Problems

Shingles asks, "Which AI product should we buy?" A better firm asks, "Which client problems, margin leaks and delivery failures are we trying to solve?" Shingles buys the tool first and invents the use case later.

Not all AI in a law firm is about producing legal advice.

In fact, some of the most useful AI may never go near a client opinion, a contract clause or a piece of advocacy. It may sit quietly in the background, helping with billing preparation, collections, client onboarding, matter opening, reporting, accounting, document administration, knowledge management, CRM and all the other operational machinery that keeps a law firm moving.

A great deal of this work is non-billable. The client does not pay for it directly. It is simply part of the cost of running the firm. Necessary, yes. Valuable, often. But still cost.

So, firms need to avoid treating all AI use as if it creates the same commercial problem.

If AI reduces the time spent on billable legal work, and the firm is still wedded to the billable hour, it may create a pricing and revenue problem. Fewer hours may mean less income, unless the firm has changed the way it prices and captures value.

But if AI reduces the cost, delay, duplication and friction in the non-billable parts of the firm, the position is very different. Profitability can improve without immediately blowing a hole in revenue. Which means the sensible starting point for many firms may not be the shiny client-facing AI tool, the clever legal product, or the system promising to remove hours from legal work. The better starting point may be much more ordinary.

- Where are we wasting time?
- Where are we duplicating effort?
- Where are we annoying clients?
- Where are we slowing down cash collection?
- Where are we frustrating lawyers?
- Where are we making support teams wrestle with processes that should have been fixed years ago?

Before asking how AI can reduce the cost of legal advice, firms should ask a more basic question.

How can AI reduce the cost of running the firm?

That may not sound as exciting as an AI tool that drafts a contract in 30 seconds, but improving intake, billing, collections, reporting and internal processes can have a direct and positive impact on margin, cash flow, client experience and staff morale.

And here is the important point. A firm that learns how to use AI safely and effectively in its non-billable operations will also build confidence, governance, habits and understanding that can later support more complex client-facing use cases. It gives the firm a lower-risk place to learn before it starts making bigger promises to clients about AI-enabled legal delivery.

So, when firms ask, "Who should we use?", perhaps the answer should not begin with a vendor list. It should begin with a business problem.

- What are we trying to improve?
- What cost are we trying to remove?
- What client experience are we trying to enhance?
- What risk are we trying to manage?
- What process is currently slow, manual, irritating or expensive?
- What are we doing repeatedly that does not require legal judgment?

This is what the managing partner at the conference in Bristol raised… how can we work better… the answer from her head of IT was blunt, "Learn to use the tools you have". It's not a bad starting point.

Because the danger is obvious. Shingles & Co. will buy the shiny thing first and work out the strategy later. A better firm will identify the problem first, understand the commercial impact, then choose the tool that helps solve it.

WORDS WITH THE WISE

Joanna Gaudoin

The first question should not be, "What AI should we buy?" It should be, "What are we trying to achieve?" Sometimes, the answer may not even be full AI. It may be a simpler piece of automation. The danger is that firms spend a lot of money on technology, people do not use it properly, or it ends up taking more time rather than less.

SHINGLES LOGIC

Shingles Buys AI

Shingles buys an expensive AI tool, announces it as transformational, then tells lawyers they must still hit exactly the same chargeable hour targets as last year. Shingles calls this innovation. It is not innovation. It is the old business model wearing a software licence.

AI IS NOT FREE MAGIC

[Apologies to the person who said this first… it's a great line. It wasn't me, but I am damned if I can remember who it was and where I read it!]

There is a dangerous myth developing around AI, and it is the idea that because the machine can produce something quickly, the work has somehow become free. It has not.

AI is not free. It is a new capability, but it is also a new cost base, and law firms need to understand both sides of that sentence.

Subscriptions cost money, tokens cost money, implementation costs money, supervision costs money, training costs money, data governance costs money, risk management costs money, infrastructure costs money, and the time spent working out how to use AI safely and effectively also costs money.

The firm may be able to produce certain outputs faster, but that does not mean the firm has no cost, no risk and no value in the process.

This is where some of the AI pricing debate becomes far too simplistic.

> **WORDS WITH THE WISE**
>
> **Andrew Allen**
>
> Do not buy AI and assume the pricing will sort itself out. Ask what AI costs, where it saves time, who gets the benefit of that saving, and how the firm recovers its investment. Otherwise, the firm spends more, records fewer hours, charges less, and leaks margin.

Law firms must learn how to earn a return on its investment in AI.

That does not mean adding a crude "AI surcharge" to every bill and hoping the client does not notice. I know some commentators and indeed managing partners are thinking this way. In most cases, AI costs should be treated as part of the firm's base cost of delivery and reflected in the overall pricing model, rather than being presented as a separate disbursement. Clients generally prefer clear, all-inclusive pricing, not a bill that says, "legal work, plus a bit for the robot."

In the Crib Sheet for this section, there are links to four articles that I recommend you read.

The first is to a paper by Josh Kubicki in his Brainyacts special briefing, *Money Spent, Earned, and Prompted: The New Economics of Legal Work in the AI Era.*[4] Kubicki argues that AI is not just changing how legal work is done; it is exposing the economics underneath it. His biggest warning for law firms is about tokens. Every prompt, document upload, model response and agentic loop consumes tokens. They may look cheap today, almost too small to worry about, but that is exactly the trap. Firms are building AI-enabled workflows without tracking token usage by matter, client or practice group. Once agentic AI starts looping, retrying tasks, calling sub-agents and expanding scope, token consumption could rise dramatically. The danger is not simply that AI costs more, the danger is that firms will not know what their AI-enabled work actually costs to produce. And if they do not know that, they cannot price confidently, defend their margins, or explain to clients what part of the fee is production, what part is judgment, and what part is just old-fashioned opacity wearing a shiny AI badge.

The second is *Build what only you can build. Don't be the OS*[5] by Christian Brown. His warning is blunt: experiment with AI, but don't accidentally turn your law firm into its own unsupported tech company. The risk is that firms build workflows without knowing the real meter is running model calls, integrations, testing, maintenance, monitoring, rework and internal time. The "DIY tax" can become very expensive.

The third is Ryan McClead's *Bride of the Token Cost Panic.*[6] It cuts through some of the current noise about AI costs in law firms. His argument is not that token costs do not matter (they do) but he makes the more important point that the token bill is only the meter reading. The bigger questions are what work the machine is now doing, what value that work creates, who captures that value, and whether the firm has the pricing and management information to understand it.

The fourth article I recommend is Alex Herrity's *Out of Tokens: Insert Coin(s) to Continue.*[7] Herrity offers a point that should make every law firm leader pause. Tokens may look like a new technical issue, but as a cost unit they have an uncomfortable resemblance to the billable hour. They measure consumption, not quality. They tell you how much has been used, not whether the client received value. Herrity also warns that token consumption is already becoming a real enterprise challenge, especially as firms move towards agentic workflows, where AI systems can loop, retry, reprocess and consume vastly more than anyone expected. His message is not "do not use AI", far from it, the message is: understand the economics before you build your future firm on assumptions that may not hold. Otherwise, we may finally escape the billable hour only to insert coins into a different machine.

Legora's June 2026 announcement that its most capable product, Agent Pro, will move to consumption-based pricing is an important signpost. It tells us that, as agents undertake more complex work, the commercial unit will move from seats bought to work done.

Think of it this way. Buying a powerful AI platform is a little like buying a Ferrari. The purchase price may get your attention, but it is the running costs that can really hurt: fuel, tyres, servicing, insurance, repairs and the rather expensive consequences of driving it badly. A Mini will also get you from A to B, but it does not consume the same resources every time you put your foot down.

The same is true of AI. A simple prompt or modest workflow may cost next to nothing. But a powerful agent working through hundreds of documents, calling sub-agents, retrying tasks, using premium models and looping through complex instructions can consume a great deal more. Firms need to understand what it costs to run the machine, not just what it costs to buy it. Otherwise, they may proudly acquire the Ferrari, hand everyone the keys, and only later discover that the fuel gauge has been falling at an alarming rate.

Firms will be able to see which matters, teams, and clients are consuming expensive agentic capacity. But the answer is not to turn around and send the client a bill for "1,847,392 tokens and three agent loops". Tokens are a cost of production, not a measure of value. The smarter firm will use that visibility to design matters better, set sensible assumptions and budgets, choose the right level of AI for the job, and price the client for the outcome, judgment, and responsibility delivered. Otherwise, we may swap one bad habit – recording every six minutes – for another: watching the meter spin while pretending that is strategy.

So, where does all this leave us? It means you need to understand your new cost base. Properly. Not vaguely. Not "Dave in IT says it is probably fine." Properly.

It also means AI strategy cannot be left to the keen lawyer who has discovered ChatGPT and is now wandering around the office like the second coming of Steve Jobs. Nor can it sit only with the innovation team. Your CIO and CFO need to be in the room. The decisions firms make now – about platforms, architecture, security, scalability, data access and governance – will shape cost and risk for years.

WORDS WITH THE WISE

Mark Barrett

Some people assume that if AI allows a task to be done more quickly, the work must automatically become cheaper. I do not think that is the right way to look at it. Yes, AI may reduce the time spent on a particular activity, but there is a lot of work that sits behind safe and effective AI use.

There is the cost of the tools. There is the cost of training. There is the cost of governance. There is the cost of compliance. There is the cost of configuring the systems. There is the cost of senior people designing, reviewing and supervising the process. There is the cost of building and maintaining the firm's knowledge and intellectual property inside the workflow. There is the cost of constant improvement.

That has to be recognised in the commercial model.

AI is not free magic. It may look like magic to the client when something happens quickly and elegantly, but the reason it works is because someone has designed the process, trained the people, built the controls and applied years of experience. A good illusionist may make the trick look effortless, but people are not paying only for the five minutes on stage. They are paying for the years of preparation, design, practice and expertise that make the five minutes possible.

BRACE YOURSELF...
incoming provocative statement

The client does not care how clever your prompt was. They care whether you helped them make a better decision.

WORDS WITH THE WISE

Mitch Kowalski

AI also changes the conversation about what should be charged to clients. To me, AI is overhead. It is the cost of doing business. It is like electricity, telephones, rent, technology systems or the tools you need to do your job. I do not want to see a separate line item for tokens. If a law firm sent me a bill with an AI token charge on it, I would go crazy. I would ask, "What are you even talking about?"

The firm should manage its pricing to cover its costs. That is what businesses do. But breaking out artificial little charges for technology usage is not helpful. It creates friction, invites challenge and makes clients wonder whether the firm is simply trying to recover its investment in a way that has nothing to do with value.

There is also a danger that token charging recreates the slowest horse problem. If one lawyer is poor at using the technology and uses more tokens, does the client pay more? That cannot be right. The client should not be penalised because the lawyer is inefficient with the tool.

The better answer is to agree the price based on the value, scope and risk of the work, and then let the firm decide how best to deliver it.

WORDS WITH THE WISE

Aku Sorainen

If you want to price properly, you still need to understand your cost base and your likely input. Value pricing does not mean guessing. It does not mean throwing away all management information. You need to know, at least as a bottom line, how much time and resource a particular type of matter is likely to require. Then you can decide how to price it.

One of the big opportunities with AI is that it can help us avoid loss-making matters. If you can see from your data that certain types of work have been profitable and others have not, you can make better decisions. You can budget better. You can price better. You can also ask better questions before you take on the work.

At the moment, around half of our work is done on fixed fees and around half on hourly rates. Some firms may already be further along the fixed-fee path, but we are moving in that direction. However, fixed fees create their own challenge. When lawyers work on a fixed fee, some of them stop recording time carefully because they think it no longer matters. Sometimes younger lawyers may stop recording time, because they might feel ashamed for having spent too much time on doing something.

That is a mistake.

Even if time is not used as the basis of the bill to the client, it still has value as management information. If you stop recording input, you lose the ability to learn. You lose the ability to understand whether the work was profitable. You lose the ability to improve budgeting. You lose the ability to see who contributed to the work and how.

There is a lot of discussion about measuring only output and results. Of course, output matters. But output is affected by many things you cannot directly control. The economy may be growing or declining. A matter may become more complicated than expected. Internal projects may take longer than planned. There are always variables you cannot know at the beginning.

That is why I do not think law firms should skip measuring input.

I am in favour of measuring inputs because they assist with budgeting properly for the future. If you record input and measure it consistently, you get better. Your tools get better. Your systems get better. Your processes get better. Your future estimates become more accurate even if the AI tools change your working processes.

WORDS WITH THE WISE

Andrew Allen

AI is not just an IT project. It has pricing consequences.

If a firm charges by the hour and AI reduces the time spent, the bill reduces. If the firm charges a fixed fee, it may keep the benefit of the saved time, but it still needs to understand the cost of the AI and whether the fixed fee was right.

There may be attempts to add AI as a separate bill line item. IT costs may now be too large simply to hide inside charge-out rates. But clients may challenge those charges, particularly if they think AI should have made the work cheaper.

The firm therefore needs to explain where the value sits: supervision, judgment, responsibility and risk.

8 PPP PENGUIN LOGIC

Clients do not buy AI. They buy clarity, confidence, progress, risk reduction, protection and better decisions. Price those things.

CLIENTS ARE REWRITING THE RULES

Clients are not waiting for law firms to work out their AI strategy, pricing model or internal politics, because some of them are already changing the rules for how outside counsel will be paid.

Meta has apparently updated its outside counsel billing guidelines to flag and refuse payment for tasks it believes could have been performed by AI. The Meta guidance was picked up by Ken Callender in his article *The Gap Is Closing: Why AI Is Breaking The Billable Hour Model*[8] which appeared in Above The Law.

Meta is not alone. Zscaler's published outside counsel billing guidelines[9] already state that any time or cost associated with AI-generated work product should not be passed on to the company. Callender's article states UBS is also reported to have updated its billing guidelines in early 2026 to include AI-specific provisions.

The message from major corporate clients is becoming very clear. If a machine can do the work, the client is increasingly unlikely to pay a lawyer's hourly rate for it.

That is important because a significant proportion of traditional associate billing has historically been built around tasks that are now within the capability of commercially available AI tools. Research summaries, first drafts, document review, chronology building, issue spotting, routine correspondence and basic analysis have all supported the leverage model for years, but clients are now starting to ask whether those activities still justify the same price when technology can perform some of them faster and more cheaply.

This is where the old model becomes exposed.

The firms most likely to thrive are the firms that have already thinking about the redesign of workflows so that AI deals with the commodity layer and lawyers charge properly for the judgment layer above it. Those firms will be able to explain what the technology did, what the lawyer checked, what judgment was applied, what risk was managed and what outcome was improved.

The firms still putting three associates on work that could largely be summarised, sorted or structured by AI may find their invoices coming back with red lines through them.

In May 2026, Revolut Bank announced it was replacing its traditional law firm panel with a dynamic model that reviews firms quarterly against performance metrics, pricing and responsiveness. Panel members need to apply every quarter.

What Revolut, Meta, Zscaler, and UBS appear to be doing is not just tinkering with billing guidelines. They are not waiting for regulators.

As Callander highlights, "The pace is accelerating with each model release. More importantly, what Meta, Zscaler and UBS are doing is something no previous technology cycle produced: clients imposing AI-efficiency standards on their outside counsel through private contract, faster and more precisely than any regulatory body could. This is the market doing what legislation cannot."

I suspect may other businesses will follow their lead.

BRACE YOURSELF…
incoming provocative statement

Time billing survived when clients could not see inside the work. AI changes that.

WORDS WITH THE WISE
Ben Weinberger

Clients are now driving this change. Some clients have already said they will not pay for work that AI could do. Clients also have access to AI tools themselves, and in some situations, they are getting a "good enough" answer without paying law firm rates.

THE PARTNERSHIP MODEL WAS BUILT FOR YESTERDAY

The billable hour is not just a pricing method; in many law firms, it is the operating system that drives staffing, leverage, supervision, partner compensation, budgeting, targets, associate career progression and the way success is measured.

Law firm economics has always depended on a fairly simple assumption: tomorrow will look enough like yesterday for the model to keep working. More people doing more work would record more hours, more hours would create more revenue, and more revenue would support partner profits.

AI puts pressure on that logic because it reduces the labour required to perform many tasks that have traditionally been billed by associates. If the work that once took ten hours now takes two, and the firm is still selling time, the economic foundation starts to wobble.

This is the burning platform for law firm leaders.

If AI can perform or assist with work that was previously used to generate associate hours, the revenue supporting partner profits comes under pressure. That does not mean lawyers become irrelevant, but it does mean the old leverage model becomes harder to defend if the firm continues to attach value to hours rather than outcomes. Activity is not value.

If your pricing model rewards activity, people will create activity. If your reporting celebrates hours, people will produce hours. If your partnership model rewards leverage, the business will become addicted to leverage. And if your culture treats busyness as proof of value, AI will feel like a threat rather than an opportunity.

But clients are not buying internal activity. They are buying outcomes, judgment, commercial insight, risk reduction, speed, certainty and accountability.

If a firm is still charging by the hour, clients know AI is being used, or soon will be used, and they will expect the hours and the bills to go down. That is entirely logical from the client's perspective, because if the stated unit of value is time, and AI reduces time, the client will expect a lower price.

The problem is not the client. The problem is the model.

If AI reduces the labour needed to achieve an outcome, the value cannot sensibly remain attached to the number of human hours recorded. The value has to migrate elsewhere. It has to move towards technology-enabled delivery, better systems, stronger processes, legal judgment, commercial acumen, strategic insight and the ability to help the client make better decisions.

That is a very different business model from simply putting more bodies on the work and billing the time.

The firms that understand this will redesign how work is scoped, staffed, delivered, priced and explained to clients. The firms that do not will try to preserve yesterday's economics with tomorrow's technology, which is unlikely to end well.

Shingles & Co. will tell itself that AI is just another tool and that the partnership model will carry on as normal.

Penguin logic says otherwise. If the work changes, the economics change. If the economics change, the model must change. And if the model must change, law firm leaders cannot leave this to the IT team.

BRACE YOURSELF…
incoming provocative statement

The partnership model was built to reward hours.
AI will reward firms that can price outcomes.

THE CLOCK IS NO LONGER THE PRODUCT: OUTCOMES ARE

Law firms need to stop thinking that they sell time, tasks, documents, cleverness or effort, because in an AI-enabled legal market many of those things will become easier to produce, easier to compare and harder to defend as the basis of price.

The future is not about selling hours. It is about selling Outcomes as a Service.

I once spoke with an immigration lawyer who believed she was selling "right to remain" certificates. During the conversation, her secretary grasped the bigger picture first: clients weren't buying forms – they were buying their future. The outcome was starting a new life, marrying, having children, or reuniting with family. Lawyers need to recognise they're not selling legal procedures – they're selling outcomes. And once you price outcomes, you leave the billable hour behind.

This is where many firms need to do some serious thinking.

- How do you differentiate your service beyond cost?
- What is the nature and depth of your relationship with the client compared with your competitors?
- Do you anticipate client needs before they have to ask?
- Are you genuinely the preferred choice for the clients you most want to act for?
- Do your rates, fees and pricing models properly reflect the value you deliver, or are you simply hoping that the client will not challenge the bill?
- Are you earning a premium for outstanding work, or are you doing premium work at commodity prices because you have never learned how to explain the value?

These are not soft questions.

They are commercial questions.

They are pricing questions.

They are survival questions.

If AI can help clients access information, generate first drafts, review documents, summarise material and produce basic legal outputs, then the value of lawyers will have to move away from simply what they know, what they can produce, how clever they are or how hard they work. Those things may still matter, but they will no longer be enough.

The value of lawyers will increasingly sit in *who* they are, *how* they relate to clients, *how* they exercise judgment, *how* they build trust, *how* they guide people through uncertainty, *how* they behave under pressure, and *how* they act as stewards, navigators and problem-solvers.

That is a very different proposition from "we record time and send you a bill".

PRICE THE MACHINE WORK DIFFERENTLY FROM THE HUMAN JUDGMENT

AUTOMATED WORK - THE WORK AI CAN HELP PRODUCE

Automated work is the specialised intellectual activity traditionally carried out by lawyers when generating legal outputs: researching, issue-spotting, summarising, synthesising, drafting, revising, comparing, reasoning and analysing.

For decades, this has made up a large part of lawyers' work and, therefore, a large part of lawyers' billed hours. In an AI-enabled legal market, much of this work will be done faster, cheaper and, in some cases, increasingly well by machines, either directly by clients, by in-house teams, or through systems and platforms that reduce the need for routine lawyer involvement.

That does not mean lawyers disappear.

It means lawyers need to be far clearer about where their real value sits.

The obvious starting point is routine, repeatable work The first draft. A first review. The long document that needs summarising. The chronology that needs building. The common issue that needs spotting. Much of that work can now be produced by AI. That does not remove the lawyer. It changes where the lawyer adds value.

None of that is the lawyer's competitive edge. In fact, much of it actively prevents senior lawyers from spending time where their edge really matters.

8 PPP PENGUIN LOGIC

If AI compresses production time, move the value conversation towards judgment, supervision, risk, accountability, speed, certainty and outcome.

So, the question for law firms is not whether automated work exists.

It does.

The better question is which parts of the firm's current work are routine enough, structured enough and low risk enough to be automated safely, and which parts must remain firmly in the hands of trained lawyers exercising judgment, accountability and commercial acumen.

BRACE YOURSELF…
incoming provocative statement

Clients will not pay premium prices for work they believe your software did and your lawyers merely glanced at.

WORDS WITH THE WISE

Mark Barrett

My central message to law firms is this: AI is not just another piece of software for the IT budget. It is a change in how work is done. That means it has to be treated as a business issue, a governance issue, a training issue, a pricing issue and a client communication issue.

Many firms have already deployed AI tools, or are about to. Some have invested in expensive legal AI platforms. Others have Microsoft Copilot sitting inside their existing environment and are not yet using it properly. In both cases, the risk is similar. Firms either assume the tool will solve the problem, or they assume their lawyers will instinctively know how to use it because they already know how to review documents, summarise matters, draft advice or conduct research.

That is a dangerous assumption.

AI changes the mechanics of the work. It changes the speed of production. It changes the review process. It changes where risk appears. It changes what junior lawyers need to learn and what senior lawyers need to supervise. It also changes the conversation with clients, because clients will increasingly want to know how AI is being used, whether it is safe, whether it improves the work and why they are being charged what they are being charged.

For law firm leaders, the question is no longer, "Should we use AI?" AI is already here. When even the Pope is talking about AI, it is difficult to pretend this is still niche, experimental or something that can be safely ignored. It has entered the mainstream, and law firms now need to decide how they will use it, govern it, explain it and price the work that flows from it.

The better question is, "What value are we trying to get from it, how do we use it safely, and how do we build that into the way we train, govern, price and explain our work?"

WHAT MUST STAY HUMAN?

As law firms become more confident using AI, there is a question they need to ask before everyone gets carried away with the shiny thing, and it is not simply, "What can we automate?" That question is too easy, because if you ask enough vendors, attend enough demos and watch enough excitable LinkedIn videos, the answer will appear to be almost everything.

The better question is, "What should we *not* automate?"

Just because a task can be pushed through a machine, accelerated by a prompt or wrapped inside a clever workflow does not mean it should be. Some parts of legal service are not valuable because they are fast; they are valuable because they are careful, contextual, human and wise.

Firms should be very cautious about automating:

Area	Why caution is needed
Final legal judgment	The lawyer must remain responsible for the final advice, recommendation and conclusion. AI can assist, but it should not be the final decision-maker.
Advice on high-risk or novel issues	Where the law is uncertain, the facts are unusual, or the consequences are serious, experience and judgment matter more, not less.
Emotional client counselling	Clients facing fear, grief, conflict, pressure or uncertainty need human understanding, not just machine-generated information.
Strategic negotiation calls	Negotiation often depends on timing, tone, leverage, trust, instinct and reading the room. That is not simply a data exercise.
Ethical decisions	Professional duties, conflicts, confidentiality, fairness and integrity require human accountability. These decisions should not be outsourced to software.
Matters requiring deep context	AI may miss the history, politics, personalities, relationships and commercial realities sitting behind the legal issue.
Decisions affecting liberty, livelihood, family, reputation or existential business risk	Where the consequences may change someone's life, business or future, the human lawyer must remain firmly in charge.

A client facing a difficult decision does not always need more information. In fact, they may already have too much information, with documents, reports, emails, advice notes, board papers, risk registers, search results and AI-generated summaries all sitting in front of them. What they need is someone with judgment who can identify the point that really matters, explain the risk that should not be ignored, challenge the tempting but dangerous option, and help them decide what to do next.

AI may help prepare the material, organise the facts, find patterns, produce a draft and suggest options, and that is all very useful if used sensibly. But the firm still has to decide where the human lawyer must remain firmly in charge, because professional responsibility, strategic advice, ethical accountability, emotional intelligence and high-consequence judgment are not things to be casually outsourced to software.

Shingles & Co. will ask, "Can we automate this?"

A better firm will ask, "Should we?" And that is a very different question.

BEWARE YOUR RABBIT WEIGHERS!

Let me explain – before you think I have completely lost the plot.

A number of years ago, I met a time and motion expert to talk about workflows in my own practice. He told me a story about some work he had done with a veterinary practice.

The process looked simple enough. An owner arrived with, a pet rabbit. Reception took the details. A nurse took the rabbit's temperature and weighed it. The information was passed to the vet. The vet came into the room, looked at the data, examined the rabbit and gave the diagnosis.

In theory, the whole process was meant to take a set number of minutes.

In practice, it always took longer.

When the time and motion expert looked at what was actually happening, he discovered the culprit. The vets kept weighing the rabbits.

Why?

Because they liked animals. More precisely, they liked holding them, cuddling them and having a little moment with them. Weighing the rabbit had become the excuse for doing the bit of the job they enjoyed, even though it was not always necessary for the process and it slowed it down.

That story has stayed with me.

In an AI world, law firm CEOs need to identify their rabbit weighers. These are the people still doing work that no longer needs to be done by them, or perhaps by anyone, because the old process gave them status, comfort, control or simply something they enjoyed. They may be lovely people, they may be excellent lawyers, they may even be doing it with the best of intentions, but if AI can remove, reduce or redesign that step, the firm has to ask the awkward question: "Are we doing this because it adds value for the client, or are we just weighing the rabbit?"

ACUMEN WORK – WHERE THE LAWYER STILL MATTERS MOST

This is where the future value of lawyers really starts to sit.

> Business acumen is learned, not inherited.
>
> **Warren Buffett**

WORDS WITH THE WISE

Wendy Jephson

The most valuable knowledge in a law firm is often the knowledge that is hardest to write down. It is the knowledge sitting inside experienced lawyers' heads. It is what they notice on a client call. It is why they pause before answering a question. It is the risk they see before anyone else sees it. It is the sense that something is missing, or that a particular line of enquiry matters, or that a client's real problem is not quite the problem they first described.

Experts often struggle to explain this because they just do it. They know what to do, but they may not immediately know how they know. You have to slow them down a little so they can unpack their own thinking.

AI can produce knowledge. It can summarise cases, review documents, draft clauses, compare contracts, extract risks, generate options and produce first-pass analysis. In some areas, it will do that faster than a human being, and in some areas, it may do it well enough for the client to start asking why a lawyer was needed at all.

So, the question becomes uncomfortable but unavoidable.

If AI can produce the information, what is the lawyer for?

The answer is not simply knowledge.

The answer is business acumen combined with legal judgment.

Lorna Khemraz makes this point beautifully in her Substack article, *The End Of The Billable Hour.*[10] Lorna gives the example of spending three weeks negotiating a master agreement with a strategic supplier. The contract eventually closed at version fourteen. But, as Lorna explains, the deal did not really turn on the redlines, it turned on a 15-minute call she made one Sunday night with the supplier's general counsel. No one talked about clauses, no one worked through a mark-up. They agreed how the two companies were going to work together for the next decade. As Lorna puts it, "The MSA codified a relationship that the call had already settled." Finance would have pointed to the redlines. The CEO would have pointed to the call. That is the gap.

And that gap is where acumen lives.

Lorna's examples are not "soft skills". They are not fluffy extras. They are acumen in action. Reading the room in a procurement negotiation, knowing which clause to give ground on because the relationship matters more than the indemnity cap. Anticipating that the CFO will ask about indemnities even though indemnities are not on the agenda. Closing down a fight between two business teams before they realise they are about to have one. Knowing when to send the one-line email and when to pick up the phone. Holding the line when the rest of the deal team has stopped noticing because they have stopped caring. Comforting a founder at midnight before a sale. That is not admin. That is not document production. That is the lawyer shaping the situation.

The problem is that the billable hour was never designed to see that work. It counted time, it counted redlines, it counted drafts, it counted activity. It did not count influence, leverage, calibration, presence or judgment operating inside a commercial relationship. For years, that did not matter quite so much because the document and the value were bundled together. Pay for the contract and you also got the relationship. Pay for the hours and you also got the judgment. But AI is now pulling those things apart. The document can be produced faster, the redline can be generated, and the first draft can be automated. What remains is the part nobody has properly labelled, developed, measured or priced: the lawyer's business acumen.

If law firms continue to price the artefact, they will be competing with tools. If they learn to price the situation they shape, the risk they reduce, the confidence they create, the judgment they bring and the commercial outcome they help deliver, they have a future. Outcomes, not hours. Acumen, not activity.

Helping clients make difficult decisions. Navigating uncertainty. Understanding context. Managing risk. Being present during some of the hardest moments in a person's life or a company's existence. Explaining not only what the law says, but what the client should sensibly do in their particular circumstances.

AI may help generate the material.

The lawyer must help make sense of it.

WORDS WITH THE WISE

Chantal McNaught

Legal services are "credence goods" – a term used by economists to explain the challenge with describing value when there is a knowledge asymmetry between the lawyer and the client. The lawyer understands the components of the work better than the client. That is not unique to law. A computer repair shop is also selling a credence good. If your laptop breaks and the repair shop quotes you more than the cost of the laptop, you may struggle to understand why. The repair shop knows what is involved. You do not.

Legal services work in a similar way. The client often cannot see the value because they cannot see the knowledge, experience and judgment required in the production of the service. That is one reason time-based billing has stuck for so long in professional services. Time became a proxy. It was a way of saying: this is how much effort went into the work.

But time is not the same thing as value.

Clients want the best possible legal outcome for their facts and circumstances, and when the law is uncertain, they want to understand the alternatives, the risks, the likely outcomes and the likely costs. They want to manage legal risk in a measured way, and they want to trust that their lawyer is bringing wisdom, experience, empathy and great judgment to the problem, not merely producing information.

So, law firms need to ask themselves some harder questions.

- Why exactly are clients paying us?
- What outcomes do they value?
- What do they need from us that AI cannot provide on its own?
- How do we help them make better decisions?
- How do we reduce risk, create certainty, protect relationships, improve commercial outcomes and bring calm to difficult situations?
- What makes us the wise, trusted, ethical expert rather than simply another producer of legal documents?

Because that is where the pricing opportunity sits.

The future is not about charging for knowledge that AI can produce. It is about charging for the acumen and judgment that make that knowledge valuable. If you don't believe me… read the quote below. It appeared in the Financial Times in an article about how Australian law firms are taking a lead on navigating best use of AI.[11]

> Pricing has to be anchored in the value we deliver to clients, not the hours we record. We're building a firm that wins on the quality of our thinking and the results we deliver for clients. That's where the real margin is.
>
> **Virginia Briggs**
> **Chief Executive MinterEllison**
> **Financial Times, 15th May 2026**

WORDS WITH THE WISE

Chantal McNaught

When AI produces something that sounds like us, lawyers can feel as though they are looking into a black mirror. It sounds like me, but it is not me. That can feel threatening. But the threat often comes from misunderstanding what clients actually buy from lawyers.

Clients are not buying the paperwork.

That is one of the most important points I would make. No one buys the paperwork. The paperwork itself is not the value. The contract, the form, the pleading, the letter, the advice note – those are often the artefacts of the work, but they are not the whole of the work.

Clients are buying assistance with reality.

They are buying the conversation in which the lawyer helps them understand what has happened, what matters, what the risks are, what choices they have, and what the consequences may be. They are buying the ability to say, "Walk me through what you think you have agreed," and then to help both sides express that agreement in terms they can live with and are less likely to dispute.

A client with a family law problem is not really buying a document. They may be frightened, distressed, confused or angry. A client in a shareholder dispute may not understand why a former business partner is acting in a particular way. A client in a transaction may not understand what still needs to happen before completion. The value is not merely in text generation. The value is in helping that client navigate the problem.

WORDS WITH THE WISE

Felix Riley

Law is an obvious target for the AI industry. It is a huge global market. It is rules-based. It is document heavy. It has precedent, process, regulation, complexity and margin. If you were designing a sector for AI vendors to go after, law would be close to perfect.

So, I understand why the noise is so loud.

But noise is not strategy.

My concern is not that law firms will use AI. Of course they will. My concern is that some firms will over-believe the hype, rush into adoption without thinking properly about return, hollow out their junior ranks, become dependent on a small number of dominant AI providers, and then discover that they have given away the very thing clients actually value.

That thing is not process.

It is judgment.

It is wisdom.

WORDS WITH THE WISE

Robert Hanna

The first thing I would say to law firms is this: do the internal audit before you go shopping.

A lot of firms are spending serious money on technology. Some of that money will be well spent. Some of it will not. The question is not simply, "Have we bought AI?" the question is, "Have we bought the right thing, for the right reason, to solve the right problem?"

I think this is where a lot of people go wrong. They have not looked properly at what they already have. They have not asked whether existing systems are being used properly. I am guilty of this myself. I probably do not know 80 per cent of what some existing tools can already do. There are powerful things already sitting inside firms that are not being used.

Then along comes a legal tech company with a very polished sales process, and firms buy something new because it sounds exciting.

That is not innovation. That is procurement with a dopamine hit.

BRACE YOURSELF…
incoming provocative statement

The task is not the value. The judgment is.

THE PRICING MODEL HAS TO CHANGE

Guess what? I am in favour of value-based pricing. "Quelle surprise", I hear you say.

But this is not because I have written books about value-based pricing, talk about value-based pricing, train law firms on value-based pricing, and occasionally bore perfectly nice people at conferences about value-based pricing. It is because AI makes the old pricing model harder to defend. The pricing model has to move from hours recorded to outcomes delivered.

When you get to the end of this book, I hope you will be convinced that pricing the value you create is something you need to do. Then guess what… you can buy *Ditch The Billable Hour!* if you have not done so already and learn how to implement value-based pricing. James, my publisher, will be delighted!

The real question for law firms is this: If you cannot sensibly bill your effort by the hour, what exactly are you asking clients to pay for?

That question takes you straight to the financial foundation of the business. A law firm still has a cost base, as we saw earlier. Even if you operate in a leaner, more virtual way, the firm still has to fund the capability required to deliver legal outcomes properly.

So let us be clear. Value-based pricing does not mean ignoring cost.

It means understanding cost, then pricing by reference to the value created for the client rather than simply adding up time spent by the lawyer.

The value you create for clients will never be captured properly by the time required to deliver it. A brilliant advocate may develop a case-changing strategy in eight hours. A commercially astute lawyer may spot the one issue in a transaction that changes the client's negotiating position. An experienced employment lawyer may prevent a dispute escalating by saying exactly the right thing at exactly the right moment. A private client lawyer may bring calm, structure and judgment to a family situation that could otherwise become destructive.

None of that value is properly measured by the clock.

The client is not buying the hours.

The client is buying the result, the confidence, the decision support, the risk reduction, the commercial protection, the strategic advantage and the reassurance that someone with judgment and acumen is helping them reach the right outcome. Indeed, a Beaton Research piece suggests clients *may well pay more.*[12] Libby Maynard reported, "The firms that can clearly articulate the upside or the avoided downside of their advice are the ones that get price uplift."

That is what law firms need to learn to price.

Value-based pricing does not mean vague pricing. In fact, it requires better scoping, not worse. The firm must define precisely what the client will receive, how many documents will be reviewed, what level of analysis will be provided, what issues will be covered, what will be excluded, what deliverables will be produced, when they will be delivered and what assumptions sit behind the price.

Clear scope protects both sides.

It helps the client understand exactly what they are buying, and it helps the firm avoid scope creep that quietly destroys margin.

This is where many firms get nervous, because hourly billing has allowed them to avoid some of the hard thinking. If the work expands, the hours expand. If the matter becomes messy, the bill grows. If the scope was never properly agreed, the time still gets recorded.

Value-based pricing forces the firm to think earlier, scope better, communicate more clearly and understand the client's desired outcome before work begins.

That is not a weakness. That is better lawyering. The pricing model has to change because the work is changing.

And if the work changes but the pricing model does not, the firm will either give away the benefits of AI to the client or try to defend a billing model that clients increasingly understand no longer makes sense.

> Lawyers must learn to accept no one has a silver bullet perfect solution that many committees seem to be waiting for.
>
> Many firms that wait for the proven perfect solution could go out of business before it arrives.
>
> **Jim Hassett, Client Value and Law Firm Profitability**

SOME SAY... THE BILLABLE HOUR WILL SURVIVE

There will be plenty of people, maybe even some in your firm, who will tell you that the billable hour is not going anywhere.

In a thoughtful and well-written article *How The Billable Hour Can Survive AI,*[13] Jonah E. Perlin, Professor of Law, Legal Practice and Senior Fellow at the Center on Ethics and the Legal Profession at Georgetown University Law Center, explains how the billable hour may survive generative AI, not because AI will leave legal work untouched, but because hourly billing is deeply embedded in law firm economics, client monitoring, internal performance measurement and the way firms organise themselves.

Perlin argues that we should not assume that faster work automatically means the end of time-based billing, and he uses his "CHRGE" equation to show that hours are only one part of a wider financial model involving rates, reductions, expenses and firm compensation.

I recommend you read the article, you will need to know the billable hours survival strategy!

I think the billable hour may become like scurvy. Once, scurvy was everywhere. Then we learned what caused it, learned how to prevent it, and it became something that properly belonged to the past. Yet even now, small pockets still appear when people ignore the basics.

The billable hour may follow the same path. In an AI-enabled legal market, it should become an outdated condition: largely eradicated, widely understood to be unhealthy, but still found in small pockets where firms have failed to change.

The cure is not vitamin C. It is better scoping, better pricing, better communication and the courage to charge for value rather than time.

You may well believe the billable hour can survive AI. But then ask the more important question: should it?

Remember, Paradigm shifters ask *why* we do things the way we do. Not preserve the status quo. Just because a model can limp on, supported by habit, infrastructure, fear and internal accounting convenience, does not mean it is the right model for clients, lawyers or the future of the profession. Generative AI gives law firms the chance to stop pricing effort and start pricing outcomes, judgment, certainty, responsibility and value.

The danger is not that the billable hour cannot survive. The danger is that it will.

REGULATORS WILL HAVE THEIR SAY

This is not a book about legal ethics, professional conduct or the detailed rules governing what lawyers can and cannot do with AI. But regulators will have their say. Some are ahead of the game. Others, including England and Wales, are not,[14]

In Texas, a recent ethics opinion on generative AI and legal billing made the point very clearly: a lawyer may charge for the time actually spent using a generative AI tool, refining its output and checking the work, but may not charge hourly fees for the time "saved" by using that tool.[15]

That is where AI changes the conversation. If AI enables a task to be completed in two hours rather than ten, the lawyer cannot simply bill the missing eight hours because that is what the work used to take. Those hours were not worked. They were saved.

Guess what? That is another push away from hourly billing.

The State of Victoria in Australia is already pointing firms in that direction. The Victorian Legal Services Board and Commissioner has published guidance on innovative pricing and agreed pricing models, including material comparing agreed pricing with hourly rates. That is the direction of travel.

Regulators may not tell every firm to adopt value-based pricing, but the message is becoming clearer: if technology changes how legal work is delivered, lawyers must think carefully about how legal work is charged.

The safer answer is not to pretend AI has no effect or wait for regulation.

The better answer is to move from billing time to pricing value.

THIS IS A BOARDROOM ISSUE

The change of business model then becomes a board issue. In legal services, the billable hour is not merely a pricing mechanism, it is the operating system on which much of the traditional law firm business model has been built.

It is not just a way of charging clients. It is a way of organising the business.

And that is precisely the problem.

The billable hour is fundamentally misaligned with the value clients receive. It rewards time spent rather than outcomes achieved, activity rather than progress, effort rather than impact, and internal leverage rather than client benefit.

That may have worked when clients had fewer alternatives, less data, less transparency and less ability to challenge how legal work was produced. But AI changes the context. It does not simply make some legal work faster. It exposes the weakness of a business model that has historically treated time as a proxy for value.

Once technology reduces the labour required to produce certain legal outputs, the old equation starts to break. More hours no longer automatically mean more value. More people on the job no longer automatically mean better service. More activity no longer justifies a bigger bill.

AI will not just speed up legal work, it will reshape the legal market. It will create new services, new competitors, new pricing models and new client expectations. The firms that thrive will not be the firms that simply "use AI" while leaving everything else untouched. They will be the firms prepared to rethink how legal work is governed, sold, priced, insured, staffed and delivered. That is a much bigger issue than technology adoption. It is about the architecture of the firm.

George Beaton in his article *Why The Era Of The Professional Services Pyramid Has Passed* [16] argued that the firms that survive will not be those that defend the old pyramid, but those that design a new architecture of professionalism, one that aligns technology, talent, economics and purpose. That phrase matters because the old pyramid was built for a world where junior labour could be leveraged, recorded and billed. AI puts pressure on that model because it reduces the need for some of that labour, while increasing the need for judgment, acumen, supervision, governance, client understanding and strategic advice.

In their 62-page paper, *Fighting the Hypothetical: Why Law Firms Should Rethink the Billable Hour in the Generative AI Era,*[17] Nancy B. Rapoport and Joseph R. Tiano Jr. explain that if GenAI weakens the old law firm pyramid, firms may need to think about very different shapes. They introduce some new and exciting models!

- A rocket model would have a smaller launch base but more powerful, technology-enabled senior expertise driving matters forward.

- A diamond model would place more emphasis on experienced mid-level lawyers, supported by fewer juniors and fewer equity partners.
- A starfish model would be more decentralised, with specialist teams forming around client needs rather than rigid hierarchy.
- A cylinder model would flatten the structure, with fewer dramatic differences between layers.

Lewis Silkin Partner, Roch Glowacki, speaking on Rob Hanna's excellent podcast *The Legally Speaking Podcast* in May 2026[18] introduces another shape – the "hourglass" career model. Juniors may move from the bottom of the hourglass towards senior, partner-level contribution far faster than under the old apprenticeship model, where years of time-recording, document production and supervised repetition were treated as the route to maturity.

In his book published in May 2026, *Law In The Era of AI*,[19] lawyer Bjarne Tellmann discusses both the diamond and hourglass model and then throws in the inverted pyramid and boutique models.

This book is (thankfully for me!) not about what shape your firm should become. Take your pick! But you will appreciate that there is lots of thought going into what needs to change in the legal sector. All of the models make the same uncomfortable point. AI is not just changing how legal work is delivered. It may change how lawyers are trained, how careers are built, and how law firms justify the shape of their businesses.

WORDS WITH THE WISE

Sam Stamp

My advice to law firm leaders is to start with the business model, not the technology.

Ask where your revenue comes from. Ask which parts are most vulnerable. Ask which client relationships are truly defensible. Ask what clients are beginning to do for themselves. Ask where legal tech providers might disintermediate you. Ask where you have knowledge that could be structured, productised, or used to create a more continuous relationship.

Then ask whether your firm has the capabilities to respond.

Do you understand product development? Do you have a sales function that can sell productised services? Do your incentives support collaboration? Do your partners know why they should contribute their knowledge? Do you have a way of getting expertise out of people's heads? Do you listen to clients properly? Do you have pricing models that reflect value rather than time?

This is not easy. It is genuinely hard. I think managing partners today are facing a bigger change than many of their predecessors had to manage. The old assumptions about leverage, utilisation, revenue and growth are under pressure at the same time as clients are becoming more sophisticated and technology providers are becoming more ambitious.

But there is also a real opportunity.

Law firms have expertise, trust, relationships, judgment and practical experience. Those things are valuable. The challenge is to package, price, communicate and deliver them in ways that make sense in an AI-enabled market.

The firms that do that well will not simply be faster versions of their old selves. They will be different kinds of businesses.

WORDS WITH THE WISE

Heather Suttie

The structure of many law firms is also under pressure. The traditional pyramid model depends on junior lawyers doing work at the bottom, with that work supporting the economics of the firm. If AI removes or reduces that work, the structure becomes difficult to sustain.

That also creates a partnership problem. Younger lawyers may ask who will buy them out in 20 years if the junior ranks have been reduced and the traditional model no longer works.

This is not just a technology issue. It is a structural issue.

David C. Baker (TRIGGER WARNING! … Baker is NOT a lawyer) in his article *If I Started A Brand New Firm* [20] asks a wonderfully dangerous question: what would you do if you were starting a professional services firm from scratch? It is a question law firm owners should spend much more time with.

Baker's answer is not to polish yesterday's model, bolt on some technology, write a few new policies and hope the structure survives. He invites a much more fundamental redesign. Who should own the firm? Who should lead it? How should it be positioned? Which clients should it serve? What should it be famous for? How should it price? What should it refuse to do? How should accountability work?

Those are not cosmetic questions. They go to the design of the enterprise.

That is the same challenge now facing law firms. The question is not: how do we preserve the firm we inherited? Nor is it: how do we add AI to the old machine without upsetting too many people? The better question is: what would we build if we were starting today, knowing what we now know about AI, client expectations, pricing pressure, talent, technology and value?

Baker says: "Surely we need some new thinking in this field?"

He is right.

Law firms need that new thinking urgently. They need the courage to stop treating the existing model as sacred and start making deliberate choices.

- Which clients do we really want?
- Which work should we do?
- Which work should we stop doing?
- What judgment do we sell?
- What data do we need?
- What technology do we trust?
- How will we price certainty, risk reduction, speed, acumen and outcomes?
- Which behaviours will we no longer tolerate?

The most powerful line in Baker's article is this: "Think bigger, my friends."

That should be pinned to every managing partner's wall or at least put on a T shirt.

Redesigning a law firm is not reckless. The reckless thing is pretending the current design will survive untouched. Brave owners will not simply bolt AI onto the billable hour and call it innovation. They will build firms that are clearer, better positioned, more accountable and more useful to clients.

So, the question is no longer: "How do we preserve the old pyramid?" The question is:

"What should replace it?"

In-house legal teams are already moving in this direction. The KPMG In-house Counsel Report 2026[21] found that legal operations are modernising, technology is improving efficiency across a wide range of legal activities, and organisations are reconsidering how legal services should be priced. Most strikingly, 87% of respondents said value or outcome-based pricing models are better aligned with their expectations than traditional time-based billing.

That is not a small signal. It is a warning light on the dashboard.

Clients are not simply asking firms to use technology. They are asking why the commercial model has not changed when the delivery model has. Law firms cannot keep telling clients that AI makes them faster, better and more efficient while pricing the work as if nothing has changed.

Firms need to move away from a default model that treats time as the central unit of value, and towards models that price outcomes, certainty, risk reduction, speed, judgment, acumen and commercial impact. That is business model redesign.

WORDS WITH THE WISE

Mitch Kowalski

I come at this from an in-house perspective, and also from inside a technology company. The internal in-house conversation is very different from the traditional law firm conversation.

In our world, the question is not, "How do we preserve the existing legal services model?" The question is, "How do we get the work done properly, manage risk, and use technology so that we do not have to keep spending so much money externally?"

At the moment, the money spent on external counsel is significantly higher than the money spent on the internal legal team. The goal is to invert that. Not by hiring hundreds of additional lawyers, but by using technology properly, building internal capability and using external lawyers only when they are truly needed.

That is the direction I think many in-house teams will eventually move in. Some will move slowly, because fear is still a big factor. But the direction of travel is clear. Clients are going to become much more disciplined about what they send out, why they send it out and what they are prepared to pay for.

The starting point for law firms is to ask a simple question: what are clients really buying from you?

From where I sit, we can do a lot ourselves. We can draft. We can review. We can summarise. We can use technology to help us understand documents, compare clauses, translate material, prepare first drafts and identify issues. Knowledge itself is not enough. Drafting itself is not enough. The paper is not the value.

The value is judgment and commerciality.

That is the sweet spot for external lawyers. If my internal team does not have the judgment, the commercial experience or the confidence to make the call, then there may be a reason to go outside. If the matter is complex enough, valuable enough or risky enough, then there may be a reason to involve external counsel. But that is a much narrower category of work than many law firms would like to believe.

For example, we may handle acquisitions and divestitures internally up to a significant level. A $50 million transaction may not need to go outside. A billion-dollar deal probably would. There is a threshold of complexity, value and risk that drives the decision. But the days when work was automatically sent to a large law firm simply because that was the safe thing to do are being challenged.

That does not mean every in-house team is already there. Many are not. There are still in-house lawyers who send work out because they are afraid. They worry that if something goes wrong, their job will be on the line. If they use a big brand firm and something goes wrong, at least they can say they chose the safe option. It is the old "nobody ever got fired for buying IBM" mentality.

That fear will not disappear overnight. It requires leadership from the general counsel or chief legal officer. Someone has to say, "Make the calls. Use the tools. Manage the risk. Of course mistakes may happen, but make sure they are not really big mistakes." Without that leadership, the old habits will continue.

But as internal legal teams become more confident, law firms need to understand the consequence. If in-house teams take back the ordinary, run-of-the-mill work, large law firms have a problem. A lot of what they currently sell is not "bet the farm" work. If clients decide they can do that work themselves, accept the risk and avoid paying a premium, then the traditional model becomes much harder to defend.

8 PPP PENGUIN LOGIC

Do not sell AI as cheap law. Sell better law, clearer law, faster insight and more useful legal judgment.

BRACE YOURSELF…
incoming provocative statement

If your price is based on hours, AI makes you cheaper. If your price is based on outcomes, AI can make you more valuable.

WORDS WITH THE WISE

Kerry Jack

I think law firms need to start by understanding that AI is not just something they buy and put into the business. It changes the way they talk about themselves, the way clients see them and the way they explain their value.

In my world, the same thing has happened in communications. Thirty years ago, I might have walked into a client's office with a big book of press cuttings and said, "Look at all this coverage we've got you." That was the proof of value. Now, clients are much more interested in whether the coverage was seen by the right people and whether it made those people act in the right way. It is less about volume and more about outcomes.

That feels very similar to what is happening in law. It is no longer enough to say, "We reviewed 20,000 documents." The client wants to know what that achieved. What problem did it solve? What outcome did it deliver? What risk did it reduce? What decision did it help them make?

That is where law firms need to move their thinking.

WORDS WITH THE WISE

Heather Suttie

The real opportunity is not only practice innovation. Using AI for legal research, document review and drafting is becoming table stakes.

The bigger question is business innovation.

Many firms appoint innovation leaders who focus on practice innovation, but the real issue is that the business model itself is changing. Transforming the model requires business expertise, not legal expertise.

The CEO, Managing Partner and senior leadership team need to place AI firmly inside the firm's business strategy. The real question is not "Which tool should we buy?" The real question is "What sort of legal business are we building?"

If the firm wants lawyers to price confidently in an AI-enabled world, those lawyers need more than enthusiasm and a login. They need structure, reliable data, clear guidance, worked examples, approved pricing options, client messaging and a firmwide position they can understand and explain.

Leaders need to ask where pricing pressure is already being felt in each practice area, where clients are challenging bills, where AI may reduce labour, where the firm is still relying on old assumptions, and where new pricing models may be needed.

They also need to understand which parts of the business create genuine client value, which parts create avoidable cost, and which parts are simply "how we have always done it".

That requires better data. The firm should be asking what its data reveals about pricing trends, client behaviour, margin leakage, matter types, scope creep, discounting habits and future opportunities. It should also ask whether predictive analytics and data visualisation can help identify pricing patterns, support better decision-making and improve operational efficiency.

But data on its own is not enough.

Leaders need governance, policy and oversight. They need to decide which pricing models are approved, when alternative fee arrangements should be used, who can approve non-standard arrangements, how AI-enabled work should be scoped, how value should be explained to clients, and how lessons learned should be captured and shared.

Some existing policies may need to be amended. Some may need to be ditched.

WORDS WITH THE WISE

Heather Suttie

Leadership matters. Many law firm leaders are not equipped to drive this kind of transformation. Some are elected because of seniority, not because they have business acumen or strategic vision.

Some leaders also avoid difficult conversations because they need to keep partners onside. That makes real change harder.

Firms need leaders who are willing to make difficult decisions about the business model, not just the technology.

Leadership will also have to make difficult decisions about which work to keep, which work to commoditise, and which work to stop doing. This will also impact people the firm employs. Law firms are not private members clubs; they are lean businesses that must be bottom-line driven to survive.

WORDS WITH THE WISE

Karolina Šilingienė

When I speak with law firms about technology and AI, I often see the same issue. Everyone hopes AI will be the silver bullet, but AI can only work with the information it can access. If a firm's operational data is sitting in old, clunky, on-premise systems, or in separate spreadsheets, Outlook folders, practice management systems and people's heads, then the AI does not have much useful intelligence to work with.

That is why I think law firms need to put their house in order. Before AI can properly help you, the firm needs to structure the information it already has. There is a lot of attention on AI tools that help lawyers draft faster, review documents faster or prepare legal advice faster. Those tools are important, but I am also interested in the back end of the law firm: the way the firm actually operates.

There are so many patterns sitting inside a law firm. Write-offs. Invoice corrections. Discounts. Old habits. The same people being staffed on the same types of work. The same teams being formed in the same way, even when there may be a more efficient way of doing the work. The data is there, but often nobody is analysing it properly.

In the *Law in the Era of AI,* Bjarne Tellmann[22] gives a warning: "Success for firms will increasingly depend on understanding the jobs they're being hired to do and configuring themselves to deliver those jobs in the best way. The key questions they should ask are:

- What are the jobs to be done for clients in the AI era?
- Which ones are we most vulnerable to being 'fired' from?
- Which new jobs will clients be unlikely to hire us for at all?"

Culture is important, too. A firm cannot build a better pricing model if its culture still worships hours, celebrates busyness, and treats innovative pricing as a dangerous hobby for the brave. Leaders need to get lawyers, finance, BD, innovation, operations, risk and knowledge teams working together, rather than operating as separate tribes with separate agendas.

The question is not simply whether the firm can create new pricing models. The question is whether the firm can get its people to use them.

That means training lawyers to articulate value, involve clients earlier, scope work properly, understand commercial outcomes, use data intelligently and stop defaulting to hourly rates because they feel safe. Pricing is not an administrative afterthought at the end of a matter. It is part of the client relationship, part of the service proposition and part of the firm's strategy.

AI has the potential to create a productivity revolution in legal services. But productivity only becomes a business advantage if the firm knows how to price, package, explain and deliver the value created.

Shingles & Co. will ask IT to buy the tool, tell lawyers to use it and then wonder why clients start asking for discounts.

Better firms will understand that AI, pricing, data, governance, culture and client value now belong in the same leadership conversation.

The billable hour may survive in some firms and for some clients. But as the default operating system for the modern legal business, it is under pressure.

And this time, the pressure is not coming from pricing consultants, conference speakers or penguins with strong opinions.

It is coming from clients.

Leaders need to lead.

Over the last five decades of studying organizational change, I've witnessed several "technological revolutions"… from the advent of the personal computer to the rise of the internet and the shift to the cloud. But the sheer velocity of Artificial Intelligence is unlike anything we have encountered before.

In my conversations with my teams and leaders around the world, I am seeing a very familiar pattern emerge. Organizations are rushing to buy licenses, launch experiments, and draft "AI strategies". The result? A massive amount of activity, but a severe lack of measurable business value.

When technology moves this fast, it triggers our hardwired "Survive" response. Your workforce is looking at AI and feeling a profound sense of uncertainty and anxiety about their roles and their future. You cannot mandate change and expect to see value in this environment.

The organizations that will lead in this era are not those with the best technology or the best tools; they are the ones that intentionally activate the "Thrive" channel and shift their teams from a mindset of fear to one of opportunity.

John Kotter, May 2026

WORDS WITH THE WISE

Sam Stamp

For many years, law firms have been able to predict their revenue with a reasonable degree of confidence. They knew how many partners they had, how many associates they had, what utilisation looked like, and how much work was likely to come in. That model was not perfect, but it was familiar. AI makes that much less certain.

The question is no longer simply, "Can we use technology to do the work faster?" The better questions are: which parts of our revenue are most at risk, which parts are defensible, what do clients really need from us, and how do we build services that keep us relevant?

That matters because law firms are not only competing with other law firms anymore. They are competing with legal technology providers, AI platforms, alternative providers and, increasingly, clients' own internal capabilities. Those competitors often understand product development and sales better than law firms do. That is a real risk.

I think law firms need to be much more deliberate about where their future revenue is going to come from.

For a long time, many firms have been able to model the future by looking at the past. They could say, "This is what our partners billed last year, this is what our associates billed, this is our utilisation, and therefore next year should look broadly similar, plus a bit of growth." That has worked for a long time.

I am not convinced it will continue to work in the same way.

We may all be overestimating how quickly things will change. It may be that next year looks a lot like this year, except with much bigger external technology costs sitting in the IT budget. But the strategic uncertainty is real. Firms are spending serious money on tools such as Harvey and Legora, yet many are not properly measuring return on investment. At a breakfast we hosted, we asked a group of law firm leaders how many of them had Harvey or Legora. They all had one of them. We then asked how many were measuring ROI. No one said they were.

That is a problem. Obviously!

If firms are going to spend heavily on AI, they need to know what it is for. Is it to reduce cost? Is it to improve margin? Is it to create new services? Is it to protect existing relationships? Is it to sell something different? Or is it simply a defensive move because everyone else appears to be doing it?

The firms that do best will be the ones that stop treating this as just an IT project and start treating it as a strategic business question.

WORDS WITH THE WISE

Aku Sorainen

A point I feel strongly about is leadership. I am surprised that so few senior law firm leaders attend legal technology conferences. You often see heads of IT and innovation people there, but not enough senior partners, managing partners or CEOs.

That is a problem because senior leadership sets the direction of the firm.

Technology is moving so quickly, and there are now so many legal tech companies, that it is very difficult for heads of IT alone to navigate the whole environment. Their natural responsibility is to keep the systems safe, manage risk and avoid unnecessary disruption. That is important, but it can also mean they become the brakes on innovation.

Senior leadership must not simply delegate the technology to the IT as that may mean they delegate a large element of the future of the firm.

The senior leaders need to understand what is happening in the technology environment. They need to decide what the firm should try, what risks it is prepared to take, what direction it wants to move in, and what responsibility leadership will accept. Innovation cannot just be an IT project. It has to be a leadership issue.

At the same time, many lawyers are still making enough money in the old way. That is one of the reasons change is difficult. The house is not burning enough yet. When firms are still profitable, it is hard to persuade partners that the business model needs to change.

But that comfort is dangerous.

The future will require firms to be more collaborative, more disciplined with data, more thoughtful about pricing and more serious about leadership. AI will not reward firms that simply add new tools on top of old habits. It will reward firms that understand their own knowledge, organise it properly, measure what matters and use technology to improve the way they serve clients.

WORDS WITH THE WISE

Robert Hanna

Leadership means very little if it is not followed by action. You can say all the right things about innovation, culture and values, but people watch what you actually do.

I heard William Peake, the Global Managing Partner of Harneys, one of the world's leading offshore law firms, make a point that stayed with me. One of the best questions you can ask is: when was a time you lost trust in your current employer, and what did they do to win it back?

That is a great question because every organisation gets things wrong. Every leader makes mistakes. The issue is not whether trust is ever dented. The issue is whether you notice, own it and rebuild it.

In law firms, this matters enormously. If leaders talk about change but avoid difficult conversations, fail to call out behaviour that contradicts the firm's values or refuse to act when the model needs to change, people notice. Trust leaks away.

The leaders who will do well in this next phase are the ones who are curious, visible, prepared to learn and willing to act. They will not just sit behind the desk. They will go to events, listen, network, shape conversations and bring ideas back into the firm.

The people I see cutting through are the ones who are out there. They are at conferences. They are at Legal Tech events. They are listening to founders, clients, technologists and other law firm leaders. They are not waiting for the future to arrive in an email.

CRIB SHEET

P#1

QR Code	Title	Author / Source	Link
READ			
	AI & Client Value: How Legal Professionals Can Transform AI Adoption into Competitive Advantage and Client Benefit	Colin Levy	https://www.colinslevy.com/post/ai-client-value
	Does AI signal the end of the billable hour?	Ken Crutchfield	https://abovethelaw.com/legal-innovation-center/2024/01/23/does-ai-signal-the-end-of-the-billable-hour/
	Money Spent, Earned, and Prompted – A Special Briefing	Brainyacts	https://thebrainyacts.beehiiv.com/products/money-spent-earned-and-prompted-a-brainyacts-special-briefing
	Build what only you can build. Don't be the OS	Christian Brown	https://www.linkedin.com/pulse/build-what-only-you-can-dont-os-christian-brown-oiatc/
	Bride of the Token Cost Panic	Ryan McClead	https://www.geeklawblog.com/2026/06/bride-of-the-token-cost-panic.html
	Out of Tokens: Insert Coin(s) to Continue	Alex Herrity	https://lawwhatsnext.substack.com/p/out-of-tokens-insert-coins-to-continue

	The Gap Is Closing: Why AI Is Breaking The Billable Hour Model	Ken Callander	https://xira.com/p/2026/04/28/the-gap-is-closing-why-ai-is-breaking-the-billable-hour-model/
	Zscaler Outside Counsel Billing Guidelines	Zscaler	https://www.zscaler.com/legal/outside-counsel-billing-guidelines
	The End of the Billable Hour	Lorna Khemraz	https://substack.com/home/post/p-195723643
	Australian law firms are taking a lead on navigating best use of AI	Financial Times	https://www.ft.com/content/63e1f03f-9b98-4c02-a268-08e6713bd561?syn-25a6b1a6=1
	Pricing trends: When clients are willing to pay more	Beaton Research	https://beatonglobal.com/when-clients-are-prepared-to-pay-more?utm_source=Linkedinpost
	How The Billable Hour Can Survive AI	Jonah Perlin	https://scholarship.law.georgetown.edu/facpub/2694/
	Tell us the rules for using AI in court, say solicitors	Law Society Gazette	https://www.lawgazette.co.uk/news/tell-us-the-rules-for-using-ai-in-court-say-solicitors/5126757.article
	Texas Bar Association – Regulation 75 (Opinion 705)	State Bar of Texas	https://www.legalethicstexas.com/resources/opinions/opinion-705/
	Why the Era of the Professional Services Pyramid has Passed	George Beaton	https://www.linkedin.com/posts/georgerbeaton_ugcPost-7434011362445443074-JU6M
	Fighting the Hypothetical: Why Law Firms Should Rethink the Billable Hour in the Generative AI Era	Nancy B. Rapoport and Joseph R. Tiano Jr.	https://papers.ssrn.com/sol3/papers.cfm?abstract_id=5080449
	Law In The Era of AI (book, Wiley)	Bjarne Tellmann	

	If I Started A Brand New Firm	David C Baker	https://www.linkedin.com/pulse/i-started-brand-new-firm-david-c-baker-qmmle/
	The Role Of Inhouse Counsel Is Changing – Global General Counsel Report 2026	KPMG	https://kpmg.com/xx/en/our-insights/transformation/global-general-counsel-outlook.html
	Our contracting standards	UBS	https://www.ubs.com/global/en/our-firm/suppliers/contracting-standards.html
WATCH			
	The State of AI Keynote 2026 – a landmark keynote on the state of AI in legal: what's real, what's hype, and what law firms must do right now to survive	Nikki Shaver, founder of LegalTech Hub	https://www.lawdroidmanifesto.com/p/the-state-of-ai-keynote-2026
LISTEN			
	The Junior Work Is Going: Roch Glowacki on AI	The Legally Speaking Podcast	https://youtu.be/rq8xbr6oiJY?si=ZfJr4zE1AQfZJCQU
	Pricing AI Credit: Activity-based costing in a hoodie [Ron Baker and Ed Kless take aim at the growing trend of token-based pricing]	The Soul of Enterprise	https://podcasts.apple.com/gb/podcast/episode-593-pricing-ai-credit-activity-based-costing/id893874169?i=1000774395485
MISCELLANY			
	Legal Tech Hub – Vendors Reports [Why? Gives you an idea of the size of the AI market!]	LegalTech Hub	https://www.legaltechnologyhub.com/contents/lth-genai-legal-tech-map-march-2026/
	Attention Is All You Need (Again) [Why? A wake-up call for training teams]	David Wang	https://www.linkedin.com/pulse/attention-all-you-need-again-david-wang-z2lof/

	Why Your AI Strategy is Like A January Gym Sign-up [Why? A wake-up call for leaders to do what may be difficult]	Andrea Foot	https://www.linkedin.com/pulse/why-your-ai-strategy-like-january-gym-sign-up-andrea-foot-djjvc/
	Brilliant Thinking: Why Lawyers Must See AI as an Opportunity, Not a Threat [Why? Learn why AI is a bicycle!]	Felix Riley – Legally Speaking Podcast	https://open.spotify.com/episode/1DYaRaTyXOP0FHzkPR7i57?si=k34UsVdpSDm78Xi99mFplQ

TIPS / CHECKLISTS

Possibility Thinking Questions To Pose

- How could we possibly explain our value if clients no longer believe time is the best measure?
- How might we possibly price work where AI reduces production time but increases the importance of supervision, risk and judgment?
- What could we possibly stop selling because AI has made it look too much like a task?
- What legal work do we currently sell as hours that could POSSIBLY become a fixed-fee product?
- What AI-enabled deliverable would a client POSSIBLY pay for every quarter?
- Which three client problems could we POSSIBLY turn into service options?

CEO Questions To Pose

- What percentage of our revenue is vulnerable if clients stop accepting time as the measure of value?
- What is our answer when clients ask why AI-enabled work costs the same?
- Are we pricing judgment, or are we still pricing production?
- Who owns AI pricing in this firm?
- What are the jobs to be done for clients in the AI era? Which ones are we most vulnerable to being ‘fired’ from?
- Which new jobs will clients be unlikely to hire us for at all?

P#2. PIONEERS: FINDING THE PEOPLE WHO WILL HELP BUILD THE FUTURE

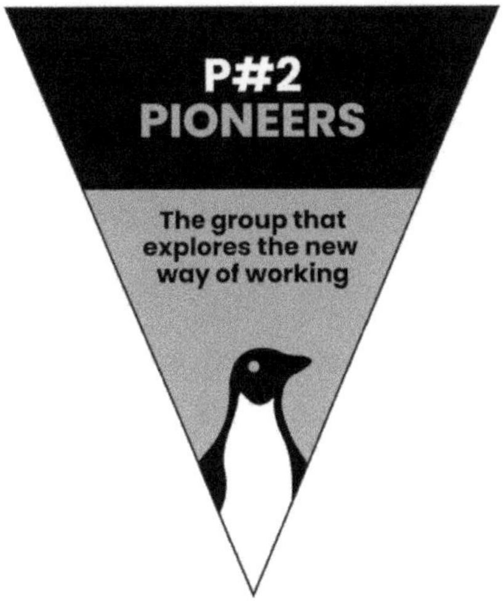

P#2. PIONEERS – THE GROUP THAT EXPLORES THE NEW WAY OF WORKING

You need help. A pilot group of Pioneer penguins who will support, deliver, and champion the change that needs to happen in your firm. You must identify key influencers and proactive members of staff who can help you plan and execute the change. You don't want Naysayer penguins in this group. You are aiming for an enthusiastic group of change agents who can inspire and persuade others in your organisation.

WELCOME TO P#2 – PIONEERS

P#2 Pioneers is about identifying the people inside the firm who are willing to explore, test, and champion AI-enabled work and value-based pricing before the whole firm is asked to change.

FIND YOUR FUTURE BUILDERS

The AI pricing revolution will not be led by committees full of cautious Naysayers, nervous spectators and people who would quite like the future to arrive after they have retired. It will be led by Pioneer Penguins.

6 MINUTES OF YOUR TIME

Watch *How to Create Change* by Simon Sinek[23]

These are the people in the firm who are curious enough to explore, brave enough to test, honest enough to say what is not working and credible enough to help others follow. They do not need to have all the answers, because nobody has all the answers, but they do need to be willing to learn, experiment, share, challenge and build confidence across the firm.

Do not start with the whole firm. If you try to change everyone at once, you will spend too much time persuading the uninterested, reassuring the frightened, managing the blockers and producing internal communications that nobody reads properly. Instead, find the curious lawyers, the commercially minded partners, the respected associates, the finance people who understand margin, the BD people who understand client language, the IT people who understand the tools, the knowledge people who understand content, the risk people who understand boundaries and the operations people who understand how work actually moves through the business.

That is your Pioneer Group.

Their job is not to sit in a room admiring the problem. Their job is to test the new way of working, build proof, create examples, listen to concerns and help the firm understand what AI-enabled pricing might look like in practice.

The Pioneer Group should explore which tasks AI can assist with, which tasks must remain lawyer-led, where judgment is most valuable, what clients actually care about, what work can be packaged as fixed-fee work, what might become subscription or retainer work, and what could become a premium advisory product. They should also identify where AI might improve speed, consistency, quality, client experience, profitability and confidence.

This is not just a finance exercise. Pricing leaders in a modern law firm need to understand more than rates and recovery. They need to understand legal work, client expectations, risk, technology, behaviour, confidence and culture. A pricing strategy that looks clever in a spreadsheet but cannot be explained by lawyers, sold to clients or delivered profitably is not a strategy. It is spreadsheet theatre.

The Pioneers also need to model the skills that now matter more than ever: asking better questions, understanding client context, spotting what really matters, communicating clearly, exercising judgment, building trust, using AI sensibly and explaining value without hiding behind time.

Why? Because the rest of the firm will copy what it can see.

If Pioneers can show colleagues how to scope an AI-assisted matter, create three sensible pricing options, explain the value of judgment, answer client questions and protect margin, the change becomes practical rather than theoretical. It stops being "the AI strategy" and starts becoming "how we now do things here".

> **WORDS WITH THE WISE**
>
> **Ben Weinberger**
>
> Change management matters. It relies on people. You need to know who the real influencers are in the firm. You cannot just assume they are the people with the biggest titles.
>
> Sometimes, the influencer is a secretary who has been there for 30 years and knows how everything really works. Sometimes, it is a long-serving partner in the corner office. These people can become your biggest supporters if you bring them with you properly.
>
> You also need to be careful about training groups. Do not put partners in a room with everyone else and expect honest learning. Partners behave differently when they are with associates or secretaries. They may pretend they understand, or they may rip the idea apart. That can kill the project.

PSYCHOLOGICAL SAFETY MATTERS

Your Pioneers will need permission to say things they might otherwise hide. They will need to be able to say, "I do not understand this yet," "I do not know how to price this," "I am worried clients will push back," "I am concerned about my targets," or "I am not sure what my role becomes if AI does the first draft."

Those are not stupid comments. They are the real comments.

If leaders do not create a safe place for those concerns to be voiced, the concerns will not disappear. They will simply move into corridors, WhatsApp groups, partner offices and quiet resistance.

That is why a pricing confidence survey should be conducted before the pilot begins. Ask lawyers whether they can explain the value they create without mentioning time, whether they can describe the judgment they bring to a matter, whether they can create three service options for a client, whether they can price an AI-assisted deliverable, and whether they can explain why the client should still pay for the outcome even if the work is delivered faster.

You need to know where confidence is low before you can build it.

The Pioneer Group should also listen carefully to the Naysayer Penguins.

In *Ditch The Billable Hour!,* the Naysayer penguins mattered because they told you where resistance, confusion and hidden objections were likely to appear. They were not always wrong. Sometimes, they were irritatingly right. The job of the Pioneer Penguins is not to ignore the Naysayers, mock them or steamroll them. Their job is to listen, decode the concern and address it properly.

When someone says, "Why are we talking about AI strategy when half the partners have not even switched Copilot on?", that may sound negative, but it is also a fair challenge. If the people signing off the strategy have not used the tools, tested them, misunderstood them, broken them and then started to understand them, they are not leading the change. They are watching it from the balcony, a spreadsheet in hand and a concerned expression on their faces.

When someone says, "Isn't this just an IT project?", the answer has to be a firm no, because AI affects recruitment, training, supervision, risk, pricing, profitability, client service, knowledge management, workflows, junior lawyer development and partner behaviour. Putting AI only in the IT budget is Shingles Logic in a shiny new wrapper.

When someone says, "Can we just buy the tool and tell people to use it?", the answer should be obvious. Buying technology feels like progress because it creates an invoice, a project name and possibly a launch email, but buying AI without educating people, creating use cases and changing behaviour is not transformation. It is shelfware with a password.

When someone says, "I have not had time to play with AI," listen very carefully, because what they may really be saying is that the business model punishes learning. If lawyers are measured almost entirely by recorded time, billed time and recovery, nobody should be surprised when experimentation, process improvement and learning fall to the bottom of the pile.

When someone says, "I do not trust the output," do not dismiss them. Blind trust in AI is dangerous, but total distrust is lazy. The real issue is whether lawyers have been trained to prompt properly, interrogate the answer, spot hallucinations, apply judgment and decide what is usable.

When someone says, "I know where the work hurts, but I do not know what AI should do about it," they may be giving you one of the most useful comments of all. Lawyers often know exactly where the pain sits: duplicated effort, clunky reporting, painful first drafts, messy inboxes, slow document review, repeated client explanations and poor handovers. What they may not know is how to turn that pain into a workable AI use case.

Pioneers translate legal pain into better workflows.

It's important to note (as already mentioned) that Naysayer Penguins are not always wrong. Sometimes, their questions are frustrating, sometimes they are designed to slow things down, and sometimes they are exactly the questions that need to be answered before a firm rushes into the next shiny thing.

Do not just answer objections. Capture them. Classify them. Act on the useful ones.

Below are some of the questions you may be confronted with from Naysayer penguins.

Naysayer Penguin question/objection	Suggested Pioneer Penguin answer
"Clients won't pay for AI-assisted work."	Clients will not pay premium prices for unexplained AI-assisted production. That is different. Clients may well pay for speed, certainty, judgment, risk reduction, better decisions and a clearer outcome. The task is not to hide AI or apologise for it. The task is to explain where the value sits.
"If AI makes the work quicker, surely the client should get a discount?"	Sometimes, yes. Sometimes, no. If AI genuinely reduces the cost of delivery and the value to the client is unchanged, that may be reflected in the price. But if AI helps the client get to an answer faster, reduce uncertainty earlier, complete a deal sooner or avoid a problem, the value may have increased. Faster is not always cheaper. Sometimes faster is more valuable.
"How can we charge the same if the work takes less time?"	That question only causes a problem if the firm is still selling time. If the firm is selling an outcome, the discussion changes. The client is not buying the hours. They are buying the result, the judgment, the checks, the risk carried, the accountability and the confidence to act.
"We can't price this unless we know how long it will take."	You need to understand cost. You do not need to make time the measure of value. There is a difference. Good pricing should understand likely effort, risk, complexity, value, client context and outcome. Time may inform the price. It should not be the only thing that creates it.
"This is an IT issue."	No, it is not. IT may help choose, secure and implement the tools, but AI pricing is a leadership issue, a client issue, a risk issue, a training issue, a

Naysayer Penguin question/objection	Suggested Pioneer Penguin answer
	supervision issue, a margin issue and a business model issue. Calling it an IT issue is a very convenient way of avoiding the harder questions.
"Our work is too complex for AI pricing."	Complex work is exactly where judgment and acumen matter most. Nobody is suggesting that AI should price the work or replace the lawyer's brain. The question is whether parts of the work can be accelerated, supported or improved by AI, and how the remaining human value should be explained and priced.
"The regulator won't like it."	The regulator will not object to a firm using technology responsibly, transparently and competently. The real regulatory risk is using AI without governance, supervision, training, accountability or proper client protection. The answer is not panic. The answer is policy, process and professional judgment.
"Our insurer won't like it."	Then speak to the insurer. Do not guess. Insurers are likely to be far more concerned about the unmanaged use of AI than its properly governed use. A firm with policies, training, supervision, audit trails and clear accountability is in a much stronger position than a firm pretending its people are not already experimenting.
"Junior lawyers won't learn if AI does the basic work."	That is a serious point, not a silly one. But the answer is not to ban AI and preserve inefficient work for training purposes. The answer is to redesign training. Juniors must learn how to think, supervise, challenge, verify, apply judgment and understand context. If AI changes the apprenticeship model, then the apprenticeship model has to change.
"Partners won't change."	Some will not. Some never do. But the firm should not design its future around the least curious people in the partnership. Find the Pioneers, run pilots, create evidence, show better outcomes and make it easier for the cautious majority to follow. Do not let the slowest penguin decide the speed of the colony.

Naysayer Penguin question/objection	Suggested Pioneer Penguin answer
"Clients will just demand discounts."	Some will, especially if the firm's own language is careless. If the firm says, "AI makes us more efficient," the client may hear, "This should be cheaper." The better message is that AI helps the firm provide faster insight, stronger checking, better options, clearer advice and more useful judgment. The discount conversation needs to be anticipated, not feared.
"We tried fixed fees before and lost money."	That usually means the firm priced badly, scoped badly, managed badly or failed to learn properly. It does not mean fixed pricing is impossible. It means the firm needs better scoping, better assumptions, better client selection, better matter management and better after-action reviews. Failure is data. Use it.
"AI hallucinates, so we should ban it."	AI can produce wrong answers. So can humans. The answer is not blind trust or blanket bans. The answer is controlled use, training, verification, supervision and clear rules about when AI can and cannot be used. The risk is real, but so is the opportunity.
"AI is overhyped."	Some of it is. There is plenty of froth, jargon and vendor fairy dust in the market. But dismissing AI because some people exaggerate its impact is lazy thinking. The sensible firm separates hype from use case, experiment from strategy and shiny object from business value.
"AI is only relevant for big firms."	No. Big firms may have bigger budgets, but smaller firms often have less bureaucracy, faster decision-making and more freedom to redesign services. AI-enabled value pricing is not only about scale. It is about clarity, courage and commercial thinking.
"AI is only relevant for small firms because big firms are too complex."	Also no. Large firms may be complex, but they also have the clients, data, talent, infrastructure and repeatable workstreams to make AI-enabled service redesign extremely powerful. The challenge for big firms is not relevance. It is coordination, incentives and leadership.

Naysayer Penguin question/objection	Suggested Pioneer Penguin answer
"Let's wait until the market settles."	That sounds sensible, but it can easily become an excuse for doing nothing. The market will not suddenly send a polite note confirming that all uncertainty has ended. Firms do not need to bet the business tomorrow. They do need to start learning now.
"We don't know which AI tool will win."	You do not need to know which tool will win before you start understanding the pricing problem. The bigger issue is not the brand of tool. It is how the firm explains value when technology changes production. Start with the business model, not the logo on the software.
"Our clients are not asking about AI yet."	They may not be asking loudly yet. That does not mean they are not thinking about it. In-house teams are using AI, reading the same reports and facing their own pressure to reduce cost and improve value. Waiting until the client asks is not leadership. It is reaction.
"We should not tell clients we are using AI."	Be careful. There may be situations where disclosure is required, expected or commercially sensible. There may also be situations where the client cares more about the outcome than the tool. The point is to have a policy and a position, not a collection of partner-by-partner improvisations.
"If clients know we use AI, they will think the work is worth less."	Only if the firm explains it badly. If the firm presents AI as a shortcut, the client may devalue the work. If the firm presents AI as part of a controlled process that improves speed, consistency, risk management and insight, the conversation changes.
"This will reduce recorded hours and damage revenue."	That may be true if the firm keeps selling hours. That is precisely the point. AI exposes the weakness in a model that rewards time rather than value. If the firm wants to protect revenue and margin, it needs to change the pricing model, not suppress the technology.
"Our finance system is built around hours."	Most are. That does not make hours sacred. It simply means the firm's systems reflect the old model. If the

Naysayer Penguin question/objection	Suggested Pioneer Penguin answer
	strategy changes, the systems, reports, dashboards and measures will need to change as well. Otherwise, the firm will claim to value outcomes while managing everyone by time.
"How do we recover the cost of AI?"	Not by adding a mysterious "AI surcharge" to everything and hoping clients do not ask questions. The firm needs to understand the cost of tools, training, supervision, governance and implementation, and then build those costs into sensible pricing models connected to client value.
"Should we charge separately for AI?"	Sometimes, perhaps. But often the better approach is to price the service, not the tool. Clients do not usually want to buy your software stack. They want a result. If AI enables a better, faster or more certain service, the value should be reflected in the overall proposition.
"What if the client uses their own AI and thinks they do not need us?"	Some clients will do more themselves. That is already happening. The opportunity for law firms is to move up the value chain: help clients verify, interpret, risk-assess and act on what AI produces. If clients have access to knowledge, the lawyer's value must move to judgment.
"What if AI makes junior work disappear?"	Then firms must rethink leverage, training and career development. Preserving inefficient junior work just to keep the pyramid alive is not a strategy. The better question is how juniors learn judgment, acumen and client context in an AI-enabled environment.
"What if we get sued because AI made a mistake?"	Then the real issue will be whether the firm had proper governance, supervision, checking, training and accountability. AI does not remove professional responsibility. It makes disciplined processes even more important.
"What if our competitors undercut us using AI?"	Some will. Some always do. Competing only on cheapness is dangerous. The better response is to be clearer about value, offer options, improve speed and

Naysayer Penguin question/objection	Suggested Pioneer Penguin answer
	certainty, and show why your judgment, accountability and outcome are worth paying for.
"This all sounds like a lot of work."	It is. Change usually is. But pretending the old model will survive untouched because the new model is hard to build is not a plan. It is wishful thinking.
"Can't we just keep billing by the hour and see what happens?"	Yes. You can. Shingles probably will. But if AI reduces the time required to do the work, and the firm still sells time, then the firm has chosen to let the business model problem arrive later, larger and with less preparation.

The big Naysayer message is this: AI adoption will not be slowed mainly by the technology. It will be slowed by old habits, old incentives, old budgets, old committees, old supervision models, old pricing structures and old partner behaviour.

That is why Pioneers matter.

They are not there to create a glossy AI brochure. They are there to help the firm learn its way into the future, one practical pilot, one better workflow, one clearer pricing option and one more confident client conversation at a time.

BRACE YOURSELF…
incoming provocative statement

The firms that struggle with AI will not struggle because the tools are too clever. They will struggle because the firm is not ready to change.

8 PPP PENGUIN LOGIC

A Naysayer Penguin may be annoying, but they may also be identifying the risk the enthusiasts have missed.
Listen first. Then decide.

FIND THE PEOPLE WHO ARE ALREADY FRUSTRATED ENOUGH TO CHANGE THINGS

Adam Grant makes a very useful point in his WorkLife episode, *The Creative Power of Misfits.*[24] Frustrated people are not always blockers. Sometimes, they are the people who can see what is broken before everyone else is prepared to admit it.

Grant refers to research showing that dissatisfied employees can be highly creative, but only where they still care about the organisation and are given feedback, support and permission to do something constructive with their frustration. Ignore them and their irritation may become corrosive. Listen to them properly and they may become allies.

When law firms start redesigning products, services and pricing models, the obvious instinct is to appoint the usual suspects. The safe partners. The committee people. The people who will not cause too much disturbance in the room. There is a place for them. But brave CEOs should also ask a more uncomfortable question:

- Who are the black sheep in this firm who have been muttering for years that the way we work makes no sense?
- Who are the lawyers who say clients hate our bills?
- Who are the associates who know exactly where the waste is?
- Who are the BD people who can see that our proposals sound like every other firm's proposals?
- Who are the finance people who know which fixed fees actually make money and which ones are just hourly billing wearing a fake moustache?
- Who are the partners who are frustrated, not because they are disloyal, but because they care enough to be annoyed?

6 MINUTES OF YOUR TIME

Watch *Angry People Make Change*[25]

Tom Peters explains the single source of innovation is angry people.

These people may not always be polished. They may not always say things in the most diplomatic way. They may occasionally make the managing partner reach for a strong coffee. But they may also be the people who can help a firm build genuinely different AI-enabled products and services, because they are not emotionally attached to the old machine.

This is where the Pioneer Penguins need to be chosen carefully. A Pioneer Penguin is not simply the most enthusiastic person in the room. Nor is it necessarily the person with the shiniest LinkedIn profile or the loudest view on ChatGPT. The best pioneers may include the constructive misfits: people who are dissatisfied with the current model, committed to the firm's future, and willing to help build something better.

AI transformation should not be imposed on them. It should be done with them.

Because in many firms, the raw material for innovation is already there. It is sitting in partner meetings. It is buried in associate grumbles. It is hiding in finance reports. It is whispered after client pitches. It is expressed in the sentence, "Why on earth do we still do it like this?"

A brave CEO will not try to silence that voice. A brave CEO will give it a job.

CRIB SHEET

P#2

	Title	Author / Source	Link
WATCH			
	How to Create Change	Simon Sinek	https://youtu.be/fDILpuiLuAI?si=UlGLgWllBLAQv1JR
	Angry People Make Change – Tom Peters explains that the single source of innovation is angry people	Tom Peters	https://youtu.be/A2EdCl-CX4Q?si=3zmK7f2vZnDIdi2H
LISTEN			
	The Creative Power of Misfits	Adam Grant	https://www.ted.com/talks/worklife_with_adam_grant_the_creative_power_of_misfits?utm_campaign=tedspread&utm_medium=referral&utm_source=tedcomshare
MISCELLANY			
	AI will End the Billable Hour and How to be Prepared [Why? A subscription lawyer's take on AI and the billable hour]	Law Subscribed – Matthew Kerbis & Stephanie Everitt (Lawyerlist)	https://podcasts.apple.com/gb/podcast/94-5-ai-will-end-the-billable-hour-and-how-to-be-prepared/id1586707101?i=1000673144745
	AI, Discounting, and the Future of Value [Why? A wake-up call for training teams]	The Soul of Enterprise	https://podcasts.apple.com/gb/podcast/the-soul-of-enterprise-business-in/id893874169?i=1000769142877&r=3248

TIPS / CHECKLISTS

Possibility Thinking Questions To Pose

- Who in our firm is already curious about AI, pricing, process improvement or better client conversations?
- Who could possibly help us translate lawyer frustration into AI use cases?
- Which Naysayer Penguin might be irritating, but right?
- How the firm could:
    - Price outcomes rather than inputs
    - Make lawyer judgment visible
    - Train juniors differently
    - Measure something other than hours
    - Use AI to improve client outcomes

CEO Questions To Pose

- Who should be in the Pioneer group if this is a business model project, not an IT project?
- Do we have pricing, finance, BD, risk, operations, KM and practising lawyers involved?
- Which people are already experimenting and should be given permission to lead?
- Which Naysayer Penguins should be listened to because they may be identifying genuine blockers?
- How will we stop the Pioneer group becoming a talking shop?

P#3. PLAN: DESIGN THE AI-ENABLED VALUE MODEL

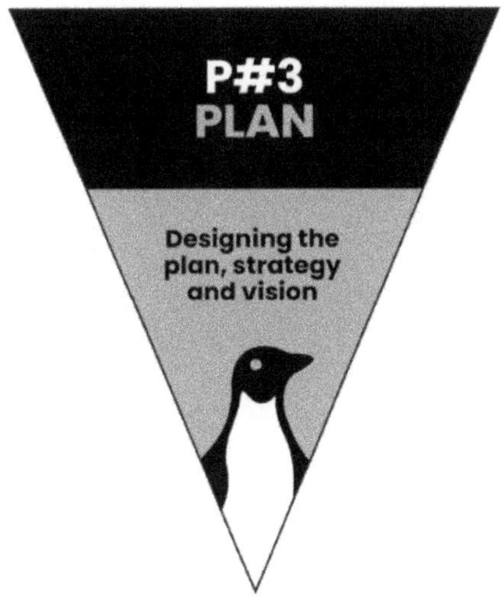

P#3. PLAN – DESIGNING THE PLAN, STRATEGY AND VISION

In this step, you are planning to create a Strategic Vision to help deliver change. A picture of the future state, the benefits to your firm, your customers and your staff and – crucially – how it looks different from your current way of doing things. Ideally, you will be able to link your Vision to your values and mission.

WELCOME TO P#3 – PLAN

P#3 Plan is where *Stop The Clock* stops being a title and becomes a project plan. It is where the firm turns the AI pricing conversation from an interesting idea into a structured business model project. It is divided into four parts: Knowledge, Tools, Vision and Plan.

P#3 – KNOWLEDGE

Do not talk about pricing until you understand value.

Before a firm can sensibly talk about AI pricing, it needs to understand value-based pricing, because if the leadership team, partners and lawyers do not understand what value-based pricing is, AI will simply make an already confused pricing conversation even more confusing.

I appreciate this may irritate my publisher, who I repeat, told me very firmly that I could not simply regurgitate my first book and expect everyone to buy it again, which is a fair point, but given that you may not have read *Ditch The Billable Hour!*, it is only right that I – briefly – explain what I mean by value-based pricing. #sozjames.

In simple terms, value-based pricing is a price that is not limited to time incurred; it is a price that is fair to those who created the value and to the client.

KNOWING WHERE TO TAP STILL HAS VALUE

The classic story is the one about the expert called out to fix a mission-critical machine in a factory. The machine has stopped working, production has stopped, people are worried, and every minute of delay is costing money. The expert arrives, studies the machine, listens carefully, takes out a hammer, taps the machine, and it is soon working again. When the bill arrives, it is not for the time spent on site. It is for knowing where to tap.

That story is often told as a joke about the engineer, the hammer, and the £1,000 invoice. Guess what… it's a true story. Allow me to introduce you to Charles Proteus Steinmetz, a brilliant electrical engineer known as the "Wizard of Schenectady". Steinmetz got Henry Ford's factory up and running. Whether told as the Steinmetz story, or as the engineer with the hammer, the lesson is the same. The value was not in the minutes spent standing next to the machine; the value was in the knowledge, experience, judgement and acumen that enabled the expert to know where to tap. Legal services are no different.

6 MINUTES OF YOUR TIME

Read the Steinmetz story in the Crib Sheet link.

You will be surprised how often you will be able to show how clever you are when people tell you the "Old Engineer" story without knowing it's actually true!

The client is not really buying the six-minute unit, the beautifully formatted attendance note, the internal email chain or the fact that three people were copied into a message. The client is buying a problem solved, a risk reduced, a deal completed, a dispute avoided, a decision made, a family protected, a business defended, a crisis managed or a commercial opportunity secured.

That is why you cannot price high-value judgment sensibly by the hour and expect the market to behave rationally. A lawyer who resolves a dispute with one carefully judged phone call may create enormous value, yet under the hourly model that lawyer may generate less revenue than one who allows the matter to drift for weeks.

That is not a pricing model, it's an incentive problem.

Value-based pricing corrects this by asking better questions.

- What is the client trying to achieve?
- What risk is being removed?
- What decision is being improved?
- What outcome is being protected?
- What would failure cost?
- What is certainty worth?
- What is speed worth?
- What is avoiding a dispute worth?
- What is getting the deal done worth?
- What is the value of a lawyer who knows exactly where to tap?

This does not mean firms take on unlimited risk, guess wildly or throw fixed fees at everything that moves. Properly structured value-based pricing requires clear scope, sensible assumptions, defined deliverables, exclusions, review points and pricing mechanisms for genuinely unpredictable work.

It is *not* a capped fee in disguise, where the firm still records time, reviews bills and hopes the cap is not exceeded. It is a different way of thinking about the commercial relationship.

Clients increasingly want budget certainty, transparency, efficiency and value. They do not want to spend time reviewing invoices to work out whether a task should have taken 1.7 hours or 2.3 hours, and in some legal departments, invoice review itself consumes valuable in-house lawyer time, which is extraordinary when you think about it. The client is spending legal time checking whether the external lawyer spent too much legal time.

AI makes that absurdity harder to ignore.

Under a properly scoped fixed fee, phased fee, subscription, retainer or other value-based arrangement, the client pays for the agreed outcome or deliverable. If the firm uses AI sensibly, supervises it properly, and applies lawyer judgment where it matters, the client benefits from a better process, and the firm benefits from efficiency.

There is no need for the strange hourly billing dilemma where the firm is almost punished for going faster.

That is the knowledge base lawyers need before they begin talking about AI pricing, because AI does not remove the need for lawyers; it removes the need for some legal work to be performed by lawyers in the old way. It changes where value sits. It forces firms to separate production from judgment, output from outcome, activity from value and hours from price.

The firms that understand this will have a much better AI pricing conversation.

The firms that do not will keep asking the wrong question: "How do we charge for the time AI has saved?"

The better question is: "How do we price the value our judgment, acumen, supervision, technology and accountability have created?"

MEASURE CONFIDENCE BEFORE YOU TRY TO CHANGE BEHAVIOUR

An internal pricing confidence survey should also be run before the pilot starts. When I work with a law firm, a typical survey asks 47 questions. I absolutely love doing the surveys and then feeding back the results to a room full of partners or Pioneer penguins. The surveys are always anonymous, so staff can answer safely, knowing it won't be career-limiting to give honest feedback on their firm's pricing.

The questions ask lawyers whether they feel confident discussing price, offering options, holding the price, dealing with AI discount requests, explaining value and saying no to badly scoped or unattractive work.

The answers for many management teams may make uncomfortable reading, but uncomfortable data is useful data! It shows where training is needed, where partners need support, where the Big Book of Usefulness needs better scripts and where the firm's stated strategy is not yet matched by lawyer confidence.

TRIGGER WARNING! Recently, one survey respondent answered the question: "When a new starter joins your team, how is the pricing induction undertaken?" with the following:

"I have recently joined a team and have been given zero training on this. I do not understand the firm or team approach, and support is very much lacking. I have asked for help but been told it comes with time – not very helpful for a new starter."

This answer is tragic. It upset me. It still upsets me. A new starter who is brave enough to ask for help gets told, *"It comes with time"*. Well, Shingles is alive and well! When the answer was shown to the Pioneer Group at the firm I was working with, there was a sharp intake of breath, and everyone hoped it was not a member of their team who felt so low and had received such comprehensively useless advice.

FYI, the most common answer to: "When a new starter joins your team, how is the pricing induction undertaken?" is "It isn't." (i.e., "We recruit new people and we let them make it up as we go along.")

The surveys have many common traits. These are the edited highlights extracted from my second book, *Ditch and Switch! 50 Value-Based Pricing Examples For Law Professionals.* Don't let my publisher, James, know I copied and pasted them in here.

Brace yourself for some uncomfortable truths!

Q: I am confident that the work we do helps and benefits our clients.

Always/Yes: ranges from 80-94%

My Take: This is brilliant! Lawyers know they add value – they just can't price it properly. If you're 90% confident you help clients, why are you so terrible at charging for that help?

Q: Which of these are issues within your firm?

Work-life balance challenges: 63%

Risk of burn-out for some individuals: 61%

Significant resources spent on time recording: 15%

Significant resources spent on chasing unpaid bills: 30%

Lack of confidence in negotiating fees at the outset of a matter: 40%

Lack of confidence when asking for an increased fee when a matter is progressing: 62%

My Take: Houston, we have another problem! Two-thirds of lawyers struggle with work-life balance, yet 62% lack confidence asking for fee increases when work gets complex. You're working yourselves into the ground whilst undercharging. That's not noble – that's barmy!

Q: I believe my firm tends to reduce prices based on what our competitors may charge.

Not at all: 35%

To some extent: 44%

Always/Yes: 21%

My Take: So, 65% of firms let competitors dictate their pricing? That's not strategy – that's surrendering control of your business to people you're supposedly competing against!

Q: My colleagues and I know how to confidently deal with price objections from clients when we receive them.

Not at all: 15%

To some extent: 65%

Always: 20%

My Take: Only 20% can confidently handle price objections? No wonder lawyers discount so quickly! You can't win a game you don't know how to play.

Q: Would you be happy for someone else to price work initially at the outset and then leave you to get on and deliver the service to the client?

Not at all: 37%

To some extent: 43%

Always: 20%

My Take: This is fascinating – 63% would welcome help with pricing, yet most firms don't provide it. There's a massive opportunity here for centralised pricing expertise.

Q: What prevents your firm from charging more for your services?

'Nothing'

'The local market/competition'

'Quality of service for clients'

'Concern about profitability, losing clients/fear'

'Referrers' fee scales'

'The customers we service can ill afford higher fees'

'Management decisions'

'Clients will leave'

'We will be too expensive'

'They will think we are ripping them off'

My Take: Look at all that fear! Most of these are assumptions, not facts. When did lawyers become mind-readers who know exactly what clients think about pricing? The real barrier isn't external, it's internal confidence.

Q: I believe that some of the clients my firm acts for should be dismissed as they are too painful and/or unprofitable to act for.

A: I have had a range of answers between 50-100%

My Take: The lowest percentage of yeses is 50%! Your own staff are telling you which clients to sack, yet most firms ignore this wisdom. If your team knows who the problem clients are, why are you still acting for them?

Q: What prevents your firm from deselecting clients?

A: Included 'Worry about our reputation', 'Inertia', and 'Partners'

My Take: "Partners" preventing client deselection – now that's revealing! And "worry about reputation" – your reputation suffers more from keeping terrible clients than from professionally parting ways with them.

Q: When someone joins your team, how is pricing training undertaken?

The answers that come back are usually mixed:

'A Partner tells them what to do'

'They are told their hourly rate'

And the vast majority of people respond, 'it isn't'

My Take: This is criminal negligence! You wouldn't let someone practice law without legal training, yet you let them price services without pricing training. No wonder confidence is so low.

Q: How are your pricing policies currently documented?

Predominantly, the answers are 'they are not'.

My Take: So, you have detailed procedures for everything else, but wing it on the thing that determines your profitability? Brilliant strategy!

Q: How is pricing set and reviewed at your firm?

Answers are usually negative, with many respondents confirming, 'I have no idea'

My Take: "I have no idea" about pricing in a business where pricing determines survival? That's like saying "I have no idea" how we breathe.

Q: What currently stops you from setting fees based on value to the client?

Answers include:

We don't know the value of our work to clients.

Partners are uncomfortable with it.

We don't have the skill sets.

Our IT systems don't allow us to do it.

My Take: Finally, some honest answers! These are all solvable problems, but only if you're willing to solve them. Most firms complain about these barriers instead of removing them.

How would your firm answer similar questions to these? I have news for you – most firms answer the same way...

These survey results paint a clear picture: lawyers know they add value, they know they should charge more, they know which clients to sack, yet they lack the confidence, training, and systems to act on this knowledge. The gap between knowing and doing is where profitability goes to die!

After the first pilot, ask again. If confidence has improved, celebrate that, too. A lawyer who becomes more confident having a value conversation is not a soft win. It is a business-model win.

PART 2 TOOLS

PRACTICE AREA PRICING POLICY / BIG BOOK OF USEFULNESS

Every practice area should have a Practice Area Pricing Policy, which should sit inside the firm's Big Book of Usefulness, or BBU. Your BBU may even be an Agentic Assistant!

The BBU is not intended to be a theoretical policy document that nobody reads, updates, or can find when they actually need it. It should be a practical operating manual that captures the team's pricing knowledge, helps lawyers scope work properly, gives them the confidence to discuss value with clients, and stops pricing know-how from living only in the heads of a few experienced partners.

A strong practice-area BBU should explain the firm's pricing philosophy, the purpose of the manual, the team's pricing objectives, and the process by which prices are set. It should make clear that value-based pricing is about outcomes, clarity, service levels, risk and value, not simply the time recorded in delivering the work.

It should also contain proper pricing governance, because lawyers need to know who can price work, who should review it, when approval is required and how the "two pairs of eyes" on every pricing process operates. The aim is not to create bureaucracy for its own sake; it is to reduce inconsistency, avoid leaving value on the table, and help lawyers feel supported when making pricing decisions.

The BBU should include guidance on client categorisation, because not every client is the right client, nor is every piece of work the right work. It should help lawyers think about profitability, strategic fit, future value, pain versus gain and whether the client is likely to respect the value the firm creates. Some clients may be better served elsewhere, and some clients may not be worth acting for at all.

It should include value conversation guidelines, because the value-based pricing conversation begins before the price is proposed. Lawyers need prompts, scripts and questions that help them understand what the client really wants, what success looks like, what risks matter, what the client will do to help the matter run efficiently and what assumptions should underpin the price.

It should contain a pricing options framework, because clients should usually be offered choices rather than a single blunt number. The BBU should include templates for Bronze/Silver/Gold, Mini/Midi/Mega, or whatever language the firm prefers, together with optional extras, service levels, payment structures and guidance on how those options should be presented to clients.

It should include risk assessment tools, because pricing the work means pricing the client, the complexity, the urgency, the opponent, the jurisdiction, the uncertainty, the resources required and the commercial context. The BBU should contain the lawyer scoring matrix, base-price guidance, and the rules for checking prices before they are quoted.

It should include a value log or Pioneer tracker, so that the firm *records* pricing experiments, options offered, outcomes achieved, feedback received and lessons learned. This creates visibility, healthy competition, accountability and peer momentum, rather than allowing every pricing experiment to disappear into a matter file and be forgotten.

It should contain calculation tools, including base-cost calculators, value questions, risk adjustments, scoping tools and objection-handling guidance, so that lawyers are not simply guessing when they propose a price.

It should deal properly with the scope of work, because value-based pricing only works if scope, exclusions and assumptions are clear. The BBU should explain what is included, what is excluded, the assumptions made, how additional services are handled, how scope creep is managed, and when re-pricing is triggered.

It should include Fixed Price Agreement templates, because the FPA is the client-facing end product of the pricing process. The BBU should explain which templates exist, where they are stored, when they should be used, what clauses matter and how stage-based or milestone pricing should be structured.

It should also include guidance on fixed-fee interviews, pro bono work, discounting, price objections, follow-up procedures, gracious-in-defeat letters, specialist areas and third-party costs, because these are the practical moments when pricing discipline is either protected or lost.

8 PPP PENGUIN LOGIC

The Big Book of Usefulness is not a nice-to-have.
It is essential.

The BBU should include communication and documentation templates, covering client updates, internal approvals, progress reporting, out-of-scope notifications and change-order requests. Good pricing is not just about setting the price at the start; it is about communicating clearly throughout the matter so the client understands what is happening, what has changed and why an additional price may be needed.

It should include a section on confidence, because value-based pricing requires lawyers to believe in the value they create. For hourly billing, you need a calculator. For value-based pricing, you need courage. The BBU should therefore capture successes, examples, stories and lessons from colleagues so lawyers can see that better pricing is possible.

Finally, the BBU should include monitoring, review, training and appendices. Pricing should be reviewed regularly through after-action reviews, team meetings, profitability analysis, client feedback and lessons learned.

The point is simple. A BBU/Practice Area Pricing Policy should not be a dusty document. It should be the place where the team captures what works, learns from what does not, supports lawyers in difficult pricing conversations and turns value-based pricing from a brave idea into a repeatable way of working.

NB: All of the above points are explained in far greater detail in *Ditch The Billable Hour!*

BRACE YOURSELF…
incoming provocative statement

If your only answer to 'Why does this still cost the same?' is 'because we are lawyers', you do not have a pricing strategy… you have a hope.

8 PPP PENGUIN LOGIC

What could you say when the client asks for the AI discount?

"You are not paying simply for the time taken to produce the document. You are paying for the outcome, the judgment applied, the checks undertaken, the risk we carry, the supervision of the process and the certainty we provide. AI may help us produce parts of the work more efficiently, but it does not replace our responsibility for getting it right."

THE AI PRICING CANVAS: WHAT IS THE CLIENT REALLY PAYING FOR?

What is the client really paying for? For years, the answer has too often been time. How long did the work take? Who worked on it? What hourly rate applies? How many units are on the clock? That may have been a convenient internal measurement, but it was never a very convincing explanation of value, and AI is now making that explanation look even weaker.

If AI can help produce research, drafts, summaries, chronologies, reviews, reports and first versions of documents more quickly, clients will quite reasonably ask why the price has not changed. That does not mean the client is right to assume the work should automatically be cheaper, but it does mean the firm needs a better answer than, "This is what we have always charged."

The Pricing Canvas is designed to force one discipline: stop pricing the hours and start identifying the outcome. Why the term "canvas"? It's because it suggests design, not calculation. It is not meant to be a rigid form, a spreadsheet, or a fee quote template. It is a working surface where you map the matter before you price it. It is a thinking tool. It helps firms avoid the very real risk of discounting too quickly, defending the old price badly, or pretending that AI has changed nothing.

Firms should consider using an AI Pricing Canvas because AI makes one question impossible to avoid. What is the client really paying for?

The Pricing Canvas helps the firm pause before it prices the work. It forces lawyers to think about the client's problem, the outcome required, the parts of the work AI can assist with, the parts that still require human judgment, the business acumen needed, the risk carried by the firm and the value created for the client.

In simple terms, it separates production from value.

Question	Why it matters
What problem is the client trying to solve?	Clients buy outcomes, not activity.
What outcome does the client need?	The price should connect to the result.
Which parts of the work can AI assist with?	Production time may reduce.
Which parts require lawyer judgment?	Judgment is where the value moves.
What business acumen is required?	The law sits inside the client's wider world.

Question	Why it matters
What risk does the firm carry?	Accountability has value.
What supervision and checking are needed?	AI output still needs responsible review.
What value does the client receive?	Value is client-specific.
What pricing options could be offered?	Clients like choice.
What will we say if the client asks for an AI discount?	That question is coming.

A firm that has used the Pricing Canvas can have a much better client conversation. It can say, with confidence, that the value of the work is not simply the time taken to produce a document.

Here is an example of a Pricing Canvas: Contract Review for a Growth Company

Canvas question	Example answer
What problem is the client solving?	Client needs to understand risk in 120 supplier contracts before the investment round.
What outcome does the client need?	Board-ready risk picture within 10 working days.
What can AI assist with?	Clause extraction, summary, risk flagging, first-pass categorisation.
What requires lawyer judgment?	Materiality assessment, negotiation priorities, board recommendations.
What acumen is required?	Understanding investor concerns, operational risk and commercial leverage.
What risk does the firm carry?	Advice relied on by the board and investors.
What pricing options?	Essential review / Board-ready report / Premium negotiation support.

Canvas question	Example answer
AI discount answer	AI improves speed and consistency, but the fee reflects judgment, risk and decision support.

Used properly, the Pricing Canvas will help a firm protect margin, improve client conversations, create pricing options, design better services and capture learning in the firm's Big Book of Usefulness. It gives lawyers a structure for explaining value at the very moment when clients are starting to question whether time is still a sensible measure. The Pricing Canvas helps the firm explain that clearly, price it sensibly and connect the fee to the outcome the client actually wants.

You will see in Appendix 1 that there are Pricing Canvas examples for another 22 legal practice areas. You can discuss them with your legal teams and improve on the scenarios. Don't let your lawyers tell you this can't be done. #youarewelcome

BUILD CLIENT TOOLS.

Some law firms are starting to understand the real AI opportunity.

It is not simply about doing the same work faster. It is not about hiding AI in the IT department, shaving a few hours off production time and hoping the client does not notice.

Colin Levy, in *AI and Client Value*, reports, "AI does not merely accelerate existing legal services. It enables the creation of entirely new service lines that generate revenue which did not exist before. These are not discounted versions of traditional legal work. They are distinct products with their own value propositions, pricing models, and delivery mechanisms."

The bigger opportunity is to become more useful.

That is why the report on 5th May 2026 about Linklaters launching a new practice to build matter-specific AI solutions is important. The significance is not that a Magic Circle firm has bought another tool – so what? The significance is that a major law firm appears to be treating AI as part of the client proposition. That is a different game.

Clients do not buy legal labour for the joy of it. They do not wake up wanting more memos, more meetings, more associates or more beautifully recorded units of time. They want to manage risk, make decisions, complete deals, avoid disasters, protect assets, satisfy regulators, reassure boards and sleep better at night.

AI gives law firms the chance to build services around those real needs.

A firm selling hours is easy to compare. Here is your rate card. Here is someone else's rate card. Procurement can do its thing. Discounts follow. The work moves.

But a firm that has helped design the workflow, structure the data, set the risk flags, apply the legal logic and embed its judgment into the way *the client actually works* is in a very different position. That firm is not just a supplier; it is part of the client's operating system.

The clever firms will not sell AI as cheap law. They will sell better outcomes, supported by technology and underpinned by legal judgment.

The less clever firms will use AI to trim time, protect the hourly model and hope the awkward pricing questions go away.

WORDS WITH THE WISE

Sam Stamp

One of the reasons legal products matter is that they can be sticky.

Legal work is often episodic. A client has a dispute, a deal, a regulatory issue, a transaction, a restructuring, a problem. The work comes in waves. Products and technology-enabled services can create a more continuous relationship. They can give the firm a reason to keep speaking to clients even when there is not a major piece of work underway.

That is valuable in two ways.

First, it helps deepen existing client relationships. When we were looking at products at Simmons, one of the early challenges was simply making sure that our own clients knew what existed. Some products were relevant only to certain types of client, but others had much wider relevance.

Second, products can create a reason to speak to clients who are not yet clients. That changes the nature of business development. Traditional law firm business development is often relationship-led. It is about who you know, what you are known for, and whether you are there at the right time. Product selling is different. It requires a pipeline, a targeted list, a clearer ideal customer profile, and a much more specific understanding of the problem being solved.

That is not necessarily how lawyers are used to selling. It is much closer to proper sales. I do not mean aggressive selling. I mean structured, disciplined, consultative selling with a clear proposition.

Law firms need to understand that because they are increasingly competing with organisations that are very good at selling products.

Legal tech companies are already selling directly to legal departments. They will look at the amount of money clients spend on law firms and say, "If we can take 20 per cent of that, that is our market."

Law firms should not assume that client relationships alone will protect them.

PART 3: VISION

CREATE A VISION THAT YOUR LAWYERS AND CLIENTS CAN UNDERSTAND

To understand what AI can do now, I recommend you read Damien Riehl's excellent article, *Beyond the Chatbot: Meet the Agentic Law Firm.*[26] It is not science fiction. It shows what is here now. Agentic AI can already plan, reason, draft, test, refine and move a legal task through several stages without waiting for a lawyer to type the next prompt. That does not remove the lawyer; it changes the work, which is why firms need a vision. Not a vague "we should use AI" statement, but a clear view of where human judgment, client value and technology *meet.* Without that vision, the firm is not leading change.

Your vision cannot be a nebulous statement about "embracing innovation" or "using technology to improve client service". That is conference brochure language. The vision needs to be more ambitious than that, because AI is not simply another tool that helps lawyers type, search, or draft faster. It changes what clients can do for themselves, what they expect from their lawyers and what they are prepared to pay for.

In *Ditch The Billable Hour!*, the Vision stage of the 8 P Point Plan is about creating a clear picture of the future state, explaining how it differs from the current way of working and linking it to the firm's values, mission and strategy. The point is not just to announce a change; it is to make the future understandable, desirable and capable of being acted upon.

For AI pricing, the vision should be built around a new client value proposition which moves the firm away from selling effort and towards selling results, certainty, risk reduction, speed, confidence, judgment and commercial impact.

If the message to clients is simply, "AI means we can do the same work faster," then clients will quite reasonably ask for the saving. If the message is, "AI helps us deliver better, faster, safer and more certain outcomes, supported by lawyer judgment and accountability," the pricing conversation becomes more sophisticated.

This is where Ron Baker's thinking is so important.

In his foreword to *Ditch & Switch!* [27] Ron Baker draws a powerful distinction between transactions and transformations. Products and services say, "Look what we can do."

Transformations say, "Look at who you can become." He argues that fee-for-service models sell outputs, while value-based pricing focuses on outcomes and impact.

AI can help produce outputs, but lawyers must focus on transformations.

The future value proposition to communicate internally to your firm could say something like this:

> *Our AI Pricing Vision.*
>
> *We will not use AI simply to do old legal work faster and then argue about discounts. We will use AI, legal expertise, commercial acumen and human judgment to help clients achieve better outcomes with greater certainty, clarity and confidence.*
>
> *We will price the value we create, not the time we record. We will use technology to improve delivery, but our clients will pay for the outcome, the judgment, the supervision, the risk management and the accountability that sit behind the work.*
>
> *We will help clients make better decisions, reduce risk, seize opportunities, protect value and move forward with confidence. Where we create a bigger pie, we will seek a fair share of the value created rather than fight over discounts on the old one.*

That vision leads naturally to better pricing conversations.

The firm is no longer saying, "Pay us for our effort." It is saying, "Pay us for helping you become safer, stronger, clearer, faster, better protected or more successful."

That is a pricing vision worth promoting.

WORDS WITH THE WISE

Noo Jones

The future of legal services will not be shaped only by technology. It will be shaped by how well law firms learn.

AI is already changing the relationship between lawyers and clients. It is changing what clients expect, what they are willing to pay for, and how they judge whether a lawyer is adding value. Some firms are responding with curiosity and urgency. Others are still acting as though AI is not relevant to their work or their clients.

That is dangerous.

For me, the starting point is not the technology itself. It is purpose. Before a firm asks, "What AI tools should we buy?" or "What skills do our lawyers need?", it should first ask, "What kind of firm are we trying to become?" and "What kind of value are we here to provide?"

Without that strategic clarity, learning becomes fragmented. People attend sessions, receive updates, download guidance, perhaps experiment with tools, but the firm does not really change. In a world where AI is altering the work, the economics and the client relationship, that is not enough.

6 MINUTES OF YOUR TIME

Watch Douwe Groenevelt's AI-generated short films.

Barney: The End of Lawyers[28] and *The Last of Them,*[29] take a deliberately tongue-in-cheek swipe at the legal profession.

The joke is that, in a future shaped by AI, traditional lawyers have either disappeared or become a lost tribe clinging to old habits, old processes and old assumptions about their own importance.

Like all good satire, it is funny because it is uncomfortable.

PART 4: PLAN

TURN THE VISION INTO BEHAVIOUR

A vision is useful only if it changes what people actually do.

If the firm's AI pricing vision is that it will use legal expertise, technology, commercial acumen and judgment to help clients achieve better outcomes, then the next question is obvious: what is the plan to make that happen?

This is where many firms will stumble. They will create an AI strategy, announce a pilot, buy some licences, run a few training sessions and then assume the business has changed.

It has not.

AI cannot be treated as a temporary innovation project, an IT experiment or a productivity toy. It is a market restructuring force. It will affect what work lawyers do, how work is produced, what clients are willing to pay for, how junior lawyers are trained, how firms differentiate themselves, how matters are staffed, how services are delivered and what clients regard as valuable.

The plan must therefore be a new business model plan, not a software roll-out plan.

BRACE YOURSELF…
incoming provocative statement

If AI reduces the time taken and your firm sells time, you have not bought productivity. You have bought a revenue problem.

START WITH CLIENT OUTCOMES

The firm should begin by moving from a "legal work" mindset to an "outcomes and experience" mindset.

That means asking what clients are really trying to achieve when they instruct the firm.

This is not a branding exercise. It is an operating model exercise.

The board should ask what outcomes clients come to the firm to achieve, which client problems the firm is really solving, what success looks like from the client's perspective, where the current experience is slow, expensive, uncertain, confusing or frustrating, and how the service could be redesigned around the client's desired destination.

A firm that maps its services only by practice area may miss the point. Clients do not wake up wanting "corporate", "employment", "litigation" or "regulatory". They want something protected, resolved, achieved, avoided or improved.

That is where the plan should start.

BUILD AI INTO THE OPERATING MODEL

The firm should not bolt AI onto the edge of the business and hope it creates transformation.

The CEO should require each practice group to identify which tasks AI can already support, which tasks are likely to be displaced, which services can be redesigned, which client problems can be solved faster or better, which risks require controls, what quality assurance is needed, and how AI affects pricing, staffing, training and client communication.

This is where the taker, shaper and maker distinction identified by McKinsey in *Rewired - The McKinsey Guide to Out Competing in the Age of Digital and AI* [30] is useful.

Most law firms will not build their own large language models. That is the "maker" route, and for most firms it will be too expensive, too technical and unnecessary. To give an example, at the top end of the spectrum in May 2026, the FT reported that Kirkland & Ellis had set aside $500 million to create its own AI platform. I suspect not many law firms will have such funds at their disposal.

Many firms will start as "takers", using available tools and subscription services to improve productivity.

The more ambitious firms will become "shapers", combining available models with proprietary data, workflows, expertise and client knowledge to create something more distinctive. That is likely to be the sweet spot for many firms. Use available tools where they make sense, but shape them around the firm's knowledge, clients, processes and value proposition.

I wasn't quite sure whether the box below should sit as a quote or as one of the incoming provocative statements. It will be quite terrifying for some. In the end, I settled on using it as a quote. But make no mistake. It is still provocative.

> Business leaders will be digitally transforming their companies for the rest of their careers.
>
> The opening sentence in *Rewired: The McKinsey Guide to Outcompeting in the Age of Digital and AI*
>
> **Eric Lamarre & Kate Smaje**

WORDS WITH THE WISE

Felix Riley

I am sceptical of the idea that every law firm needs to be seen as being at the absolute cutting edge of AI. I am not saying ignore it. I am saying do not be stampeded. Take the obvious quick wins. Use the tools where they help. But do not confuse adoption with strategy.

There is no glory in buying technology if you cannot show the return. There is no intelligence in copying another firm just because FOMO has taken over the partnership.

STOP SELLING TIME AS THE MAIN PRODUCT

> Talking about target hours feels like you're in the Middle Ages now. We need to move to measure people on output and productivity.
>
> **Renae Lattey, Chief Executive, Mallesons, Financial Times, 15th May 2026**

Global consultancies are already changing their business models to reflect the shift from activity to outcomes, so do not let colleagues tell you that law firms cannot do the same.

The Times of India,[31] reporting on the Financial Times, says McKinsey is rethinking its partner compensation structure through "Project Acorn", partly because clients are becoming less willing to pay simply for hours worked and increasingly demanding fees linked to value, results and measurable outcomes.

That is worth pausing on because McKinsey is not a tiny disruptor shouting from the sidelines; it is one of the most established professional services firms in the world.

If firms like McKinsey can see that AI, client pressure and outcome-based expectations require changes to pricing, rewards, capital structure and partner behaviour, then law firms cannot hide behind the tired excuse that "our work is different" or "clients will not accept it". Of course, law is different. So is consulting. So is audit. So is every professional discipline when viewed from the inside. But the commercial direction of travel is clear: clients are challenging payment for effort and are asking instead what has been achieved, what risk has been reduced, what decision has been improved and what value has been created.

The question for law firm owners is no longer whether outcome-based thinking can be done. It is whether they are brave enough to start redesigning the firm before their clients force the redesign upon them.

Armando Hernandez, Founder and CEO of H&CO, examines the issue with pleasing bluntness in his article, *The Billable Hour Is Dead. AI Just Signed the Death Certificate.*[32] He states: "Price the outcome. Not the hours." Hernandez is not writing as a law firm pricing consultant. He is writing as the leader of a professional services firm that has already had to face the commercial reality of AI.

His point is simple: "Clients never wanted hours. They wanted outcomes." That is the sentence law firm owners need to sit with. Time was merely the old measuring stick.

Hernandez says that, at H&CO, they have: "already moved to outcome-based pricing" across global compliance and tax services, with "fixed fees", "defined deliverables" and "no timesheets." He also says they "charge for access, insight, and outcomes, not hours."

MAKE AI VALUE VISIBLE

If AI improves delivery, clients need to see the value. Indeed, don't even assume clients see the value; *tell them* what it is.

AI can help produce the analysis, but the lawyer must explain what matters, what is dangerous, what has been missed, what the trade-offs are, and what the client should do next.

That is where the professional value sits.

The plan should therefore include standard templates for client-facing deliverables, report formats, briefing notes and value summaries. These should be properly designed, written in client language, and linked to business outcomes.

A text-heavy memo full of legal caveats is not always the best way to demonstrate value.

- Sometimes the client needs a one-page risk summary.
- Sometimes the client needs a board-ready decision paper.
- Sometimes the client just needs a call.

WORDS WITH THE WISE

Shaun Jardine!

(I promoted myself!)

Value is slippery. It is not fixed, rational or neat. It sits in the eye of the client, not the lawyer. One client values speed, and another values reassurance. Another wants status, certainty, control, kindness, discretion, or simply the feeling that someone capable has taken the problem off their shoulders. That is why a bottle of water costs next to nothing at home, more at a service station, more again in a smart restaurant, and a fortune if you are thirsty enough. It is the same water. The context changes the value.

The same is true of legal work. A letter sent in 20 minutes on a Friday afternoon may be worth far more to the client than a carefully itemised bill showing how long it took. The client is not buying the inputs; they are buying the outcome, the relief, the speed, the confidence and the feeling that the problem is being dealt with.

I explored this in much greater detail in *Ditch the Billable Hour!*, but the point needs repeating here: if value is subjective, contextual and emotional, then lawyers cannot discover it by staring at a timesheet. They have to ask better questions, listen properly, understand what matters to the client, and then offer choices. Different options. Different levels of service. Different prices. Let the client decide what they value because clients have never really been interested in an hourly rate. They are interested in what matters to them.

LAW SCHOOLS HAVE A ROLE TO PLAY

I am sure you will have heard the mutterings. One or two voices (perhaps more than one or two) raising concerns about how prospective lawyers are being trained at law school. And, frankly, they have a point.

But it is simply not good enough to sit there, arms folded, saying, "It wasn't like that in my day." Of course it wasn't. That is the point.

Helpfully, in his book *Law in the Era of AI*, Bjarne Tellmann gives proper thought to what the lawyers of tomorrow should actually be learning at law school today.

Tellmann breaks this down into two broad areas. First, learning to "Think Like a Lawyer", where subjects such as property, contract, torts, Civil Procedure and criminal law remain core subjects. Second, "Excel as Professionals", where Tellmann lists new skills that should be taught, including:

- Business literacy, strategy and leadership
- Technological and digital fluency and
- Creativity, design thinking and interdisciplinary problem solving

Now, I don't know about you, but that sounds rather more attractive than the legal education many of us signed up for. More relevant too.

A law degree that still teaches students how to think like lawyers but also prepares them to operate as professionals in an AI world. A world of clients, businesses, technology, leadership, creativity, judgment and change.

Not the old world of dusty textbooks, terrified tutorials and the occasional Latin phrase thrown in to make everyone feel inadequate.

WORDS WITH THE WISE

Abby Winkworth

We need to rethink legal education and lawyer identity

One thing that worries me is legal education.

I have a child studying law at university, and I do not think he is being taught the things that will be most useful to when he enters the job market.

Our future lawyers need more than pure legal knowledge. They need to be taught how to be commercial, curious and entrepreneurial, how to show their genuine interest and concern for the people they are working with. They need to know how to help people find solutions.

The law is a tool they can use. It is not all they are.

That may be a fundamental change. I was speaking recently to a Law firm leader and lawyer about how he identified himself as a law firm leader. He said, "No, I am an entrepreneur. I just happen to be a law firm leader." I thought that was exactly the mindset we need more of.

I fear but am equally energised by the sense that the legal world is not going to stand still long enough for people to define themselves only as lawyers.

AI has the power to be democratising if we decide to use it well. We are already seeing people carve themselves out of larger firms and start boutiques. That may continue. It may not simply be the death of big law. It may be the rise of a post-industrial legal industry, structured in a very different way.

REDESIGN TALENT, TRAINING AND DEVELOPMENT

A firm's plan must also address the issue of lawyer development.

For generations, junior lawyers learned through labour-intensive tasks: research, drafting, due diligence, bundling, reviewing, summarising and preparing first drafts. If AI performs more of that work, the firm needs to ask how junior lawyers will develop judgment, confidence, commercial awareness and professional wisdom.

This is not just an HR issue; it is a future capability issue.

WORDS WITH THE WISE

Wendy Jephson

If law firms only use AI for automation, they risk removing some of the very experiences through which lawyers learn judgment, develop expertise and understand risk.

Used well, AI can do something much more valuable. It can help lawyers reveal the thinking that usually stays hidden. It can help experienced lawyers unpack what they notice, why they act, how they make decisions and what they are predicting might happen next. That thinking can then be shared with junior lawyers, used to brief teams, improve supervision, create better records and explain value more clearly to clients.

That matters because the future of legal pricing will not only depend on whether firms can produce documents more efficiently. It will depend on whether they can explain the value of the thinking behind those documents.

The firm should create a lawyer development framework built around mentoring, AI supervision, legal judgment, client communication, commercial awareness, ethical decision-making, project management, pricing literacy, relationship building, problem diagnosis, risk assessment and conducting After Action Reviews.

Lawyers will need to be trained for the work they will actually be paid for in the future, not merely the work they historically performed on the way to becoming senior.

That means earlier exposure to clients, negotiation dynamics, commercial context, pricing conversations and decision-making. It means teaching lawyers how to supervise AI outputs, spot weak reasoning, challenge conclusions and understand consequences. It means promotion criteria that value judgment, influence, trust, client empathy and commercial acumen, not just output and stamina.

WORDS WITH THE WISE

Noo Jones

I have a real dislike of the word "training" when it is used too narrowly. Continuous learning is a better description.

Training can sound like something that is done to people. It can sound like a course, a webinar, a box to tick, or a way of making people complete tasks faster. Of course, there will always be technical knowledge that lawyers need to acquire. But the bigger issue now is continuous learning.

Law firms need to build learning into the way they operate. That means helping people develop judgment, adaptability, commercial awareness, critical thinking, client understanding and confidence with digital practice. It also means helping lawyers understand risk, value, pricing and the commercial context in which their clients operate.

Those capabilities do not appear because someone attended a one-hour session. They develop when a firm has a clear purpose, a coherent strategy and managers who support learning through everyday conversations.

In my view, firms should begin with the foundations. What is our purpose? What are our values? What do we want our lawyers to be capable of doing? How do we want clients to experience working with us? What does good judgment look like here? What does responsible AI use look like here?

Only then should the firm design the learning.

> The soul of the lawyer can't be killed by AI. The disciplined, professional attention of someone trained to see what matters will be more valuable than ever, because the supply of this insight, this judgement, will be static, and the supply of information that requires this understanding will be exploding exponentially. Ironically, this will mean that talent management, talent development, and talent retention will become core economic pillars for AI-enabled legal service delivery.
>
> **David Wang, Attention Is All You Need (Again)**

WORDS WITH THE WISE

Chantal McNaught

Generative AI is dangerously compelling because it can sound confident. Human beings tend to associate confidence with competence. That creates danger. A junior lawyer, or someone at the beginning of their learning journey, may be more susceptible to accepting AI-generated material because they do not yet have the subject matter expertise to spot what is wrong.

That is why lawyers remain so important. In matters of law, lawyers are "BS" detectors.

WORDS WITH THE WISE

Mark Barrett

If you have already deployed AI, the next logical step is to train and enable people properly. At the same time, you need to build compliance into the process. Not as a heavy, clunky overlay that slows everyone down, but as something as frictionless as possible. Good governance should not sit outside the work. It should be baked into the way the work is done.

That means building in human oversight and review points. It means making sure the information, the updates, the checks and the audit trail are part of the workflow. The more you can engineer those things into the process, the less you are relying on busy people remembering to do the right thing at the end. Removing friction is a key principle.

One of the biggest mistakes I see is firms giving lawyers an AI tool and assuming that, because those lawyers already know how to review a document, conduct research or produce a matter summary, they will know how to do those tasks with AI. They will not necessarily know. It is a different way of working.

AI is a probability engine. It gives probabilistic responses. It may give a slightly different answer each time. So, lawyers need to learn how to instruct it, how to give it context, how to define the output they want and how to challenge what comes back.

The organisation also needs to think about how it configures AI so that the output gets closer to the consistent, declarative result the firm needs. That means baking in the firm's process, its intellectual property, its quality standards, its experience and its domain knowledge. That is where the firm's real value sits.

This is not simply a matter of asking AI a better question. It is about embedding the firm's way of working into the tool, and then using the tool in a way that reflects the firm's risk profile, client obligations and professional standards.

WORDS WITH THE WISE

Abby Winkworth

The junior lawyer problem is real.

There is another issue that firms need to confront honestly: what happens to junior lawyers?

For years, junior lawyers spent time doing tasks that technology has already reduced or removed. I can remember hovering over photocopiers, removing staples, putting them back in again, collating documents and checking bundles and being paid for it. Enormous chunks of time disappeared into that sort of work, and now it has just disappeared.

I admit that I do get a bit fed up with the way chargeable hours are used to manage junior lawyers: "You should be recording seven or eight chargeable hours a day," we say, while taking away many of the tasks that used to fill their time. They are supposed to replace that time with more meaningful work, but their partners are not always giving them that meaningful work.

There is a simple solution: Give them more client management responsibility. It's a win-win. We know that clients expect to spend more time with junior lawyers and, in any event, do not want to pay for a senior lawyer or partner on simple work, but they find junior lawyers lack commerciality and the skills of curiosity and listening.

And why is that? It is because we do not teach it to them. They are often trying to work out how to make a difference to their firm and their client without the leadership, skills, knowledge and recognition that makes such ambition achievable.

As AI removes routine work, firms need to think much more carefully about training, supervision, work allocation, commercial education and the development of judgment. It doesn't help the firm, the individual or the industry to say, "AI will make everyone more efficient," and leave juniors to work out how to navigate the empty space.

WORDS WITH THE WISE

Joanna Gaudoin

There are some generic skills that everybody needs. Building rapport is one example. Lawyers need that internally and externally. But there are also situation-specific skills. How do you network at an event? How do you develop an existing client relationship? How do you have a conversation with a colleague in another department about cross-referrals? How do you start becoming a trusted adviser rather than just the person who does a transaction?

Lawyers need to understand why they are being asked to do something, what they need to do and how to do it. If lawyers do not know how to tackle something, they often stay away from it. That is not necessarily because they are unwilling. It is often because lawyers hate not knowing.

THE MILLION DOLLAR PROBLEM

It is not just training that should concern law firms. It is also the rate at which associates are leaving.

In its 2025 report, *Navigating the Million Dollar Problem,*[33] BigHand reported that replacing each lost associate can cost up to $1 million in lost revenue, recruitment costs and training fees. BigHand asked the very relevant question:

"How many can you afford to lose?"

One of the key findings in the report was that the number of associates, both junior and senior, leaving the profession has almost doubled in the last 12 months. In 2024, the figure was 9% for both junior and senior associates. In 2025, it had risen to 16% for junior associates and 17% for senior associates.

To be honest, I am not surprised.

Earlier in this book, in the section 'Measure Confidence Before You Try To Change Behaviour', I showed you the results of surveys I have run with law firm staff over a number of years. They have been telling me, consistently and clearly, that there are issues inside their firms. Once more:

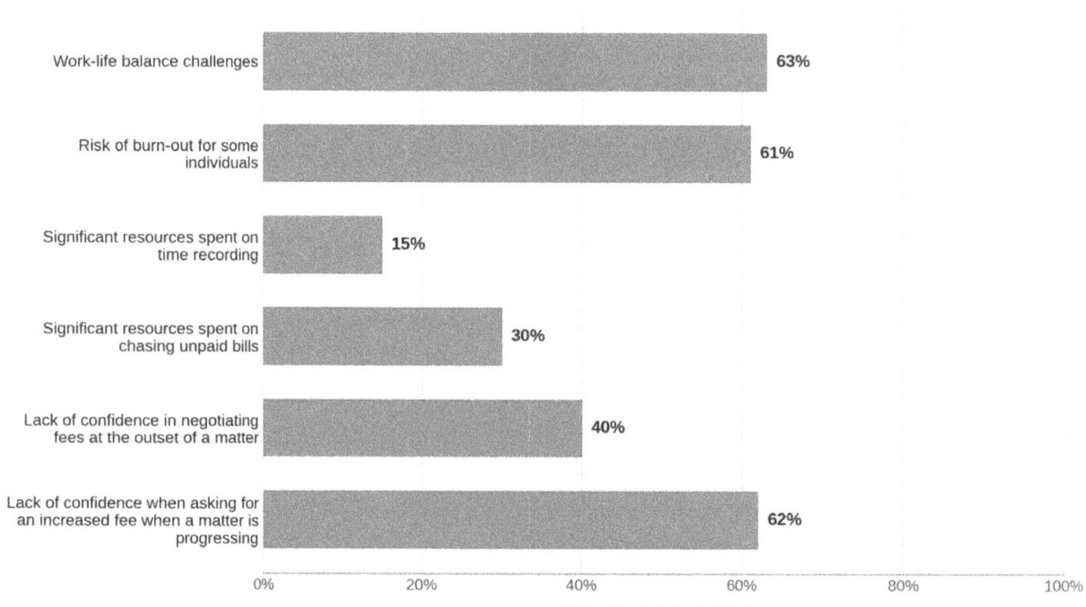

So, what happens to the staff?

- They work harder.
- They absorb the pain.
- They do more than they priced for.

- They avoid the awkward fee conversation.
- And then everyone wonders why they are exhausted.

If replacing one lost associate can cost up to $1 million, then perhaps the better question is not just, "How many can you afford to lose?"

It is this: What are you doing to stop them from leaving in the first place?

WORDS WITH THE WISE

Robert Hanna

Law firms can go out and buy all the AI tools they want, but they still have to ask: what is in the heads of our experienced lawyers, and how is that being transferred?

That judgment, wisdom and knowledge is incredibly valuable. It is also vulnerable. What happens if one of your rainmaker partners is tapped on the shoulder, gets a big offer and leaves? Their cognitive thinking walks out of the door with them.

Firms need to think seriously about how they capture and protect that cognitive capital. How do they train the next generation? How do they make sure juniors still develop judgment in an AI world where the nature of their training will be very different? How do they avoid losing the very thing clients are actually prepared to pay for?

That is not a soft issue. It is a business issue. It is a pricing issue. It is a risk issue.

8 PPP PENGUIN LOGIC

If lawyers lack confidence, train them.

SHINGLES LOGIC

Training Is Not Transformation

Shingles celebrates that 87% of people attended AI training. Unfortunately, nobody has changed a workflow, improved a client conversation, created a pricing option, reduced write-offs or launched a new service.

WORDS WITH THE WISE

Joanna Gaudoin

Technical knowledge still matters, of course, but it is no longer enough on its own. Every law firm says it has good technical lawyers.

Many firms also say they have great client service. But the question is: how is that actually demonstrated?

The real differentiator will be how lawyers apply their knowledge to the client's specific situation. That requires judgment. It requires commercial understanding. It requires the ability to listen properly, ask better questions and build trust.

This is why I think law firms need to take soft skills much more seriously. I know "soft skills" can sound vague, but I do not mean anything fluffy. I mean the practical skills lawyers need to build rapport, develop existing clients, work with introducers, network properly, collaborate across departments and become more useful to clients.

BUILD DIFFERENT TEAMS

The future AI-enabled legal service team will not always look like the traditional partner-associate pyramid. We discussed the myriad shapes available earlier in this book. Let's consider who will actually be working in the new businesses.

It may include lawyers, legal engineers, data analysts, product managers, project managers, pricing specialists, process designers, technologists, knowledge lawyers, client success managers and risk specialists.

This does not diminish lawyers. It puts lawyers where they add most value: judgment, ethics, accountability, risk assessment, client understanding and strategic advice.

The CEO should require each strategic AI project to identify the right team, rather than defaulting automatically to the traditional staffing model. If the old pyramid depended on leveraging junior labour, and AI reduces the need for some of that labour, then the structure has to be reconsidered.

WORDS WITH THE WISE

Heather Suttie

Artificial intelligence, pricing, and transience of the legal service sector's workforce will cause the traditional law firm pyramid structure to rollover like an upending iceberg, and by 2030, global legal services will operate much differently than they do now.

BRACE YOURSELF…
incoming provocative statement

A firm cannot say it wants an AI-enabled future while preserving every feature of a pre-AI staffing model.

REVIEW THE CLIENT BASE

AI will make some legal work easier to automate, commoditise or move elsewhere. Deeper relationships will be harder to displace. The plan should therefore include a proper client deselection process. You won't be surprised to learn this was covered in *Ditch The Billable Hour!*

Let me start by challenging a few myths:

- All clients are good clients.
- All clients are the same.
- Fixed pricing is impossible because you do not know what will happen.
- Clients are always shopping around for the cheapest quote.
- Competitors charge less, so we must too.
- There is a fixed "market rate".
- Clients will not pay more.
- Clients are not interested in VBP.

If you are serious about pricing, your client base will change. Good. As Ron Baker says, "Bad clients drive out good clients."

So, part of your vision should be deciding which clients to deselect, which clients to pursue, how to work more collaboratively, how to deliver better service and how to make the firm a better place to work.

That is not soft. It is sensible.

In *Ditch the Billable Hour!* I wrote about the phrase "the trusted advisor". I pointed out that most law firm websites say some version of the same thing: that the firm is client-focused, puts clients at the centre of everything it does, and that its lawyers are trusted advisors. I also said that I understood why lawyers liked the label. It has kudos. It sounds valuable. It suggests a deeper relationship than simply being instructed to do a piece of legal work. And, commercially, it makes sense because clients will often pay a premium where trust is genuinely high.

But I also made a more uncomfortable point. In the main, many lawyers are not trusted advisors. They are suppliers.

That is not meant as an insult. A supplier may be competent, professional, responsive and useful. A supplier may do good legal work. A supplier may be instructed regularly. But trusted advisor status is different. It has to be earned. It is not achieved because the marketing team put the words on the website, or because a partner says it in a pitch, or because the firm has acted for the client for a long time.

In *Ditch the Billable Hour!*, I asked lawyers to test the point by thinking about one of their best clients and then asking whether they really knew them. Did they know their spouse or partner's name? Their birthday? Their wider family position? Their business strategy? Their financial worries? Their exit plan? Whether they had a shareholders' agreement? Whether they had made a will? When was the last time they called the client when there was no live piece of work to discuss? The chances are that many lawyers could not answer those questions positively.

That was the point then. It remains the point now.

In an AI world, lawyers have to become trusted advisors, but we should not kid ourselves that the profession is already there. Trust is not a slogan. It is not a website claim. It is not a directory ranking. It is earned by showing interest, understanding the client, asking better questions, listening properly, giving judgment, taking responsibility and helping the client make better decisions.

AI will produce information. AI will produce drafts. AI will produce summaries. AI will produce options. The lawyer's opportunity is to become *the person* the client trusts to make sense of all of that.

But first, we have to gain the right.

WORDS WITH THE WISE

Karolina Šilingienė

One of the biggest issues is that law firms often do not really know their clients as a firm. A partner may know one part of the relationship, but the wider firm does not have the full picture. In a larger firm, the real estate partner may only know the real estate work. They may go into a client meeting without knowing that the litigation team has recently advised the same client, or that an IP consultant has worked on a brand registration, or that there are compliance issues handled by someone else in the firm.

That makes the firm look less joined-up than it should. It also weakens the claim that the firm is a trusted adviser. How can you be the trusted legal adviser if you are not even aware of what is happening with that client in another department?

DECIDE WHAT BELONGS INSIDE OR OUTSIDE THE PARTNERSHIP

Some AI-enabled services may not fit naturally inside the existing partnership structure.

The CEO should lead the debate on whether certain services should be delivered through the existing LLP, a wholly owned subsidiary, an alternative business structure, a joint venture, a technology company, a consultancy arm or a separate product business.

A separate structure may allow the firm to employ non-lawyer leaders more naturally, create different incentives, use product-style governance, accept external investment, separate risk, build different terms and pricing, or stop the partnership machine from suffocating the idea.

Not every innovation needs a new structure. But some might. The plan should at least ask the question.

CREATE THE PRICING ARCHITECTURE

The plan must set out the pricing architecture the firm wants to build and tools which may help. That should include value-based pricing and possibly even subscriptions. It should also include the scoping rules that protect margin, and the variables for creating options.

When creating options, think beyond the legal task itself. The differences might include who does the work, access to senior lawyers, response times, payment terms, use of technology, meetings, site visits, access to other teams, client training, legal audits, seminars, network introductions, service guarantees, capped abortive costs or even insured risk. The point is to design choices that reflect what different clients value, rather than simply offering the same service at three different prices.

THE IMPLEMENTATION RISKS AND HOW TO MANAGE THEM

Value-based pricing sounds sensible in theory. Most lawyers will nod along when you say clients want certainty, transparency and value. They will agree that AI changes the economics of legal work. They may even accept that the billable hour is looking a little wobbly. Then you ask them to change how they scope, price, sell, deliver and review work. That is when the penguins start looking nervous.

Implementation is where good ideas either become part of the firm or quietly disappear into the drawer marked "interesting initiative we must revisit at some point". The risk is not that value-based pricing is too complicated to understand. The risk is that firms underestimate the practical, cultural and commercial barriers that sit between understanding the idea and actually changing behaviour.

Managing partners need to be honest about those barriers from the start. This is not negativity; it is preparation. Lawyers are trained to spot risk, so use that skill properly. Identify the likely obstacles, discuss them openly and decide what the firm will do when they appear.

Here are some of the main implementation risks and how to manage them.

Implementation risk	What it looks like in practice	How to manage it
Partner resistance	Partners say they support value-based pricing, but continue to price by hours, discounts and gut feel. They worry about losing autonomy, profit or control.	Involve partners early. Explain the commercial case, not just the theory. Use examples from their own matters. Show how better scoping and pricing can protect margin rather than reduce it.
The "my work is different" objection	Each department insists that value-based pricing might work elsewhere, but not in litigation, not in family, not in corporate, not in private client, not in anything they personally do.	Use practice-area examples. Start with work that is repeatable enough to price sensibly. Do not begin with the most complex, unusual matter in the building. Build confidence through pilots.
Poor scoping	The firm agrees a fixed or value-based price without clearly defining assumptions, exclusions, client responsibilities, stages, or change controls. Scope creep then eats the profit.	Make scoping non-negotiable. Use written assumptions and exclusions. Train lawyers to identify what is included, what is not included, and what happens if the client changes the brief.

Implementation risk	What it looks like in practice	How to manage it
Pricing by fear	Lawyers set fixed fees too low because they are frightened the client will say no. They convert hourly anxiety into fixed-fee under-pricing.	Give lawyers pricing guidance, precedent examples, options and authority. Review early matters. Teach them that value-based pricing is not discounting with nicer stationery.
Lack of management information	The firm does not know which work is profitable, where write-offs occur, which clients cause scope creep or how much AI-enabled delivery actually costs.	Improve pricing data. Track estimated cost, price, margin, write-offs, client changes, AI tool costs and lessons learned. Feed the learning into the Big Book of Usefulness.
Incentives still reward hours	Lawyers are told to price for value but are still measured mainly by chargeable hours, utilisation and recorded time.	Align incentives with the new model. Measure margin, client satisfaction, pricing confidence, write-offs avoided, scope discipline, cash collection and successful use of pricing options.
AI cost confusion	The firm uses AI tools but does not understand subscriptions, token usage, implementation costs, supervision time, rework, governance or support costs.	Bring the CFO, CIO, risk team and practice leaders into the conversation. Treat AI as part of the cost of delivery. Do not assume faster automatically means cheaper or more profitable.
Client confusion	Clients do not understand what they are being charged for if AI has helped produce part of the work. They may assume AI means the work should be almost free.	Explain the value clearly. Separate production from judgment. Show what AI assisted with, what the lawyer supervised, what risk was managed and what outcome the client is buying.

Implementation risk	What it looks like in practice	How to manage it
No change control	The client asks for "just one more thing", the matter expands, and the lawyer absorbs the extra work because they feel awkward raising the price.	Build change control into every fixed-price or value-based proposal. Train lawyers to say: "That is outside the agreed scope, but we can price that additional work for you."
Internal inconsistency	One partner offers options, another gives a single fixed fee, another discounts hourly rates, and another tells the client the firm is "still working all this out".	Create a common pricing language. Use templates, examples, crib sheets and internal guidance. The aim is not robotic uniformity, but clients should not receive completely different messages from the same firm.
Overcomplication	The firm turns value-based pricing into a giant internal project with committees, spreadsheets, approval layers and no actual client conversations.	Start small. Pick pilot areas. Create simple tools. Test, learn and improve. Do not wait until the system is perfect. It never will be.
Failure to train lawyers to sell the price	The price may be sensible, but the lawyer cannot explain it confidently to the client. The lawyer then retreats to hourly billing or apologises for the fee.	Train lawyers in value conversations. Give them words, scripts and examples. Pricing confidence is a skill. It improves with practice.
Ignoring junior lawyer development	AI removes or reduces some traditional junior tasks, but the firm has no replacement method for training judgment, pattern recognition and commercial sense.	Design new learning pathways. Use supervised AI collaboration, matter debriefs, pricing reviews, client context discussions and judgment training. Do not leave development to accident.

Implementation risk	What it looks like in practice	How to manage it
Leadership loses interest	The managing partner launches the initiative, everyone gets excited, and six months later, the firm is back to hours, write-offs and old habits.	Keep the change visible. Review progress regularly. Celebrate quick wins. Share examples. Make pricing part of management meetings, department reviews and strategy discussions.
No one owns the project	Everyone agrees that value-based pricing matters, but nobody is responsible for making it happen.	Appoint owners. Create Pioneer Penguins. Give them authority, time and support. Pricing transformation cannot be run entirely by goodwill and enthusiasm.

The point is not to scare you. The point is to stop you being surprised.

Every one of these risks can be managed if the firm is willing to look at them properly. None of them is a reason to stay stuck in the old model. In fact, many of them are reasons to change. If your firm cannot scope properly, does not understand matter profitability, relies on discounts, rewards hours over outcomes and has no idea how AI affects cost, margin or client value, then the problem is not value-based pricing. The problem is that the current model has been hiding weaknesses that need to be fixed now.

That is why implementation matters.

Value-based pricing is not a slogan, nor a new line in a proposal, nor a clever way of saying "fixed fee". It is a different way of thinking about the relationship between value, price, risk, delivery and profit.

AI makes that work more urgent because it changes the relationship between effort and output. But the firms that succeed will not be the firms that simply say, "we use AI" or "we offer fixed fees". The firms that succeed will be the firms that build the habits, tools, data, confidence and culture needed to price outcomes properly.

So do not pretend the risks are not there.

Name them. Plan for them. Manage them. Then keep going.

BRACE YOURSELF…
incoming provocative statement

The firms that win with AI will not be the firms that adopted it first.

They will be the firms that adopted it properly, redesigned the business model around client value, trained their people for the work that will matter, and priced the outcome rather than the hours that disappeared.

CRIB SHEET

P#3

	Title	Author / Source	Link
READ			
	Charles Proteus Steinmetz – read about the original engineer with a hammer…although in this case it was a piece of chalk!	Smithsonian Magazine	https://www.smithsonianmag.com/history/charles-proteus-steinmetz-the-wizard-of-schenectady-51912022/
	Beyond the Chatbot: Meet the Agentic Law Firm	Damien Riehl	https://mnbars.org/?pg=BenchBarofMinnesota&pubAction=viewIssue&pubIssueID=69276&pubIssueItemID=459569
	Ditch & Switch – 50 Value-Based Pricing Examples For Law Professionals (book)	Shaun Jardine	

	Rewired: The McKinsey Guide to Outcompeting in the Age of Digital and AI (book)	Eric Lamarre & Kate Smaje	
	McKinsey is rethinking its pay structure because clients are no longer paying for hours	The Times of India	http://timesofindia.indiatimes.com/articleshow/131131220.cms?utm_source=contentofinterest&utm_medium=text&utm_campaign=cppst
	The Billable Hour Is Dead. AI Just Signed the Death Certificate.	Armando Hernandez	https://www.linkedin.com/pulse/billable-hour-dead-ai-just-signed-death-certificate-armando-hernandez-gzozf/
	Navigating The Million Dollar Problem	BigHand	https://www.bighand.com/en-us/resources/whitepapers/navigating-the-million-dollar-problem/
WATCH			
	Barney – The End of Lawyers	Douwe Groenevelt	https://youtu.be/c_OMFSCUyZA?si=q3p_U4_SQjZeCt6I
	The Last of Them	Douwe Groenevelt	https://youtu.be/ndGaqdYYX30?si=uz1JCl5OhqTvUcF6
MISCELLANY			
	Is This The End Of Leverage?	George Beaton	https://www.linkedin.com/pulse/end-leverage-george-beaton-ng5xc/
	Linklaters Launches New Practice to Build Matter-Specific AI Solutions	Law.com	https://www.law.com/international-edition/2026/05/08/linklaters-launches-new-practice-to-build-matter-specific-ai-solutions-/
	The Law Firm Pyramid Rollover	Heather Suttie	https://heathersuttie.ca/insights/the-law-firm-pyramid-rollover/
	3 Things that Make a MEANINGFUL Vision	Simon Sinek	https://youtu.be/zpzZumZCdWA?si=beUfxZhtOkj8B_sD

TIPS / CHECKLISTS

Possibility Thinking Questions To Pose

- How could we possibly separate automated work, lawyer judgment and business acumen in our pricing model?
- What new AI-enabled products could we create if we stopped thinking in terms of hourly rates?
- How might we possibly create three pricing options for an AI-assisted matter?
- What could we possibly say when the client asks for the AI discount?

CEO Questions To Pose

- What client problems are we trying to solve with AI?
- What new products, services or pricing options could AI allow us to create?
- Where does AI reduce production time, and where does lawyer judgment remain non-negotiable?
- What does our AI-enabled pricing process look like from the first client conversation to the final bill?
- Where will we capture examples, lessons, client responses and pricing decisions in the BBU?

P#4. PROMOTE: EXPLAIN THE NEW STORY INTERNALLY AND EXTERNALLY

P#4. PROMOTE – COMMUNICATING AND GETTING PEOPLE BEHIND THE PROJECT

One absolutely crucial step is to communicate the Vision to the whole firm and stakeholders. This is where many plans fail.

Depending on the size of your firm, you will use a variety of channels to engage with your audience. The Vision in P#3 must be reinforced by both the leadership/Pioneer Group's actions and behaviours. Through effective communication, you will get buy-in and create enthusiasm and commitment to the change.

WELCOME TO P#4 – PROMOTE

P#4 Promote is about communicating the AI-enabled value-based pricing project clearly, repeatedly, and in language that clients, lawyers and the wider firm can understand.

LAWYERS MEASURE WORK DIFFERENTLY FROM CLIENTS

Client metrics are not lawyer metrics.

Before we get too carried away with AI and pricing models, we need to confront a more basic problem. Lawyers and clients have not always understood each other very well. That was true before AI. It is even more important now.

In *Ditch The Billable Hour!* I referred to the LexisNexis report, *The Riddle of Perception,*[34] authored by Jon Whittle. The report explored the legal market and, in particular, the gap between what lawyers thought clients valued and what clients actually valued. It was difficult reading then, and it is even more difficult in an AI-enabled legal market.

The central point was simple. Lawyers thought they knew what clients wanted, but the evidence suggested otherwise. That is why the P#4 Promote stage is so important.

So, before we look at how to promote an AI pricing project, it is worth reading the wise words of Jon Whittle. Because the lesson from *The Riddle of Perception* is still the same, never assume you know what the client values. Ask. Listen. Then price and communicate accordingly.

WORDS WITH THE WISE

Jon Whittle, Jon Whittle Consulting Ltd

One of the reasons LexisNexis decided to compile the report was because, whilst we were specialists in providing law firms with comprehensive legal research and legal productivity tools, we thought it would be illuminating to have a better understanding of how lawyers interacted with their own clients.

If we understood the needs of Law Firm clients, it would help LexisNexis improve the quality of the services it provided to law firms. So, we did some market research to help LexisNexis with their understanding of how law firms worked with their clients – to get under the bonnet of what law firms actually did!

When we started the work, we began to unearth a huge disconnect between what a client thought a good relationship with their law firm looked like, and what lawyers thought made up a good lawyer-client relationship.

We were working with 122 law firms and got access to 108 clients and really drilled into both parties' respective perceptions of value. The client's perception and the lawyer's perception. It immediately became apparent that there was a problem – 77% of lawyers thought the legal service they gave represented good or excellent value for money. However, only 26% of clients thought they got good or excellent value in the service they received from their lawyers. This was one of the widest gaps in perception of value between a provider and a customer that I have seen in any of the professions.

As a follow-up piece, when we asked if lawyers worked in a service industry, all of those surveyed said yes, but caveated their answer by saying that they did not think their colleagues did. This translated into a statistic which states that 77% of other lawyers did not believe they were in a service industry. If 77% of lawyers are not in a service industry, what industry are they in? I think this mindset is a crucial window into the mindset that causes so many challenges in the relationship between lawyers and their clients.

The question I wanted to explore as a consequence of these research results was to understand why lawyers' perceptions of value were so different from those of their clients. My conclusion was that its roots lie in a very simple observation: which is that the whole point of being a lawyer is to deliver high-quality, robust, secure, dependable legal advice. The fundamental requirement to deliver good law trumps all other considerations.

Furthermore, everything the law firm does is driven by that objective. It's critical. The rule of law matters more than anything else. Which is why law firms invest, first and foremost, in legal processes, technology, systems and information, all of which are designed to support the delivery of that high-quality advice. Customer care and customer service will, by definition, always come second to the delivery of good quality advice.

If you talk to law firms about improving their law firms, it usually revolves around getting more lawyers – good ones – then it's about process, technology, information and how they can make their law firm better at delivering law.

This then tips over into how law firms choose to promote themselves and their service. The focus is all about the quality of law.

If you look at any law firm's website, there will be a lot of information about what they do (their legal offering), who their people are, how many of them there are, how many of them have over 30 years' experience. It's all about them. Law Firms seem compelled to talk about what they do rather than how it helps their clients. To demonstrate this, I took the 'about us' page from ten different law firm websites, removed all the identifiers (names, locations, etc.) and showed them all to the Managing Partners of those ten law firms. Not one could pick out their own website. If a solicitor can't spot their own firm from what they're saying about their own business, then how would they expect a prospective client to choose to work with them?

So, why do clients have such a poor perception of value from law firms? It's because clients start from a very different place when they engage a law firm. They make an assumption that the legal advice they're going to get will be good. They assume this because the law firm is regulated, the law firm is trading, and the solicitor they're briefing is qualified and certified. Why, in the client's mind, would they not get good law? The client is only interested in outcomes – and that is because they are on a journey. They start at Point A with an issue, and their only objective – when going to a law firm – is to get to Point B where there is a solution to their issue. If a lawyer, when taking that matter on, does not know what Point B looks like, or why Point B matters, then you can get the disconnect regarding value. What lawyers forget is that Point B has nothing to do with the law. For example, Point B can be:

- Getting into the new house before the baby is born.
- Getting probate sorted so Granny has some money to live on.
- Getting the new factory premises bought before the machinery we've bought arrives from Germany.

So, if the lawyers have not got their heads around what matters to the client, then there is a real danger that the matter becomes just about legal process and not about real-life human issues. Lawyers are, rightly, obsessed with inputs, whereas clients, reasonably, only care about outputs. Lawyers who forget the crushing importance of the output are the ones who find themselves at the wrong end of the value perception.

If you go to the dentist with terrible toothache, you don't ask the dentist to prove their successful track record in teeth extractions. You assume because they are a dentist, because it says 'dentist' above the door, and because there is a big chair with a light on it, that the dentist knows what he/she is doing and will be able to take away the pain. As a patient of a dentist, you are in real, actual pain. You will know you are in pain because you are eating porridge, and you want to eat steak! The value is all about the pain relief, and at that point, most people will pay whatever it costs to have that pain alleviated.

It's the same with the law – it's only about the money if the value is missing.

And that final point is important. In all the research we did, we found that price was rarely important to clients. Price was at the bottom of their list. Value was what was important. To demonstrate this, we asked clients who had fixed-price engagements to express their sense of value. We found that 89% of clients on fixed-price engagements were satisfied with the outcomes, whilst clients who were on open-ended hourly rates only recorded a 26% satisfied rating. Price does matter. Value matters more.

If lawyers can focus on what really drives value in a lawyer-client relationship, and can learn to take away questions about price, then you will have happy and repeat clients.

Lawyers often judge service by the things they can see and measure internally: technical accuracy, diligence, hours worked, pages written, risks identified and points protected. Clients judge service very differently. They ask whether the lawyer understood the real problem, made life easier, helped them make a decision, removed uncertainty and gave them confidence. That is the communications gap. A lawyer may think the value lies in the legal process. The client may think the value sits in the outcome.

Jon's interview explains a critical distinction between lawyer metrics and client metrics. You can see the difference in thinking in the table below. Look at what is most important to the client – a clear understanding of my particular needs. Look at what is bottom of the table, coming in 14th.

	Lawyer Perceptions	**Client Perceptions**
1	Provides Clear Indication of Costs/Fixed Fees	Clear Understanding of My Particular Needs
2	Clear Understanding of My Particular Needs	Efficient
3	Provides Good Customer Service	Keeps To Timetable/Avoids Case Dragging On
4	Easy To Get in Touch With	Keeps Me Informed Along the Way
5	Keeps Me Informed Along the Way	Provides Clear Indication of Costs/Fixed Fee
6	Keeps To Timetable /Avoids Case Dragging On	Easy To Get in Touch With
7	Makes Me Feel Valued as A Client	Provides Good Customer Service
8	Speaks Plainly, Not Too Much Jargon	Value For Money
9	Efficient	Does not Overcomplicate
10	Value For Money	Speaks Plainly, Not Too Much Jargon

11	Delivers Added Value	Makes Me Feel Valued as A Client
12	Does not Overcomplicate	Choice Of Pricing/Service Level
13	Choice Of Pricing/Service Level	Delivers Added Value
14	Lower Prices Than Others	Lower Prices Than Others

WORDS WITH THE WISE

Abby Winkworth

I think AI is currently at a point where it is less about money than it is about time.

That is quite an odd thing to say in a book about pricing, but in a market where often clients don't really understand the value of the service they are buying – a lot of the time what they are looking for is things to happen faster. So, for instance, when clients are buying or selling their house, what they care about most is how quickly they can move from where they are to where they want to be They want progress. They want certainty about how long it is going to take. They want the thing to happen. They take for granted that it will all go according to plan, so speed is their measure.

So, although the industry is a little obsessed with whether AI can make service delivery cheaper to produce. For the client, it is about whether we can remove delay, get things started sooner, speed up institutions and processes that have historically relied on slow, non-technological answers, and create a better experience.

That is why I think the most interesting use cases of AI are not the ones that make lawyers faster. They are the ones that help firms understand what is driving client behaviour and serve them better.

WORDS WITH THE WISE

Joanna Gaudoin

Good client service is not just about doing the legal task. I sometimes ask lawyers to think about a service they have bought recently. It could be getting a car serviced, having a bike repaired, or buying some other service. What was good? What was bad? Would they recommend that provider? Why?

Very often, the answer is not about price. It is about how the service was delivered. The car was ready early. Someone called with an update. They remembered that timing mattered. They made the client feel understood.

That is the point lawyers need to absorb. It is not just the matter. It is the "how". It is the communication, the understanding and the feeling that the client matters.

BRACE YOURSELF…
incoming provocative statement

Some legal advice is designed to protect the lawyer, not the client… but the client pays for it.

CLIENTS WANT JUDGMENT, NOT FENCE-SITTING

I often say that clients do not laugh at lawyer jokes because they think they are funny; they laugh because they suspect they are true. If you are a lawyer, that should worry you more than it amuses you.

There is one old joke that makes the point particularly well. A client says he is looking for a one-armed lawyer and insists that, under no circumstances, will he instruct a lawyer with two arms. When asked why, he replies: "Because I am tired of lawyers saying, 'On the one hand this', and then, 'On the other hand that.'"

Like many lawyer jokes, it lands because there is a grain of truth in it.

Clients do not want a memo written to prove how clever the lawyer is. They do not want a beautiful parade of caveats, qualifications, exceptions, risks, authorities and professional self-protection. They want help making a decision. They want to know what matters, what does not matter, what could go wrong, what is likely to happen, what the options are and what the lawyer recommends.

That matters enormously in an AI-enabled world, because if AI can produce more information, more analysis, more drafts and more options, then the lawyer's role is not to bury the client under even more material! The lawyer's role is to help the client make sense of it.

Chances are, you don't have enough one-armed lawyers in your business.

COMMUNICATE THE VISION

Whatever your future Vision is, it must be communicated clearly, repeatedly and in language people understand. In any change management project, communication is not a soft extra; it is one of the main ways the change succeeds or fails.

For AI pricing, the message has to be tailored to different audiences inside and outside the firm. Partners, associates, finance, IT, HR, marketing, risk and clients all need to hear the story, but they do not all need to hear exactly the same story.

Partners need to understand that this is about protecting future profitability, because AI will reduce some traditional hours, client expectations are changing quickly, pricing must move towards value, and compensation models may eventually need to reflect something more intelligent than recorded time.

Associates need to understand that their future is not based on typing faster than AI. Their future lies in judgment, supervision, client empathy, commercial sense, curiosity, confidence and the ability to use technology intelligently. AI should remove drudgery, not remove purpose.

Clients need to understand that the firm uses technology responsibly, supervises outputs carefully, provides human judgment, prices transparently, offers meaningful choices and focuses on outcomes rather than process for the sake of process.

Marketing teams also need to change the language. The firm should stop saying things such as, "We are innovative", "We use AI" and "We are efficient" as though those statements are compelling in themselves. They are not. They are rapidly becoming minimum requirements.

The better language is client language: here is the decision we help you make; here is the risk we help you manage; here is the outcome we help you achieve; here are your options; here is how we make your life easier; and here is how we help you move forward with confidence.

That is the message.

HOW TO TALK TO CLIENTS ABOUT AI WITHOUT SOUNDING DEFENSIVE

Firms should create simple, consistent client-facing language explaining how AI fits into the service. Lawyers should not be left to invent their own answers every time a client asks whether AI is being used, whether the work is being checked or whether the price should be lower.

Useful language might include:

- AI assists the production layer. Our lawyers provide the judgment layer.
- You are not paying for machine output. You are paying for legal interpretation, risk calibration, supervision, accountability and advice.
- The price reflects the value of the result, not the number of minutes taken to produce it.

This is not about hiding AI. It is about explaining it properly.

8 PPP PENGUIN LOGIC

THE ONE-SENTENCE TEST

Here is a simple test.

Can every lawyer in the firm explain why the client should pay the price being sought without mentioning hours?

If they cannot, the firm has a communication problem. The lawyer should be able to say, in plain English, that the price reflects the outcome, the risk being managed, the judgment being applied, the supervision involved, the responsibility being accepted and the certainty being provided.

If the only explanation is "that is how long it took", the firm has not moved far enough. We need to price the outcome, the judgment, the risk we carry and the certainty we provide – not simply the hours spent getting there.

PUT THE NEW VALUE STORY INTO EVERY PITCH

The way law firms describe their AI capabilities in proposals, pitches and tender responses will have a direct impact on whether clients believe them.

Vague claims about innovation are not enough, and clients are becoming more sophisticated. They want to know which tools the firm uses, how those tools are integrated into workflows, what quality controls are in place, and how the firm's AI capability creates a specific benefit for their matter.

A good AI section in a tender response should be specific, credible and connected to client value. It should explain what the firm is actually doing today, not what it hopes to do at some unspecified point in the future.

Colin Levy makes this point well in his work on *AI And Client Value*. Firms should name the specific AI tools and platforms they use, explain how AI fits into the relevant workflow, describe where human review takes place, quantify the impact where possible, and explain the governance framework that sits around AI use. That means talking about data handling, quality review, ethical guidelines and human oversight, not simply sprinkling the word "innovation" across the pitch document and hoping for the best.

The rule is simple: be specific, not aspirational.

Every AI capability mentioned in a proposal should be linked to a client need. If the client has asked about speed, explain how AI improves turnaround. If the client has asked about risk, explain how AI supports better issue spotting and supervision. If the client has asked about cost certainty, explain how AI helps the firm offer clearer scope and better pricing options.

Technology for its own sake is not a value proposition.

WORDS WITH THE WISE

Kerry Jack

If AI takes some of the process away, then the law firm needs to explain what remains. In my view, what remains is judgment, confidence and reassurance. Clients are buying confidence. They want to know that the lawyer will get them where they need to get to. They are buying judgment. They are buying reassurance.

That is why education is so important. Law firms need to educate clients about how AI can help, but they also need to demonstrate where the lawyers add value. The firms that are best able to explain why human judgment matters will be the ones that come out of this well.

I have not yet seen many firms do that properly. I have seen firms talk about being tech-savvy. I have seen them talk about innovation. I have seen the usual AI-washing. But I have not seen many firms really take the bull by the horns and explain their AI story in a way that makes clients feel more confident, rather than just making clients think the work should be cheaper.

The messaging needs to move away from cost. It should be about how AI helps the firm be better. How it helps the client get more out of the relationship. How it improves the quality of the work, the experience and the outcome.

WHAT ARE YOU REALLY PROMISING?

The KPMG Global General Counsel Report 2026[35] highlighted how GC expectations of legal providers' technology capabilities are rising. As legal operations modernise, general counsel are upping their expectations, with a full two-thirds of respondents expecting a greater focus on technology-enabled services, and 82 percent now expecting law firms to clearly explain how AI is used in their work.

That is a very direct challenge. What are you telling clients?

BRACE YOURSELF…
incoming provocative statement

If you cannot explain your value without mentioning time, you have homework to do.

The Juro *State of In-House 2026* [36] survey offers even more uneasy reading for panel law firms. According to Juro, only 7% of respondents said their law firms had adopted AI tools and had been open about doing so. More than three-quarters either believed their firms were using AI without disclosing it, or said they had no visibility into AI use at all. That is not a small transparency gap. It is a trust issue.

If AI is reducing effort and turnaround times, clients will reasonably expect firms to explain how that affects delivery, supervision, pricing and value. Silence is not a strategy, particularly when in-house legal teams are already wondering whether AI savings are being kept by firms rather than shared fairly with clients.

This is not only a legal sector issue. Professional service firms generally will need to explain what is being sold when AI is involved. Clients will ask. Better firms will answer before they are asked.

SHINGLES LOGIC

Shingles tells clients, "We are using AI to become more efficient." The client hears, "Excellent, my bills should be lower." Shingles then looks surprised. Words matter. Especially when clients are listening.

GIVE LAWYERS THE WORDS BEFORE CLIENTS ASK

Client communications should feature in the BBU, covering AI use, value-based pricing, fixed fees, options, scope changes, price objections, supervision, and service guarantees.

Template letters should be prepared, but they should not sound like lifeless templates. They should help lawyers maintain relationships, explain value and protect pricing integrity.

Clients do not need a lecture on large language models, tokens, prompts or training data, but they do need reassurance that AI is being used carefully, confidentially and responsibly, that privilege is not being casually put at risk, and that human legal judgment remains firmly in charge.

Role play becomes important here. Lawyers should practise difficult pricing and AI conversations, receive feedback, refine the wording and then capture the best answers in the BBU. If someone in the firm finds a good way to answer a difficult client question, that answer should not disappear into the air after the meeting. Write it down. Share it. Improve it. Use it again.

Every value-based engagement should also include an After-Action Review (AAR) at completion, documenting what was delivered, the risks identified, the decisions supported, what went well, and what would be changed. This reinforces the value proposition for future engagements and helps clients understand what they received beyond a document, a meeting or an email.

SHINGLES LOGIC

Every Partner Invents An Answer

A client asks whether AI means the price should be lower. One partner says yes, one says no, one says it depends, one says AI was not used, and one sends the question to IT. Shingles calls this partner autonomy.
The client calls it confusion.

8 PPP PENGUIN LOGIC

Make your firm's AI use policy publicly available.

WORDS WITH THE WISE

Kerry Jack

The internal piece is just as important as the external piece. If a client asks five partners about the firm's approach to AI and gets five different answers, that is a problem. If one partner says the firm does not really use AI, another says they use it all the time, another gives a discount and another cannot explain the policy at all, the firm has lost control of the message.

Law firms need one hymn sheet. They need to know what they say to clients. They need to know what they say to their own people. They need to know how AI fits with their pricing, their risk management, their client service and their values.

There is also a real opportunity here for firms that are prepared to communicate honestly. I am tired of law firms telling people they are innovative and that they really care about client service. I have been hearing that for 30 years. My advice is the same now as it was then: do not tell me, show me.

If more than 9,000 law firms in England and Wales are all saying the same thing, how can any of them stand out? AI could be a genuine differentiator for some firms, but only if they are brave and bold enough to explain what they are doing in a meaningful way.

CRIB SHEET

P#4

	Title	Author / Source	Link
READ			
	The Riddle of Perception – the section on what lawyers think clients want, and what clients actually want, is illuminating	LexisNexis	https://www.lexisnexis.co.uk/bellwether/assets/pdfs/Lexis-nexis-report-2016_interactive%20version03.pdf
	The KPMG Global General Counsel Report 2026	KPMG	https://kpmg.com/xx/en/our-insights/transformation/global-general-counsel-outlook.html
	State of In-House 2026	Juro	https://www.linkedin.com/posts/juro_the-state-of-in-house-2026-report-is-now-activity-7425562153954349056-vdpq/
	KPMG pressed its auditor to pass on AI cost savings	Financial Times (Feb 2026)	https://www.ft.com/content/c891c47c-b21f-4e0f-84b3-b80c794eff3d?syn-25a6b1a6=1
MISCELLANY			
	Communicating a Vision for Change	John Kotter	https://youtu.be/bGVe3wRKmH0?si=qrFjnOD0GH6f1fV9

	Your Customers Probably Aren't Paying You What You're Worth – pricing consultant Casey Brown shares stories and learnings to help you communicate your value and get paid for your excellence	Casey Brown	https://www.ted.com/talks/casey_brown_know_your_worth_and_then_ask_for_it?referrer=playlist-get_paid_what_you_re_worth&autoplay=true
	The Change Process – Emotions when Reacting to Change – Kim Tasso eloquently explains the emotions people experience when dealing with change	Kim Tasso	https://www.youtube.com/watch?v=XN5R_jePWJk

TIPS / CHECKLISTS

Possibility Thinking Questions To Pose

- How could we possibly explain AI to clients without accidentally training them to ask for a discount?
- What language should we stop using immediately?
- What client questions are we not yet ready to answer?

CEO Questions To Pose

The CEO may wish to use these questions in a partner strategy session.

- What do our clients actually buy from us?
- Which parts of our work will clients soon expect AI to perform?
- Where are we still charging for effort rather than value?
- Which services are most vulnerable to automation or commoditisation?
- Which client relationships are deep enough to survive AI disruption?
- Which clients only use us transactionally?
- What would it mean to become a legal solutions and experience provider?
- How do we help clients achieve better outcomes, not just complete legal tasks?
- How should we train lawyers when AI does much of the first-pass work?
- Where can we price outcomes rather than hours?
- What should we stop doing?
- What should we do more deeply?
- What should we build now before the market forces us to?
- What story are we telling our people about AI: cheaper law or better value?

- What story are we telling clients about AI, judgment, risk, supervision and outcomes?
- Are we using language that accidentally invites clients to ask for discounts?
- Who is allowed to speak to clients about AI pricing, and have they been trained?
- What internal communication rhythm will keep the project visible?

P#5. PERMIT: GIVE LAWYERS PERMISSION TO THINK AND PRICE DIFFERENTLY

P#5. PERMIT – GIVING PEOPLE THE AUTHORITY TO ACT

The fifth step is to give authority and permission to your team and stakeholders. Any barriers, policies, or behaviours that impede the change that needs to happen need to be removed. Resources and support need to be provided to the team to facilitate the change. You need to enable the team to take ownership and responsibility for the change.

WELCOME TO P#5 – PERMIT

P#5 Permit is about giving lawyers the authority, confidence and protection they need to use AI responsibly and price differently.

This is the point in the AI and pricing journey where the firm has to stop talking about change and start allowing people to behave differently. That sounds obvious, but in law firms it is often the point where good intentions begin to wobble, because firms are very good at launching projects, forming committees, buying licences, arranging webinars, issuing strategy papers and telling everyone that AI is going to be important. They are less good at answering the much more practical questions that most lawyers will be quietly asking themselves.

What am I actually allowed to do? Who is supervising me and checking the outputs?

These questions matter enormously, because unless lawyers know what they are allowed to do, what they are not allowed to do, who will check the work, who will approve the price, who carries the risk, what needs to be said to the client and whether the firm will back them when they price differently, most of them will return to the safest place they know… the billable hour.

It may be unloved, illogical, unpopular with clients and increasingly exposed by technology, but to many lawyers it still feels familiar, defensible and safe. It gives them something to point at. It gives them something to record. It gives them something to justify. Lawyers like safe, and if a firm wants them to move away from safe, it must do more than tell them to be innovative. *It must give them permission.*

GIVE LAWYERS PERMISSION TO LEAVE THE CLOCK BEHIND

If lawyers are going to use AI properly, they need permission, training, guardrails, confidence, pricing know-how, supervision models, client language and a clear understanding of where responsibility sits. They also need to know that if they price the value of the outcome rather than the time spent producing the work, the firm will stand behind them.

If you want different behaviour, you have to create the conditions in which different behaviour is possible. That is what #P5 Permit is about.

Lawyers need permission to use AI safely, offer fixed fees, present options, price judgment, scope more tightly, use change control, stop billing every tiny unit of effort, have better value conversations, say no to bad work and explain to clients why faster does not automatically mean cheaper. Lawyers need permission to say – confidently and without apology – that the client is buying outcomes, not hours.

They also need permission to supervise differently, train junior lawyers differently and challenge old assumptions about what legal work is, how it is delivered and what clients are really buying.

REMOVE THE CONTRADICTIONS

There is one contradiction that will destroy an AI project in a law firm faster than almost anything else. It is the contradiction between telling lawyers to use AI to become more efficient, while at the same time insisting that they hit the same chargeable-hours targets as before.

8 PPP PENGUIN LOGIC

If you want lawyers to adopt AI, remove the contradiction.

Do not ask them to become more efficient while rewarding only recorded hours.

If you reward people for recording time, do not be surprised when they record time. If you punish people for reducing hours, do not be surprised when they hide efficiencies. If you tell lawyers that AI is the future, but measure them as though nothing has changed, do not be surprised when nothing changes.

The troops are not stupid. They will work out what the firm really values, and what the firm really values is usually found on the bonus sheet, not in the strategy document.

This is why P#5 Permit cannot be separated from the business model. If the firm says that AI should improve productivity, quality, speed and client outcomes, but continues to manage the business as though the only valuable thing lawyers produce is recorded time, *then the firm has not embraced AI at all.* It has merely bought some software and added another contradiction to the lives of its lawyers.

HOWEVER, Time recording may still be useful in a law firm. There. I have said it.

Used properly, time recording can help a firm understand base costs, capacity, scope, and risk. It can show how much human lawyer time is still needed once AI has done the first pass. It can reveal which work types are being transformed by AI and which are not. It can help identify where lawyers are failing to use the tools, failing to supervise, failing to review work, where matters are taking longer than expected, and where fixed-fee work is becoming unprofitable.

In that sense, time recording acts like a smoke alarm.

It may flag scope creep. It may identify bottlenecks. It may show that a client is consuming far more resources than expected. It may help the firm compare estimated time with actual time, track AI adoption, improve processes and understand base cost.

That is useful management information.

But only if the data is honest.

Some lawyers do not really believe they are worth their own hourly rate. So, they discount what they do. Indeed, discounting is everywhere. In *Timeshift*, Phil Wedgwood uses the phrase "quintuple discounting" to describe what happens when time is written off at several stages:

- The lawyer does not record the time at all
- The lawyer records it inaccurately, or chooses to under-record it
- Time is discounted when the bill is prepared
- The partner discounts the draft bill again
- The client then challenges the bill and receives a further point-of-sale discount.

Sound familiar?

Many CFOs know that vast amounts of time never make it onto a timesheet in the first place. The usual explanations are also familiar:

- "I went down a few dead ends, so I have not charged for that."
- "I was training someone."
- "I was correcting another lawyer's drafting, and they had already recorded a lot of time, so I did not bother recording mine."

What is interesting is what those explanations reveal. Lawyers know, instinctively, that not every hour recorded under the billable hour model creates value for the client. That is why they hesitate to record it. That is why they write it off. And that is why the model itself deserves to be challenged.

The firms that learn how to capture, interpret and use data sensibly will have a significant advantage. The firms that rely on guesswork, folklore and "what we charged last time" may find that AI has simply made their old weaknesses easier to see.

8 PPP PENGUIN LOGIC

Permission without guardrails is chaos.

Guardrails without permission is paralysis.

The job of the leadership team is to find the sensible middle, where people have enough freedom to act differently and enough structure to know where the edges are.

BUILD THE BBU BEFORE EVERYONE MAKES IT UP

If AI is going to change the way legal work is produced, the firm's Big Book of Usefulness becomes even more important. It should be the practical home for the firm's pricing, scoping, supervision, AI and client-conversation know-how.

It should contain the approved pricing policy. That policy should explain:

- What work can be AI-assisted
- What work must be human-reviewed
- What must never be delegated to AI
- How AI costs are recovered
- How prices are approved
- How client disclosures are handled
- How value is explained
- What must be recorded
- When work must be escalated
- Who has the authority to approve new approaches

The BBU should also contain details of AI tools, approved prompts, sample scopes, service-level options, precedent price options, client scripts, objection-handling responses, AI risk checklists, human review checklists, value summaries, pricing calculator examples, change-control wording and examples of occasions when the firm held its price because the value was in the judgment, responsibility and outcome rather than the time taken to produce the first draft.

Do not leave this knowledge inside the heads of a few confident partners. That may have worked, just about, when legal work moved more slowly and the apprenticeship model had more room to breathe. It will not be enough in an AI-enabled firm where knowledge, judgment and pricing confidence need to be captured, systemised and shared.

1. Capture it.
2. Systemise it.
3. Share it.

That is how firms become scalable. That is how judgment gets taught. That is how lawyers become more confident when clients ask difficult questions.

If the firm does not give lawyers the answer, lawyers will invent their own. Some will discount too quickly. Some will over-explain. Some will under-explain. Some will say the firm does not use AI even when it does! Some will promise that the work will obviously be cheaper before anyone has worked out whether that is right.

PREPARE LAWYERS FOR THE AWKWARD CLIENT QUESTIONS

Clients are going to ask awkward questions about AI. Good. They should. If clients know that technology can now help produce documents, summaries, contracts, chronologies and research more quickly, it is perfectly reasonable for them to ask how that affects price.

They may ask why the fee is still £X if AI helped. They may ask whether they are paying for software. They may ask for a discount because the work took less time. They may ask how they know the output has been checked. They may ask why they should pay a premium for something that appears to have been produced more quickly.

Do not leave lawyers to answer these questions while staring nervously at their shoes.

Give them the words.

A sensible answer may be:

> "Where AI helps us work more efficiently, we will take that into account. But the price is not based only on the time taken to produce the work. It reflects the outcome you need, the judgment applied, the checks we carry out, the responsibility we accept and the certainty we provide. AI may assist the process, but the accountability always remains with us."

That answer is calm, reasonable and fair. It does not pretend that AI makes no difference, but it also does not throw the firm's value into the discount bin the moment a client mentions technology.

THE ACCOUNTABILITY GAP – AI DOES NOT REMOVE RESPONSIBILITY

In the suggested wording above, I mentioned "accountability always remains with us", and it does. We know that. AI does not have a practising certificate, licence, professional indemnity insurance, a reputation, a mortgage, a regulator or a managing partner waiting outside its office asking what on earth happened. The lawyer does. The firm does.

That is the accountability gap, and every law firm thinking seriously about AI and pricing needs to understand it. When AI is used in legal work, responsibility does not transfer to the tool, the vendor, the model, the prompt or the software licence. The client will not sue the chatbot. The regulator will not discipline the algorithm. The professional duty remains with the people who chose the tool, used the tool, reviewed the output and sent the advice.

This is why AI does not make lawyers less valuable. It moves the value.

The value is no longer simply in producing the first draft, summarising the document or generating the words. The value is in knowing whether the output is right, whether it is safe, whether it is commercially sensible, whether it answers the real question and whether it helps the client make a better decision.

BRACE YOURSELF…
incoming provocative statement

AI may sit in the workflow…
it should not sit on the hook.

8 PPP PENGUIN LOGIC

The pricing question should not be, 'How long did this take?' The better question is, 'What value did this create and what risk did we carry?'

NEW SERVICES NEED NEW RULES

AI will not simply make existing legal work faster. It will create new services, new products, new subscriptions, new platforms and new ways of helping clients before they even instruct the firm on a traditional matter. That is exciting, but it is also uncomfortable, because the moment a firm creates something new, lawyers will begin to ask sensible questions.

- Which partner supervises it?
- Which department owns it?
- How do we record the time?
- What time should be recorded?
- Which client will buy it?
- Has the committee approved it?
- What if it cannibalises existing work?
- How do we price it?
- Does our insurance cover it?
- Does the partnership agreement allow it?
- Who gets credit for the revenue?

These are not stupid questions; they are good questions. But if every good question becomes a roadblock, the firm will never build anything new. Innovation will die in committee, quite slowly, probably with minutes, action points and a follow-up meeting scheduled for six weeks' time.

This is why the leadership team must carefully consider permission before sending the Pioneer Penguins off to explore AI-enabled pricing and new services. The board needs to decide whether AI is used merely to make existing work faster or to create services that clients could not previously buy. It needs to ask what work should become a product, subscription or platform; which governance processes would kill a new business model; whether the firm has the right non-lawyer skills to build, price and sell AI-enabled services; whether insurance covers what the firm says it wants to offer; and whether partners are financially incentivised to create services that may reduce billable hours.

Those questions may be uncomfortable. Good. The future usually is.

DO NOT LET AI SHIFT RISK SILENTLY ONTO THE FIRM

Clients are going to use AI. That is not the issue. The issue is what happens next.

A client may use AI to draft a contract, summarise documents, prepare a chronology, review a lease, compare clauses, produce a board note or generate a proposed legal position. It may look impressive. It may be fluent. It may even be mostly right. Then it lands with the lawyer with a deceptively simple instruction.

"Can you just check this?"

Beware the word "just".

"Just checking" may become one of the most dangerous phrases in legal pricing, because the client is not simply asking the lawyer to read something. They are asking the lawyer to stand behind it, to find what AI missed, to spot what looks right but is wrong, to test the assumptions, to understand the commercial context, to apply judgment and to carry the risk.

That is not a clerical task. It is not a quick favour. Professional accountability is being transferred to the law firm.

If a client has used AI to reduce its own internal cost, that does not mean the law firm should absorb the validation risk at a bargain-basement price. In fact, the opposite may be true. The more machine-generated material the lawyer is asked to approve, the more important the lawyer's judgment becomes.

In his article, *I Said It Would Escalate. It Has,*[37] Josh Kubicki makes an important point for law firms: the entry point has changed. Clients are no longer always arriving at the lawyer's door with a blank sheet of paper, asking, "What do I do?" Increasingly, they may already have used AI to understand the issue, frame the problem, identify possible options and even test the likely advice. That changes the pricing conversation.

The old model allowed firms to charge for diagnosis, orientation and early-stage sorting out. But if the client has already done some of that work, the lawyer's value moves elsewhere. It sits in judgment, validation, and risk assessment. In knowing what the AI missed, what matters, what is dangerous, and what should be ignored. The warning is clear. If the entry point has moved, the pricing model has to move with it.

The value is not the time spent looking at the document. The value is knowing whether the document is safe. It is knowing what is missing. It is knowing whether the AI has misunderstood the facts, overstated the law, ignored the human dynamics, missed the commercial risk or produced something beautifully written but legally dangerous.

A sensible response to the client may be:

"Of course we can review AI-generated material, but our role is not to rubber-stamp it. Once we advise on it, amend it or approve it, we are applying professional judgment and accepting responsibility for the risk. Our price reflects that judgment, the checks we undertake, the accountability we carry and the certainty we provide. It is not simply a charge for the time taken to read the document."

That is the shift.

BRACE YOURSELF…
incoming provocative statement

"Just checking" may be the client's phrase.

"Professional accountability" should be the lawyer's price.

WORDS WITH THE WISE

Sam Stamp

Checking clients' AI homework is a real opportunity.

One very practical opportunity is helping clients check work they have created using AI.

Clients are already using AI. They will increasingly come to lawyers and say, "I have produced this contract," or "I have drafted these terms and conditions," or "I have created this policy. Can you check it?"

That is a very obvious fixed-fee service.

A firm could say, "If you have used AI to draft an employment contract, we have a price to review it, check it, advise on the risks and sign it off." The price may vary depending on scope and risk, but it is much better suited to fixed pricing than hourly billing.

There is value there because the lawyer is taking responsibility. The client is not just paying for time. They are paying for assurance, expertise, risk assessment and, in many cases, the comfort of the firm's insurance and professional judgment.

Over time, firms may use their own AI tools to support that review work. They may learn what client-generated documents tend to get wrong. They may build more efficient review processes. That could make the work more profitable.

But it needs to be designed properly. Firms will need to ask questions such as: what did the client put into the AI tool? What source material was used? Was confidential information uploaded? Was someone else's document copied? What risks are hidden in the prompt or the process, not just in the output?

This is a good example of how AI creates new legal work, but not necessarily in the old form.

SHINGLES LOGIC

AI Innovation, Old Law Style

Shingles bought AI. Obviously, it did.

There had been a partners' meeting, a consultant had used the words "existential threat", someone from IT had shown a slide with a robot on it, and three clients had already asked whether AI would make their legal work cheaper. This created urgency.

Not enough urgency to rethink the business model, pricing strategy, client proposition, governance structure, partner behaviours or reward systems. But enough urgency to buy some licences. So, Shingles bought AI and called it innovation.

The managing partner announced that the firm was "embracing the future". The IT director sent out a helpful email explaining where to click. A few partners nodded gravely and said things like, "We need to be at the cutting edge", before returning to their offices and asking their secretaries to print the AI policy.

Then came the first problem. A lawyer used AI sensibly, carefully and appropriately. A task that might previously have taken six hours took two. This was good news. Except it was not good news at Shingles, because Shingles still measured success by recorded time. The lawyer was quietly reminded that, whilst the firm was committed to innovation, nobody should be "reckless" about reducing hours. After all, utilisation mattered. Recovery mattered. Targets mattered. The spreadsheet mattered. The client's outcome mattered too, of course. But not enough to disturb the spreadsheet.

So, the message spread quickly. Use AI, but do not let it reduce the time. Be more efficient, but not in a way that damages utilisation. Embrace the future but keep recording the past.

Then, clients started asking awkward questions. "If you are using AI, will our fees come down?" This would have been an excellent moment for Shingles to produce a pricing policy. It could have explained how the firm priced outcomes, judgment, risk, responsibility, speed, certainty and accountability. It could have helped partners answer confidently and consistently. But Shingles did not have a pricing policy. Shingles had partner discretion, which is a polite way of saying that every partner made it up differently.

One partner told clients AI was irrelevant to price because "we charge for expertise". Another offered a discount before being asked. A third said AI was just like email and therefore none of the client's business. A fourth tried to create an "AI technology charge" because the license cost money. A fifth avoided the conversation entirely and hoped nobody noticed.

Naturally, the clients noticed. Internally, this was described as "flexibility". Externally, it looked like confusion.

Meanwhile, Shingles continued to celebrate its AI journey. There was a LinkedIn post. There was a lunch-and-learn. There was a photograph of serious-looking people standing beside a screen with the word "innovation" on it.

But nothing fundamental had changed.

The firm had bought AI, but it had not changed its pricing model. It had accelerated the work but protected the hours. It had given lawyers new tools, but no commercial script. It had exposed partners to difficult client questions but offered them no shared answer.

And then, with magnificent confidence, Shingles called this innovation.

BRACE YOURSELF…
incoming provocative statement

The firms most at risk are not the firms that ignore AI. They are the firms that buy AI, keep the billable hour charge by time, and then discount the saving away.

CRIB SHEET

P#5

	Title	Author / Source	Link
READ			
	I Said It Would Escalate. It Has.	Josh Kubicki	https://thebrainyacts.beehiiv.com/p/282-i-said-it-would-escalate-it-has
WATCH			
	The Best Leaders Are The Best Followers	Simon Sinek	https://www.youtube.com/watch?v=V5wtzze9L_M
MISCELLANY			
	For Smarter Decisions, Empower Your Employees	Aaron De Smet, Caitlin Hewes & Leigh Weiss (McKinsey)	https://www.mckinsey.com/capabilities/people-and-organizational-performance/our-insights/for-smarter-decisions-empower-your-employees
	Why You Shouldn't Treat AI Agents Like Employees	Matthew Kropp, Julie Bedard, Emma Wiles, Megan Hsu & Lisa Krayer (HBR)	https://hbr.org/2026/05/research-why-you-shouldnt-treat-ai-agents-like-employees
TIPS / CHECKLISTS			

Possibility Thinking Questions To Pose

- What permission do lawyers need before they will price differently?
- What policies currently stop people behaving in the way the strategy says we want them to behave?
- How could we possibly make experimentation safe?

CEO Questions To Pose

- Are we telling lawyers to innovate while still rewarding only recorded hours?
- What permission do lawyers need to offer AI-enabled pricing options?
- Do our current policies help people act differently, or do they protect the old model?
- Have we trained lawyers to explain the value of supervision, judgment and accountability?
- What obstacles must the board remove if it wants behaviour to change?

P#6. PRIZES: CREATE QUICK WINS THAT PROVE THE MODEL

P#6. PRIZES – CREATING SOME QUICK WINS

It's fundamentally important to celebrate and generate quick wins that demonstrate the value of the change and its success.

Conscious efforts will have to be made to celebrate milestones, plus recognise and reward team members; this will help build momentum and confidence in the change underway.

6 MINUTES OF YOUR TIME

Watch *Celebrate Good Times* [38]

Kool & The Gang/Ziggy Mack

WELCOME TO P#6 – PRIZES

P#6 Prizes is about creating early, visible proof that AI-enabled value-based pricing can work in practice.

It is about quick wins, celebrating milestones and building confidence. It is the stage where the firm has to show that AI-enabled value-based pricing is not just another clever idea being discussed by enthusiastic people in a meeting room, but something that can improve the client experience, protect margin and help lawyers become more confident when talking about value.

Lawyers need proof. Boards need proof. Clients need proof. Naysayer penguins definitely need proof.

Quick wins could include:

- One AI-assisted matter priced as a fixed fee with three options
- One client-facing AI explanation script approved by risk
- One pricing council review of AI-enabled work
- One team trained to answer the AI discount question
- One process map showing what AI does and what lawyers check
- One client report improved using AI, but priced around outcome
- One write-off reduction avoided through better scoping
- One new AI-enabled product launched as a pilot
- One client saying, "That was clearer/faster/more useful"

The early wins do not need to be dramatic, but they do need to be visible, practical and capable of being repeated. A win might be a better fixed price, a clearer client conversation, an improved process, a junior lawyer being trained differently, or a client saying, "That was useful." *Do not underestimate that last point*; if a client says the work was useful, clear, reassuring, fast or helped them make a better decision, that is value in action.

The important point is that value demonstration should begin at the start of the engagement, not at the end. If you want to celebrate a win, you need to know what the baseline was before you started. What did clients previously pay? How long did the work usually take? Where did write-offs arise? Where did scope creep happen? What parts of the work created frustration for clients or lawyers? What did the old process look like? Without that baseline, the firm may have a nice story, but it will not have proof.

The sensible place to start is with matter types where the scope can be controlled, there is enough volume to learn from, AI can assist safely, clients value speed or certainty, lawyers can create options, and the work can be measured. This is not the moment to choose the most complicated, bespoke, awkward matter in the firm and announce it as the flagship pilot. That is not brave. That is daft.

Good quick-win candidates may include employment settlement agreements, commercial contract reviews, lease reports, conveyancing options, data protection audits, will review packages, debt recovery stages, and repeatable transactions where AI tools can assist with creation review, comparison and issue-spotting.

The question is not simply, "Can AI do this task faster?" The better question is, "Can AI safely assist the process so that our lawyers spend more time applying judgment, helping the client make decisions and explaining value?"

That is a very different question.

The firm should also ask questions to find out from clients what they actually value. Not what the partners assume they value. Not what the lawyers think they ought to value. What they actually value. Some clients will value speed. Some will value certainty. Some will value options. Some will value a dashboard. Some will value a board-ready summary. Some will value knowing what they do not need to worry about. Some will value a lawyer who helps them make a decision rather than sending them a long explanation of the law. One client I spoke with a number of years ago told me that she and her husband would have paid up to three times the price they had been quoted for a conveyancing transaction… if the lawyer would return their calls!

Here is a radical thought. To find out what clients value… ask them.

Every quick win should become a value story. Not a long case study written in marketing language that nobody reads, but a clear internal story that explains what happened, what changed and why it matters. For example, the client chose the premium option because they wanted board-level comfort. AI reduced production time, but lawyer judgment identified the real risk. The client paid more than the old hourly estimate because the value was clear. The matter had no write-off because the scope, options and change-control process were agreed at the start.

These stories matter because they create internal proof. They show lawyers that the new approach can work. They give partners better language. They give juniors confidence. They give the Board evidence. They give the Naysayer penguins less room to flap.

I also like the idea of a Prize Board. Make the wins visible. Celebrate the first AI-enabled fixed fee, the first three-option proposal, the first subscription product, the first client dashboard, the first matter where a write-off was eliminated and the first client testimonial about certainty. Celebrate the first junior lawyer who used AI responsibly and then explained the risk better than expected. Celebrate the first matter where the firm protected its margin without selling time. Celebrate the first client who said, "That helped us make the decision."

Do not just celebrate more revenue. Celebrate better behaviour, better outcomes, better conversations and better confidence.

That matters because people repeat what gets noticed. If the firm celebrates hours, it will get more hours. If the firm celebrates better client outcomes, protected margin, clearer scopes, stronger judgment and confident value conversations, it will get more of those behaviours instead.

8 PPP PENGUIN LOGIC

Quick wins are not the end of the project. They are evidence that the project is worth continuing.

Use them to build confidence, create stories, silence objections and show the firm that AI-enabled value-based pricing is not theoretical. It works.

BRACE YOURSELF…
incoming provocative statement

A quick win is not recording more hours.

A quick win is proving that the client received more value, and the firm protected its margin without selling time.

QUICK WINS PROVE THIS IS REAL

P#6 Prizes is where the firm starts to build belief. The early wins do not need to be perfect, but they do need to be visible, honest, measurable and useful. Pick the right matter types, capture the baseline, ask clients what they value, train lawyers to have better conversations, produce value summaries and celebrate the behaviours you want repeated.

Because in an AI-enabled legal world, the firms that win will not be the firms that merely become faster.

They will be the firms that can prove they are more valuable.

CRIB SHEET

P#6

	Title	Author / Source	Link
WATCH			
	Celebrate Good Times [Why? Makes you smile]	Kool & The Gang / Ziggy Mack	https://youtu.be/3GwjfUFyY6M?si=dZEXEuvI8Ga9Qwym
	Celebrate Those That Do	Simon Sinek	https://youtube.com/shorts/yTotCREiTRU?si=hLz85eqN5JNP5wUj
	How do you celebrate success?	TED Ideas Studio	https://youtu.be/HtThmuswK8E?si=inkGj9UJ8cOMKPnl
READ			
	Celebrating success: Why recognition matters in business	Angela De Souza	https://elitebusinessmagazine.co.uk/sales-marketing/audience/item/celebrating-success-why-recognition-matters-in-business

TIPS / CHECKLISTS

Possibility Thinking Questions To Pose

- What would count as a quick win in 30 days?
- Which client, team, matter type or workflow gives us the best chance of proving the model?

- What small success would make the Naysayer penguins slightly quieter?

CEO Questions To Pose

- What quick wins would prove this project is real?
- Which pilot could show better client value, better margin or better pricing confidence quickly?
- Are we measuring adoption, or are we measuring behaviour change?
- How will we celebrate teams who create better client outcomes, not just more recorded time?
- What evidence would persuade sceptical partners that the model can work?

P#7. PERSEVERE: EMBED THE NEW OPERATING MODEL

P#7. PERSEVERE – KEEP GOING

The seventh step is to build on the success of the changes you have implemented. It is looking at gaps and the opportunities for improvement. – the changes you have designed and undertaken need to become embedded into your systems and processes.

WELCOME TO P#7 – PERSEVERE

P#7 Persevere is about making sure AI-enabled value-based pricing does not remain a pilot, gimmick, BD campaign or innovation story. The firm must embed the new model into Finance, HR, IT, knowledge management, client onboarding, matter management, supervision, dashboards and partner compensation. Otherwise, the old hourly model will quietly reassert itself.

KEEP GOING WHEN THE FIRST BURST OF ENTHUSIASM HAS WORN OFF

This is the point in the AI pricing journey where the excitement has probably started to fade, the launch emails have been sent, the early adopters have had their moment, the board has nodded sagely at a dashboard, and the firm now faces the much harder question.

Are we actually changing how we work?

This is where many law firms will struggle, because running an AI pricing pilot is not the same as changing the business model. A pilot can feel exciting. It can involve a small group of enthusiastic people, a new tool, a few impressive examples, a client willing to try something different, and perhaps even a celebratory internal post announcing that the firm is "embracing the future". All very nice. But a pilot is not a transformation.

The danger is that AI pricing becomes a gimmick, a business development campaign, an innovation story or a small island of good practice surrounded by the old ocean of hourly billing, old partner behaviours, old targets, old reporting, old compensation structures and old assumptions about what clients should pay for.

Persevering is about refusing to let that happen. It is about making sure AI-enabled value-based pricing does not live only in the innovation team's slide deck, but becomes part of how the firm scopes, prices, delivers, reviews and improves legal work.

This is not a "launch it and leave it" exercise.

It is a keep-going exercise.

It is not enough to run one AI pricing pilot and then announce victory. The firm has to keep working through the real tensions that AI creates:

- Efficiency vs Revenue
- Speed vs Supervision
- Automation vs Judgment
- Client expectations vs Firm profitability
- Technology-enabled delivery vs Junior lawyer development

This is where firms will get tired.

Clients will demand efficiency. Partners will worry about profit. Juniors will worry about training. Finance will worry about margin. Risk will worry about governance. BD will worry about messaging. Management will need to keep everyone moving roughly in the same direction without pretending that the answers are easy.

That is leadership.

Persevering does not mean stubbornly sticking to the first version of the plan when the evidence shows it is not working. Persevering means monitoring what is happening, listening to the market, reviewing the data, learning from client conversations, spotting the unintended consequences and making sensible course corrections as the firm learns. The firms that succeed will not be the firms that set a new pricing strategy once and then frame it. They will be the firms that build dynamic, responsive and transparent pricing disciplines supported by communication, technology, training, review and accountability.

In other words, the plan must be alive.

BRACE YOURSELF…
incoming provocative statement

Clients never wanted your hours. They tolerated them because you gave them no better option.

> Given the scale and speed of change now underway, few firms will remain untouched. As these pressures intensify, the traditional law firm model will struggle to remain competitive without significant reform.
>
> **Bjarne Tellmann, *Law in the Era of AI***

HOW DO JUNIOR LAWYERS LEARN WHEN AI DOES THE FIRST DRAFT?

One of the biggest issues firms will need to address is junior lawyer development.

The old training model cannot simply be preserved because it feels familiar, and it certainly cannot be preserved for nostalgia. For decades, junior lawyers have learned by doing much of the labour-intensive work that now sits directly in AI's firing line: research, first drafts, document review, summarising, bundling, chronology building, comparison exercises and process-heavy legal grunt work.

That work was not always glamorous. In fact, much of it was deeply dull. But it did provide repetition, exposure, pattern recognition and the slow accumulation of legal instinct.

If AI now removes or reduces some of that work, firms cannot simply shrug and hope junior lawyers somehow become excellent by osmosis. They need a new development path.

Junior lawyers are not merely revenue generators. They are the profession's future capability. If firms allow AI to strip out the work that used to train them, without designing new ways to teach judgment, client understanding, commercial acumen, supervision and risk assessment, then the profession may save some time today and create a competence problem tomorrow.

That would be a very poor bargain.

The answer is not to make juniors do pointless manual work simply because "that is how I learned". That is Shingles Logic! The answer is to design new learning loops deliberately:

- Supervised AI review
- Flawed-output exercises
- Client simulations
- Pricing conversations
- Risk discussions
- After-action reviews
- Judgment workshops
- Earlier exposure to the real context behind the legal work

AI may remove some of the old friction; firms must deliberately build better learning.

In May 2026, LinkedIn nearly exploded when a case in England hit the legal headlines for all the wrong reasons. Journalist Neil Rose from Legal Futures reported on the case[39] and the facts were these. A junior solicitor at Pinsent Masons used AI to help draft two letters to the High Court in a routine transfer application. The letters referred to legal provisions that had not been properly checked and were misleading. The judge said the junior had *"almost entirely outsourced the thinking process"* to AI. The AI tool had warned that the material needed checking, but it wasn't checked.

That is the story, but the real issue is not AI. It is training, judgment and supervision.

The uncomfortable point for Pinsent Masons is that this happened inside a large, sophisticated, well-resourced firm. The supervising senior associate accepted that there had been a failure to supervise and review the drafts properly. The partner had limited involvement but still approved one of the letters. Nobody had properly checked the statutory references before they went to court.

Rose reported, "Judge Mullen decided that leading law firm Pinsent Masons' self-referral to the Solicitors Regulation Authority (SRA), alongside the public admonishment of a published ruling, was a sufficient sanction."

This was not a complex, high-stakes AI experiment. It was routine work! "Boxwork". The sort of thing that moves around firms every day. And that is where the danger sits. Not just in the big AI strategy projects, but in the ordinary, dull, supposedly low-risk work where everyone assumes someone else has checked it.

BRACE YOURSELF…
incoming provocative statement

"That's how I learned" is not a training strategy.

SHINGLES LOGIC

Shingles says junior lawyers must learn by doing routine work manually. It does not ask whether the routine work was ever good training, whether the client should pay for it, or whether judgment can be taught in a better way.

LEARN FROM EVERY PRICE, EVERY MATTER, EVERY MISTAKE

After-Action Reviews (AAR's) are essential. For a start, you get feedback on outcomes (see above).

> Being ashamed of our mistakes
> makes them a crime.
>
> **Confucius**

If a firm is serious about AI-enabled value-based pricing, it needs to learn from what actually happened… not what everyone hoped would happen when the pilot was launched.

At the end of each matter, the team should ask:

- Whether the pricing model worked
- Whether the scope was clear
- Whether AI reduced cost or created additional review burden

- Whether supervision took longer than expected
- Whether the client understood the value
- Whether the firm protected margin
- Whether the matter generated write-offs
- Whether the client raised objections
- Whether the same model should be used again

This is not bureaucracy. This is learning.

It is also how the Big Book of Usefulness stays useful. If the firm learns something from a matter and fails to capture it, the learning vanishes into the air. If someone finds a good way to explain AI value to a client, it should go into the BBU. If a scope clause worked well, it should go into the BBU. If a pricing assumption was wrong, it should go into the BBU. If a client pushed back and the lawyer handled it brilliantly, that wording should go into the BBU.

The firm should not keep relearning the same lessons at great expense.

8 PPP PENGUIN LOGIC

Capture examples, prompts, pricing language, client objections, supervision rules and lessons learned before they disappear into inboxes.

THE PROBLEMS THAT WILL NOT GO AWAY BY THEMSELVES

Every AI pricing project should have a Persevere Problem List. This is not a failure list. It is an honesty list.

The list should include the things that will quietly drag the project back to the old model if nobody pays attention:

- Partners reverting to hourly rates
- Associates worrying about targets
- Clients asking for AI discounts
- Finance reporting the wrong metrics
- Inconsistent scoping
- Poor AI output quality

- Lack of matter reviews
- Weak supervision
- No one updating the BBU
- Absence of leadership communications

Do not hide these problems. Name them.

If you name them, you can manage them. If you pretend they are not happening, they will become the culture.

The Naysayer penguins will also be watching closely at this stage. They will not necessarily object loudly. They may simply wait for the project to lose momentum and then quietly say, "I told you this would never work."

Do not give them that gift.

THE QUESTIONS THE CEO MUST KEEP ASKING

The CEO and leadership team need to keep asking whether the firm's systems are helping or hindering change.

You will recall that at the end of each section of this book, CEO questions have been listed. Are you/your CEO prepared to grasp some of the nettles? Partner compensation should be reviewed. Does it reward hours or value? Does it penalise AI efficiency? Does it encourage partners to hoard work? Does it reward product development, client satisfaction, better scoping, protected margin and value creation?

Associate targets should also be reviewed. If juniors are still measured almost entirely by chargeable hours, do not be surprised when AI learning, judgment development, knowledge capture and pricing contribution are treated as second-class activities. The firm may need fewer pure chargeable-hour targets and more focus on output quality, client feedback, AI supervision, commercial understanding, pricing literacy and contribution to the firm's knowledge assets.

BRACE YOURSELF…
incoming provocative statement

If your compensation system still worships hours, your AI pricing strategy is probably just theatre.

WORDS WITH THE WISE

Noo Jones

I also think law firms need to stop relying on serendipity as their main learning model. Too much professional development has historically depended on who you sit near, which partner you work for, what kind of matter happens to land on your desk, or whether someone has time to explain things properly. That is not enough in a rapidly changing environment.

The SQE process in England and Wales, with its focus on practical learning and outcomes, reflects a broader point. Lawyers need to be able to evidence and reflect on what they are learning, not simply attend sessions. Firms should be helping people build capability through structured pathways, meaningful feedback, manager support and regular development conversations.

Managers are central to this. A firm-wide learning strategy will not work if managers do not support it. People need routine check-ins. They need help connecting their development to the firm's strategy and to client value. They need to understand not only what they are learning, but why it matters.

The firms that do this well will not try to implement twenty initiatives at once. They will build carefully. They will start with purpose, then capability, then learning pathways, then support structures. They will help people take reasoned decisions and calculated risks. They will create the conditions in which lawyers can grow.

New roles will be created. In some of the larger firms, you will find new professionals working in the industry; Shingles lawyers will refer to them as "non-lawyers " (I hate that term… it's like referring to nurses as non-doctors. Call it out. Rant over).

These new roles could be AI workflow supervisors, legal product owners, pricing champions, matter design leads, client value analysts, legal knowledge engineers and AI risk reviewers. Some firms may prefer gentler titles: matter planning leads, service design leads, AI assurance reviewers, value pricing leads, legal workflow specialists or knowledge design leads. Fine. Call them what you like. The title matters less than the fact that someone is finally asking: how should legal work be designed, priced, delivered, checked and improved in an AI-enabled world?

And yes, some lawyers will find these roles alarming. That may be a very good sign. It may mean the firm is finally asking the right questions.

Training must also become continuous. AI literacy, prompt discipline, verification, professional judgment, value conversations, pricing options, scoping, risk communication and client empathy are not one-off training topics. They are the new skill base.

The firm should embed AI pricing into onboarding scripts, client care letters, fixed-price agreements, matter opening, pricing approval, project management, after-action reviews, precedent banks and management dashboards.

If AI pricing sits outside the firm's systems, the old model will win.

The old model always knows where the shortcuts are.

BRACE YOURSELF…
incoming provocative statement

A lawyer who cannot explain their judgment will struggle to price it.

CREATE A PRICING STEERING GROUP

The firm should create a Pricing Steering Group with enough authority to do more than discuss interesting things.

Its job should be to monitor pricing models, review AI-enabled matters, track margin, look at client feedback, identify where lawyers need more support, make sure the BBU is updated, spot inconsistency across practice groups and keep the leadership team focused on the commercial implications of AI.

This group should not be a talking shop. It should have data, authority, deadlines and responsibility.

It should also include people beyond the usual suspects. Finance, BD, Risk, knowledge, operations, IT and lawyers all need to be in the conversation because AI pricing is not one department's problem. It is a business model issue.

8 PPP PENGUIN LOGIC

A Pricing Steering Group can stop every partner from inventing a different answer to the same client question.

SHINGLES LOGIC

Shingles creates an AI Steering Committee made up entirely of people who have not used AI, do not like AI, do not trust AI, and who think ChatGPT is something their children use to cheat at homework.

Shingles sends an internal email saying the future has arrived.

Shingles then leaves the hourly targets untouched, keeps the same partner reward system, forgets to update the BBU, fails to review the matters, does not train juniors differently, and lets everyone drift back to the old way of working.

Six months later, Shingles announces that AI pricing "did not really catch on."

PERSEVERE IS WHERE THE PROJECT BECOMES REAL

P#7 Persevere is where the firm proves whether it is serious.

It is easy to be excited at the beginning. It is easy to run a pilot. It is easy to create a few slides, tell a few stories and show a few early wins. The harder work is embedding the change into the parts of the firm that actually shape behaviour: Finance, HR, IT, knowledge, training, supervision, client onboarding, matter management, pricing approval, dashboards and partner compensation.

That is where the project either becomes real or quietly dies.

AI-enabled value-based pricing will not succeed because a firm bought tools, launched pilots or produced a clever pricing policy. It will succeed because the firm kept going, kept measuring, kept learning, kept training, kept refining and kept asking whether the client received value and the firm captured a fair share of that value.

Persevere. Not because the first plan was perfect. Because the destination matters.

SHINGLES LOGIC

How To Launch An AI Pricing Project And Make Absolutely Sure Nothing Really Changes

Shingles & Co. decides it needs an AI pricing strategy, mainly because three clients have asked awkward questions, two competitors have put "AI-enabled delivery" on their website, and one partner has returned from a conference saying, "I think we need a chatbot."

The board agrees this is a strategic priority.

Obviously, this means asking IT to buy something.

After several demos, a few lunches, a procurement process nobody fully understands, and a spreadsheet with red, amber and green boxes, Shingles buys a sparkling AI tool. It is very pretty. It has a dashboard. It has a vendor who uses the word "transformational" a lot. It may even have a logo involving a hexagon.

The firm announces the launch with great excitement.

"Shingles & Co. is delighted to embrace the future of legal services."

Nobody mentions pricing.

Nobody mentions partner compensation.

Nobody mentions hourly targets.

Nobody mentions supervision.

Nobody mentions whether clients will be told.

Nobody mentions whether the tool has actually been tested on a live matter.

But there is a launch email, so progress has clearly happened.

The Managing Partner records a short internal video saying AI will "free our lawyers to focus on higher-value work." Unfortunately, the same lawyers are then reminded by Finance that their chargeable-hours targets remain exactly the same, their recovery rates will still be reviewed monthly, and anyone falling behind should "have a word with their supervisor."

This is called alignment.

In the first month, a few keen lawyers use the tool. They produce some impressive-looking drafts, summaries and issue lists. One associate saves six hours on a contract review and, being young, optimistic and still in possession of a soul, tells the partner.

The partner looks alarmed.

"Excellent," says the partner. "But where are the six hours going?"

The associate learns an important lesson.

Efficiency is encouraged in theory, but not necessarily in the timesheet.

Meanwhile, the Innovation Committee meets to discuss AI adoption. The meeting lasts two hours. Nobody uses AI to summarise it. The minutes are circulated three weeks later and contain twelve action points, seven of which begin with "consider whether".

One partner asks whether AI will reduce write-offs. Another asks whether clients will expect discounts. A third asks whether the firm should create value-based AI pricing options. There is then a thoughtful pause before someone suggests forming a subcommittee.

The subcommittee is approved.

This is also called progress.

In month two, a client asks whether AI was used on their matter and whether the fee should be lower as a result. The partner has not been trained to answer this question, so decides to improvise, which is always exciting in a regulated profession.

"Well," says the partner, "we do use technology where appropriate."

The client asks again.

The partner says the firm's position is "evolving".

The client hears "discount".

The partner panics and knocks 15% off the bill.

Finance records this as a commercial write-off, not as a failure of strategy, training, communication, pricing confidence, client education and leadership courage.

Very tidy.

By month three, different departments have invented different answers. Corporate says AI is included in the price. Employment says AI is not used unless the client asks. Litigation says AI is used but only "administratively", whatever that means. Private Client says it is too risky. Real Estate says it is waiting for guidance. The guidance is being drafted by Risk, reviewed by IT, amended by Compliance and then sent to a partner who is on holiday for three weeks.

Naturally, the BBU has not been updated.

In fact, nobody has opened the BBU since the launch webinar, where it was described as "central to our knowledge strategy." It contains no approved AI pricing language, no client scripts, no worked examples, no scope clauses, no AI review terms, no value summaries and no explanation of how to deal with the phrase "Can you just check this?"

But it does contain a very nice PDF from 2019 about file naming conventions.

So that is reassuring.

By month four, the first AI pricing pilot is declared a success because "the client seemed happy" and "the team felt it went well". Nobody has compared margin against the old model. Nobody has checked whether supervision took longer than expected. Nobody has measured client perception of value. Nobody has asked whether the fixed fee was too low. Nobody has captured the scope assumptions. Nobody has worked out whether the firm gave away the efficiency gain.

But the client paid the bill.

So, champagne is considered.

The junior lawyers, meanwhile, are confused. They are told AI will remove drudgery, but they are not told how they will now learn the instincts that drudgery used to create. They are asked to verify AI output, but not properly trained to know what good verification looks like. They are encouraged to be curious but not given time to learn. They are told to be commercially aware but not invited to pricing conversations.

Then, at appraisal time, they are marked down for not recording enough hours.

This is called talent development.

By month six, the original enthusiasm has faded. The AI tool is still there, but usage is patchy. The keen people are still keen, the sceptics are still sceptical, and the vast middle of the firm is waiting to see whether this is a real change or just another initiative that will quietly disappear, like the client journey mapping project, the cross-selling strategy, and the values refresh.

The Naysayer penguins begin to emerge.

"I told you clients would just ask for discounts."

"I told you AI was overhyped."

"I told you fixed fees were dangerous."

"I told you lawyers would not use it."

"I told you this was just an IT project."

The annoying thing is that they now have some evidence, because Shingles has done the one thing guaranteed to prove the Naysayers right. It launched the pilot and forgot to change the firm.

The hourly targets remained. The compensation system remained. The dashboards remained. The pricing approval process remained. The client letters remained. The matter-opening process remained. The training model remained. The BBU remained unloved. The after-action reviews did not happen. The value stories were not captured. The learning disappeared into thin air.

Then the board asks why AI pricing has not scaled.

8 PPP PENGUIN LOGIC

Shingles believes the work is done when the pilot is launched.

Pioneer Penguins know the work begins when the pilot ends.

That is when the firm must update its pricing policy, change the dashboards, train the lawyers, review the matters, capture the learning, revise the scopes, improve the client language, challenge the compensation model and keep going until the new behaviour becomes normal.

WORDS WITH THE WISE

Felix Riley

My view is that, when the dust settles, a lot of AI tools will become fairly standard. They will be useful. They will be normal. They will be expected. But they will not, by themselves, be much of a differentiator.

AI may become like Excel for accountants.

Useful? Absolutely.

Important? Of course.

A reason to choose one accountant over another? Not really.

You do not choose the accountant because they have Excel. You choose the accountant because they know what the numbers mean.

The same will be true of lawyers.

CRIB SHEET

P#7

	Title	Author / Source	Link
READ			
	Junior solicitor used AI to draft misleading letters to court	Neil Rose	https://www.legalfutures.co.uk/latest-news/junior-solicitor-used-ai-to-draft-misleading-letters-to-court
WATCH			
	Why Do Change Efforts Lose Momentum?	John Kotter	https://youtu.be/u1417S5AolU?si=cbbjq_cXPF3tHzwP
	Embracing Change	Jason Clarke (TEDx Perth)	https://www.youtube.com/watch?v=vPhM8lxibSU

TIPS / CHECKLISTS

Possibility Thinking Questions To Pose

- How could we possibly stop this from becoming another forgotten initiative?
- What needs to be measured every month?
- Who needs to keep asking awkward questions?

CEO Questions To Pose

- Who owns the project after the excitement of launch has faded?
- What will be reviewed monthly: pricing, margin, client response, write-offs, AI use, risk and training?
- How will we turn pilot learning into a repeatable process?
- What will happen if partners drift back to hourly billing by habit?
- Which governance group has the authority to keep making course corrections?

P#8. PASSION: CREATE THE NEW CULTURE

P#8. PASSION – CREATING THE NEW CULTURE

The eighth and final step is to embed the change into your business.

By the time you get to this stage, you need to align and integrate the changes with your vision, goals, and values and embed them. Your leadership and management need to have totally bought into the process and be leading by example.

WELCOME TO P#8 – PASSION

P#8 Passion is where AI-enabled value-based pricing stops being a project and becomes part of the firm's culture.

Passion is key. You must create excitement about implementing change.

PASSION IS WHEN THE CLOCK LOSES ITS POWER

P#8 Passion is where the change becomes the culture.

By this stage, AI-enabled value-based pricing should not feel like a side project, a pilot, an innovation experiment or something that only a few enthusiastic Pioneer Penguins understand. It should be visible in how the firm operates with AI, prices, scopes, trains, supervises, communicates, rewards, reviews, and talks about value.

The firms that thrive will not be the ones that cling to time because it feels safe. They will be the firms that understand what clients really buy and have the confidence to price it.

- Clients buy outcomes.
- Clients buy judgment.
- Clients buy certainty.
- Clients buy reassurance.
- Clients buy the ability to make better decisions when the answer is not obvious.
- The lawyer's acumen is sold.
- That is where the value has moved.
- That is where the culture must move, too.

When the culture has changed, *Stop The Clock* will no longer be the title of a book. It will be the way the firm thinks.

6 MINUTES OF YOUR TIME

Watch *How to Start a Cultural Change?*

by Simon Sinek[40]

RETIRING THE OLD CULTURAL SYMBOLS

Every culture has symbols, and law firms are no different. The traditional law firm has worshipped at the altar of chargeable hours, utilisation, write-offs, discounts, recovery rates, "we are very busy", "we cannot know what it will cost", and that much-loved lawyer phrase, "it depends".

Now, before anyone in Finance has a panic attack, I am not suggesting firms should stop measuring important financial data. Of course, firms need to understand cost, profitability, recovery, margin and cash flow. Sensible financial discipline is essential.

But there is a difference between measuring something and worshipping it.

If the firm's heroes are the people who record the most hours, the culture will produce more hours. If the firm celebrates those who are constantly busy, the culture will produce busyness. If the firm quietly admires the partner who keeps every matter open, every task bespoke, and every answer dependent on more time being spent, the culture will produce more of that behaviour.

Do not be surprised when people repeat what the firm rewards.

The old cultural symbols need to be challenged. The new cultural symbols should be:

- Outcome clarity
- Client confidence
- Risk reduction
- Decision support
- No surprises
- Service options
- Value summaries
- Reusable knowledge
- AI-enabled insight

That is culture.

Culture is not the words on the wall. Culture is what gets noticed, rewarded, repeated and defended when the pressure is on.

8 PPP PENGUIN LOGIC

Culture changes when the firm's rewards, language, systems, training and client stories all point in the same direction.

THE TASK IS NOT THE VALUE

The task is not the value. Judgment and acumen are.

That sentence should probably be printed and posted prominently in every law firm serious about AI and pricing. The task may still matter, of course – a document still needs to be drafted, a contract still needs to be reviewed, a chronology still needs to be prepared, a report still needs to be produced – but tasks are becoming easier to automate, accelerate, compare and challenge. Judgment is not.

The lawyer's future value lies in knowing which task matters, which risk is real, which issue is noise, which option is sensible, which client concern is unspoken, which commercial reality changes the legal answer, and which recommendation will actually help the client move forward.

That is the work clients will pay for, provided lawyers learn to name it, package it, explain it and price it.

THE FIRMS THAT WIN WILL LOOK DIFFERENT

Winning firms will not simply be the firms with AI tools. Let us get that out of the way immediately. Having AI tools will not make a firm special any more than having email, a document management system, or a website. The issue will not be whether the firm has bought technology; the issue will be whether the firm has changed how it thinks.

The winning firms will organise around:

- Client needs
- Price on value
- Understand outcomes
- Build deliberate talent programmes
- Use AI responsibly
- Communicate transparently
- Take accountability seriously
- Develop deeper relationships
- Adapt as the market changes

They will not treat AI as an add-on to the old model. They will use AI as a catalyst to ask better questions about what the firm sells, how it delivers, what clients value and how lawyers should be trained for the work that will matter in the future.

That is a cultural change.

In the new culture, lawyers understand value and ask better questions. They use AI responsibly, value price outcomes, and explain judgment. They give clients choices, are proud of certainty, and stop equating busyness with importance.

For too long, some lawyers have behaved as though being busy is the same as being valuable. It is not. A lawyer can be very busy doing work that the client does not value, does not understand, and does not want to pay for. Equally, a lawyer can create enormous value in a single, short conversation because they have the experience, judgment and commercial acumen to know what the client should do next.

Time is not the value. Time is just the thing we use to count.

> The choice is stark. Remain a guild that reveres the clock or rise as a calling that reveres the client. One path leads to moral injury and irrelevance. The other, to moral courage and reinvention.
>
> **Ron Baker, Writing in the foreword to Ditch & Switch!**

WORDS WITH THE WISE

Abby Winkworth

The opportunity is bigger than efficiency.

For me, the big themes are these.

First, the focus on efficiency is too narrow. You cannot grow your way into the future through cost savings.

Second, the role of junior staff and their education needs serious attention. Everyone is thinking about it, but not enough firms are doing enough about it.

Third, client experience has to become central. Firms need to understand what clients value now and what they will value in the future.

Fourth, firms need to create revenue opportunities outside the simple promise of efficiency.

Law is very good at sticking its feet firmly in the ground and refusing to move. But it is getting harder and harder to do that now.

I am glad to be working in the legal industry while this is happening. It is a more exciting place to work now than it has been for much of my career, because people are finally asking the big questions.

What is law for? How do we create value? How do we sustain a future in this industry?

Those are much more interesting questions than, "How do we make the same old work happen a bit faster?"

That is where law firms should be putting their energy.

OUTCOMES AS A SERVICE – WHAT CLIENTS WERE BUYING ALL ALONG

The future law firm sells outcomes as a service.

I appreciate this may upset those who still believe the product of a law firm is "legal work", but clients do not usually wake up in the morning desperate to buy legal work. They contact lawyers because something needs to happen, stop happening, be protected, be achieved, be avoided or be resolved.

- A will is not merely a document; it is peace of mind for a family.
- A merger is not paperwork; it is the birth of a new enterprise.
- A defence is not a bundle, a chronology or an attendance note; it may be reputation, liberty or livelihood.
- A divorce is not a process; it is a route to a new life.
- A conveyance is not a file full of searches, enquiries and undertakings; it is a family moving home.
- An employment dispute is not just about pleadings, correspondence and settlement wording; it may involve dignity, risk, future security and the ability of people to move on.

That is the point.

Law is not merely a transaction. It is often one of the routes by which human beings and businesses move from painful, risky, uncertain or stuck places to somewhere better.

If that is what lawyers are really helping clients to do, why on earth would the profession define its value by the number of hours spent on the way?

The culture you are trying to build is one where lawyers are proud to sell outcomes rather than hours. That does not mean being reckless, it does not mean ignoring risk, and it does not mean guaranteeing things that cannot be guaranteed. It does not mean pretending every matter can be priced in exactly the same way.

It means the firm understands that clients want progress, certainty, confidence, reduced risk, good decisions and fair value. It means lawyers are trained to ask better value-based questions at the start, scope properly, give options, explain assumptions, communicate clearly, use AI responsibly and produce value summaries that show the client what has been achieved.

It means the firm stops apologising for charging for judgment and acumen.

It means partners stop treating value-based pricing as a brave exception and start treating it as a serious commercial discipline. It means juniors learn that their future is not in working slower than a machine, but in becoming better at judgment, context, client understanding and commercial sense. It means Finance stops seeing value-based pricing as a mysterious dark art and starts helping lawyers understand cost, margin, risk and value. It means marketing stops shouting "we use AI" and starts explaining how the firm helps clients achieve better outcomes.

Above all, it means the firm moves from being a producer of legal output to being a guide, adviser, risk manager, decision supporter and outcome creator.

That is a better place to be.

8 PPP PENGUIN LOGIC

If AI does the task, lawyers must price the judgment.

If judgment is valuable, name it, package it and sell it.

If clients want choice, give them options.

If lawyers lack confidence, train them.

If clients value outcomes, price outcomes.

If AI changes production, pricing must change.

If the firm rewards hours, do not be surprised when lawyers protect hours.

And if you want culture change, change the systems first.

CRIB SHEET

P#8

	Title	Author / Source	Link
READ			
	Five Steps to Making Business Change Stick	Jenna Phillips & Edward Wallace (PA Consulting)	https://www.paconsulting.com/insights/five-steps-to-making-business-change-stick/
WATCH			
	How to Start a Cultural Change?	Simon Sinek	https://youtu.be/zClAdLw4yRI?si=OFwq7eTiv43gKwpz

TIPS / CHECKLISTS

Possibility Thinking Questions To Pose

- What would our firm look like if we genuinely priced outcomes rather than effort?
- What old cultural symbols need to be retired?
- What do we want junior lawyers to believe value means?

CEO Questions To Pose

- What will show us that AI-enabled value-based pricing has become part of the culture?
- Do our rewards, partner conversations, dashboards and promotion criteria support the new model?
- What do we want junior lawyers to learn about value, judgment and client outcomes?
- What old symbols of success need to change?
- How will clients experience the cultural change?

CONCLUSION

SO, WHAT ARE YOU GOING TO DO?

We have reached the end of Part 1, but not the end of the problem. In fact, if I have done my job properly, I hope this is the point at which you are now slightly uncomfortable, mildly energised, and possibly wondering whether the economic model underlying your law firm is quite as sturdy as everyone has been pretending. That, to be honest, would not be a bad outcome.

The message of this book is not that AI will destroy lawyers. I do not believe that. Clients will still need lawyers, businesses will still need lawyers, and families will still need lawyers. People in trouble, under pressure, facing risk, making decisions, doing deals, resolving disputes, protecting assets, managing relationships and navigating uncertainty will still need lawyers.

But they may not need lawyers in quite the same way.

AI will change how legal work is produced. In many places, it already has. It will reduce the value of some things lawyers have historically charged for, including research time, drafting time, review time, process time, and routine correspondence. The work that kept people busy, filled timesheets and supported the old leverage model may not disappear overnight, but its value is going to be questioned, challenged and – in some cases – removed. That does not mean lawyers become less valuable. It means the value moves.

The value moves towards judgment, business acumen, discernment, supervision, accountability, empathy, courage, ethics, context and the ability to help clients make better decisions when the answer is not obvious. It moves towards knowing what matters, what does not, what can be safely ignored, what needs to be escalated, what the client really wants and what the client should sensibly do next.

That is not a small shift. That is a paradigm shift.

FROM SAAS TO OAAS

Law firms will, whether they like it or not, embrace more technology. Software as a Service will become part of the daily fabric of legal work. AI tools, workflow tools, document tools, data tools, dashboards, portals, and platforms will increasingly sit at the heart of how firms operate.

Fine.

But SaaS is not enough.

The future law firm must also embrace OaaS… Outcomes as a Service.

That means the firm stops defining itself by the hours it records and starts defining itself by the outcomes it helps clients achieve. It means the firm stops selling effort and starts selling progress, certainty, risk reduction, reassurance, commercial advantage, better decisions and peace of mind.

So, the question is simple. Will your firm keep defending hours, or will it learn to price outcomes?

Lawyers often take comfort in being members of a profession. I understand that. There is pride in it, and rightly so. A profession carries duties, standards, ethics, obligations and privileges.

But here is the uncomfortable truth.

A profession gives you the privilege to practise.

A professional services industry determines whether clients will still choose you.

- Why should the client pay us?
- What are we uniquely needed for?
- What value do we create?
- How do we capture that value?
- How do we build lawyers who are trusted guides, not just task performers?
- How do we become indispensable when technical production is increasingly abundant?

AI is making production faster, clients are becoming more informed, regulators are paying attention, and the old habit of treating time as value is becoming harder to defend. The firms that understand this will redesign their model. The firms that do not will carry on polishing the clock while the market quietly walks past them.

Clients have more information, more tools, more options and more confidence to challenge old assumptions. They may respect the profession, but they will not keep paying for a model that no longer makes sense to them. Change it.

If this book has done its job, and if you identify as a rabbit, you will have seen the lights. You will understand what is coming. And, more importantly, you will know it is time to move.

Not backwards into the comfort of hours. Forwards into outcomes.

> It is not necessary to change.
> Survival is not mandatory.
>
> **W. Edwards Deming**

PART 2
WORDS WITH THE WISE

Part 2 of this book includes the full interview summaries from the wise people I spoke to while researching this book. These are not decorative extras, and they are not there simply to prove that I have been busy having interesting conversations.

The people featured in Words With The Wise have looked at AI, pricing, leadership, law firm structure, governance, technology, client value and professional services from different angles. Some have run firms. Some advise firms. Some build technology. Some think deeply about legal markets, behaviour, strategy and change. They do not all say the same thing, and that is one of the reasons I have included them.

Readers should take on board what the Wise have said. Not because every word should be accepted without question, but because their comments provide warnings, prompts, examples and practical insights that can help law firm leaders think more clearly about what is coming.

Read them properly. Argue with them if you need to. Highlight the bits that make you uncomfortable. Share the most useful parts with your Pioneer Penguins. Use them in partner meetings, strategy sessions, pricing workshops and awkward conversations with NoNo Penguins.

The point of Words With The Wise is not just to give you more content. It is to give you other voices, other experiences and other ways of seeing the same iceberg.

And if several wise people are pointing at the same iceberg, it might be sensible to look.

WORDS WITH THE WISE

QUENTIN SOLT

Introduction

Quentin Solt is a UK solicitor, legal consultant, futurist and writer of the *Facts Are Friends* Substack, where he explores AI, legal services, work, society and the uncomfortable truths the profession cannot afford to ignore. He writes with clarity, curiosity and a willingness to challenge easy assumptions – particularly around how AI may reshape legal work, law firm economics and the future role of lawyers. His forthcoming book, *AI, Abundance and the Future of Work* (working title), looks beyond legal technology hype and asks a much bigger question: what happens to professional work when the old certainties start to wobble?

Core Advice from Quentin Solt

You have asked me about the future of the legal profession. I speak from the perspective of my corporate finance and commercial background. I tend to polarise to make points.

I start from a blunt place. Law firms, as we know them today, are moribund.

That is not a comfortable thing to say. It is not a comfortable thing for lawyers to hear either. But I think the legal profession has to stop pretending that AI is just another tool that can be absorbed into the current model.

It is not. At least, I do not think it is.

My view is that the legal profession is, in many situations, interference. Lawyers do not like that. Of course they do not. The profession has spent years, decades, centuries even, persuading itself that it sits at the centre of legal transactions. They have traditionally been a necessary layer in the relationship between clients and their counterparts.

The client has a problem. The lawyer receives the instruction. The lawyer applies the law. The lawyer gives the answer. The lawyer sends the bill.

That is the story lawyers tell themselves. Increasingly, it is not the story clients believe.

The comparison I use is the chemist. We still call some pharmacies chemists. But they do no chemistry. The name has survived. The function has changed. I think the same thing may happen to law firms. We may still call some organisations law firms. They may still have people who call themselves lawyers. They may still use the language of law.

But will they do law in the way lawyers understand it today?

I doubt it.

This is relevant because you cannot price something properly if you misunderstand what is happening to it. And I think a lot of law firms are still trying to price the old model while the new one is arriving underneath them.

The utility model

The law will increasingly be sold as a utility.

That is where I think this is going.

But the real threat may not come wearing a lawyer's suit. It may arrive inside the tools clients already use. It may arrive with tokens, usage limits and an insurance wrapper.

Think about your old mobile phone contract. You bought minutes. Texts. Data. You had a bundle. If you used more, you paid for more. I can see legal going the same way. HR and legal support bundled into a utility contract. A basic allowance. More units if you go over. A practical answer when you need it. Not a partner opening a file and starting the clock.

A commodity.

Now, lawyers will say: "But what about quality?"

They always do. But, frankly, the quality many lawyers give today is questionable – that goes to value. If you don't believe me, listen to the horror stories people tell about dealing with lawyers.

They will say: "AI hallucinates."

Yes. It does. That is today's problem. It will be tomorrow's joke. I do not mean hallucination is irrelevant – mistakes matter, systems matter, checking matters. But lawyers make mistakes too. And some of the recent examples people point to are not really stories about AI. They are stories about human failure. A junior did something. A senior failed to check it. The tool said, "Check what I am doing," and nobody did.

That is not an argument for the permanent survival of the old legal model. It is an argument for better systems.

"Good enough" – and why it matters

The bigger point is this: AI is becoming "good enough".

That phrase matters. And "good enough" is not a fixed point. It is moving up the food chain. What is good enough for low-value, high-volume transactions today becomes good enough for more complex work tomorrow. The threshold keeps rising.

Lawyers tend to compare AI with the best possible lawyer doing the best possible job. Clients do not always make that comparison. Clients compare AI with the actual experience of using lawyers.

Delay. Uncertainty. A lack of clarity. A bill that could be £3, £300 or £30,000. A result that could take three hours, three days or three months.

If I go to AI, I get an answer quickly. Maybe instantly. Maybe in twenty minutes. I know roughly what I am getting. I know what it costs. And for a lot of work, that may be good enough.

I sit on boards. I hear people saying it already: "We did this one by AI." Not because they hate lawyers. Not because they are trying to be clever. Because they know their own business. They know the pitfalls. They know the scale of the deal. And for that piece of work, they do not need a lawyer in the middle.

The consumption paradox

That is where the consumption paradox comes in.

Everyone gets lawyered. But they do not need lawyers.

AI may increase the consumption of legal capability while reducing the consumption of lawyers. More people may get legal assistance. More businesses may get legal answers. More transactions may have legal input. But the work may never arrive at the law firm.

That is the bit law firms really need to understand.

The optimistic story says cheaper legal work means more legal work, and therefore more opportunity for lawyers. I am not convinced. Cheaper legal capability may mean the client does the work themselves. Or the commercial team does it. Or the tool does it inside the business workflow. Or the intelligent agent deals with it before it becomes a legal instruction.

The client still gets the benefit. The lawyer does not get the work.

That is the consumption paradox in its simplest form. It is not just that law becomes cheaper. It is that demand moves. Some of it goes in-house. Some of it goes into the machine. Some of it disappears before the lawyer ever sees it.

And if the instruction never arrives, it cannot be repriced.

The castle and the water supply

My car analogy explains part of this. A hundred years ago, my grandfather had a motor car. He had a chauffeur. You and I think of a chauffeur as the man who drives the car. But the chauffeur was really a mechanic. He kept the car running. He understood the engine. The spark plugs. The bearings. The grease. He tinkered with it. He made sure it worked.

Today I drive an electric car. I do not need a chauffeur. I barely need a mechanic in the old sense. The car tells me when it needs attention. I take it to a garage. They plug it into a diagnostic bed. Often, nothing much needs doing.

Many garages do not like that. They like tinkering. They like the old craft. That is where many lawyers are. They like complexity. They like being necessary. But businesses can be retrofitted in a way cars cannot. The change may be slow for a while. Nothing happens. Nothing happens. Nothing happens. Then suddenly the work has gone.

That brings me to the castle.

I went to St George's Castle in Lisbon. It sits above the city. It had a moat. It had three walls. It looked impenetrable. It was the centre of the Portuguese Empire.

The walls were never penetrated. And yet it was defeated. By something nobody had anticipated.

That is where law firms are now.

The castle is the law firm. The partners are the kings and queens. The associates are the knights. The post room, reprographics, support teams and infrastructure are the farmers, milkmaids and everyone else who keeps the castle alive. But they all depend on one thing. Food and water coming into the castle. In law firm terms, that is client instruction and client payment.

So, what are the law firm's defensive moats?

The first was knowledge. That moat has drained. The corpus of law is available on the internet. If it is available on the internet, AI has it. Or soon will. The second was client relationships. That is under pressure too. The third was judgment – clever pattern recognition drawn from experience. But AI has a larger corpus of experience, and we know about the value of pattern recognition applied to big data.

There is a fourth moat that is rarely discussed, and it matters enormously. Lawyers did not just apply knowledge. They accumulated embedded judgment – contextual understanding built through transactional immersion. They knew the players, the history, the pressure points. That understanding was acquired by being in the room, doing the mechanics, absorbing the texture of a deal as it developed.

AI threatens that too. But not in the way most lawyers assume.

If AI handles the mechanics – the drafting, the research, the first-pass review – the lawyer no longer gets the immersive experience that generated the embedded judgment in the first place. They arrive later in the process. The context has been built by the machine. The catch-up required to contribute meaningfully erodes the very differentiator they were relying on. And the uncomfortable truth is that someone else – a well-briefed executive, a non-lawyer agent, a competitor armed with the same tools – could do that catch-up equally well.

AI-first law firms and AI-first providers have an unfair advantage in this environment. They do not have the legacy. They do not have the partnership to feed. They do not have all the associates. They do not have the real estate. The only thing they apparently do not have is the client relationship.

But the rainmakers are beginning to see something. They are carrying a lot of luggage. That luggage helped them get where they are. It gave them status. It gave them structure. But it may be wholly unnecessary now.

And that is why I do not see this as a drone attack on the castle. A drone attack is positive – it is someone attacking you. I do not think anyone is necessarily saying:

"Let's put lawyers out of business." In fact, for now, many of the AI providers are keeping lawyers in business. But they are also building their own reservoir upstream.

They are saying: "We can provide the food and water directly. We do not need to go through the lawyers." So, they build a dam.

That is what will kill the lawyers. Not an assault on the walls. A diversion of the water.

And the uncomfortable part is that law firms may have helped this happen. They have continued charging the client in ways the client increasingly resents or does not understand. They look at their current profits and say, "We are doing very well." Yes. For now. Many clients are currently implementing AI and need help. Many law firms have not properly implemented AI themselves, so the effect has not fully hit them.

But wait.

When the client has implemented it, when the tools are embedded, when the systems are working, the volume of instruction reduces. The requirement for the traditional lawyer evaporates. Maybe not everywhere. But enough.

What does the client actually need?

That is why the pricing conversation has to start much earlier than price.

What is the client actually trying to achieve?

In corporate and commercial law, which is the world I know best, the client does not go to a lawyer because they want a contract. They go to a lawyer because they want a sustainable business relationship. The contract is the thing we produce. The relationship is the thing they need.

That distinction matters. It is like going to a doctor. You do not go to the doctor because you want a conversation. You go because you want to be healthy. You do not take medicine because you like the taste. You take it because you want to get better or stay well.

Medicine is not for diagnoses. It is for health outcomes. And contracts are not for documents. They are for sustainable commercial relationships. That reframing matters because it shifts the disruption threshold. The question is not whether AI can produce a document to the standard of an excellent lawyer. The question is whether AI can get the client to the outcome they actually need. And that bar is lower, and falling faster, than lawyers want to admit.

The contract problem

Today's contract is a static risk allocation mechanism. It memorialises the deal and then tries to work out what happens if we deviate from it.

We use keyboards instead of quills. Screens instead of parchment. But someone from 700 years ago would recognise what we are doing. We are still creating static documents because the parties do not fully trust one another.

That is what contracts are about. A lack of trust. Human beings are competitive. We try to advance our own position. So, we write everything down. We sign it. Then, often, we put it in a drawer and do not look at it again until something goes wrong.

Then what? Litigation. And once we reach litigation, who is guaranteed to win? The lawyers. Nobody else really wins. One party may notionally win. The other loses. But under English law, very often, the winner is put back into the position they would have been in had the breach not occurred.

I do not call that winning.

You have spent thousands, maybe hundreds of thousands, on lawyers. You have lost years. You have destroyed a relationship. And if you are lucky, you end up where you should have been at the start. That is mad.

There is also huge risk in the way lawyers are instructed. When you brief your lawyer, you give the lawyer the facts as you see them. You filter the story through your own understanding. Then the lawyer filters it again. The lawyer decides what matters, what is relevant, what is important.

The other side may see a completely different picture. They may have facts you do not have. They may know they have no real leg to stand on, but they may run the argument anyway. Why? Because they can. Because they think you may run out of money. Or lose your nerve. Or settle.

This is not a great system if the real objective is a sustainable business relationship. And it is built on information asymmetry – the condition that adversarial contracting was designed to exploit. That condition is about to change.

From risk to relationship

That is where intelligent agents become interesting – and where I think the most significant disruption actually lies.

Enterprise management information systems know more and more about what is going on inside a business. The letters. The emails. The supply chain issue. The payment record. The operational reality. The stuff that matters.

In the future, the lawyer may not be a lawyer in the traditional sense. It may be an intelligent agent. Your intelligent agent. In-house. With transparency. Mine too.

And those agents may have one objective: to build and maintain a sustainable business relationship. So, if you come to me and say, "I want to buy widgets," my agent may say, "Quentin, you cannot do this," or "There is a risk here." We then have that discussion at the start.

And as we move forward, day by day, if I have a supply chain issue, my agent sees it. It can talk to your agent. It can say: "We have a problem. How do we resolve it?" Because you may still want me to be in business next year. Maybe we wind the arrangement down before anyone sues. Maybe you only need 80 widgets instead of 100. Maybe you need all 100, but we adjust the payment profile. Maybe we find another way through.

That is not litigation. That is good-faith negotiation. That is relationship management.

The technical infrastructure for this already exists. Automated performance monitoring. Real-time data exchange. Continuous alignment checks against each party's position. None of this is theoretical. When both sides have complete information and aligned incentives, risk allocation becomes redundant. The contract stops being a document designed to allocate blame when things go wrong. It becomes a living instrument – one that defines what good looks like for both parties and monitors its own performance against those parameters continuously.

The question the contract answers shifts. From "who is liable if this fails?" to "how do we ensure this succeeds?" That is not a refinement of the existing contract model. That is a different document entirely.

People say this could not possibly work. I am not so sure. Look at the alliances between Nvidia and TSMC, or Apple and Corning. While these multi-billion-dollar partnerships are eventually formalised in agreements, they are fundamentally trust-derived and relationship-based. In these ecosystems, the legal contract is not the driver of behaviour. The contract is a formalisation of a strategic interdependence. These companies invest decades of R&D and billions in capital before the ink is even dry on specific purchase orders, relying on a mutual commitment to shared survival that no legal clause could ever fully enforce.

That is where I think we are going. Not everywhere. Not immediately. But the direction of travel is clear.

What the lawyer of the future looks like

The lawyer may still be valuable. But perhaps not because they know the law in the way we currently train them to know the law.

The lawyer of the future may facilitate deals without needing the kind of training law school currently provides, at least not for the role I am describing. The value may be elsewhere: in understanding relationships, risk, trust, systems, behaviour, and commercial reality. Designing the framework – the parameters, the thresholds, the escalation triggers and the shared definitions of success – is skilled work. It requires judgment, commercial understanding and legal architecture capability of a high order. But it is a one-time task per relationship. Not a recurring advisory engagement.

That is a very different proposition from the traditional law firm model.

The pricing conversation starts before the price

So, my message to lawyers on pricing is simple.

Do not assume the client wants to buy your time. Do not even assume the client wants to buy your legal output. In many cases, the client wants certainty. Speed. Protection. A relationship that works. A way to avoid disputes before they happen. A way to get business done without being dragged into a static document and then into litigation when the document fails.

If legal capability becomes a utility, and if the client can get good enough legal assistance inside the business, with insurance, at predictable cost, then the law firm has a problem.

Not a pricing problem.

A relevance problem.

The castle may still look impressive. Its walls standing proud. The kings and queens may still be inside. The knights may still be polishing their armour.

But if the food and water stop coming in, the castle starves.

And the client may not even notice.

They will still be lawyered.

They just may not need lawyers.

WORDS WITH THE WISE

SAM STAMP

Introduction

Sam Stamp is the co-founder and CEO of Legal Engine, a business focused on voice-first agentic AI for professional services and law firms. Before founding Legal Engine, Sam was Head of Innovation and New Business at Simmons & Simmons, where he worked on legal products, technology-enabled services, client-facing tools and new ways of taking legal expertise to market.

Sam brings an unusual and valuable perspective to the pricing debate because he has sat at the intersection of innovation, legal technology, product development, sales, business development and law firm change. He understands both the opportunity and the operational difficulty of turning legal knowledge into something clients will actually buy, use and value.

Core Advice from Sam Stamp

My central message is that law firms cannot just think about AI as a delivery tool. They also need to think about how AI changes what they sell, how they sell it, how they organise themselves, how they price their work and how they maintain relationships with clients.

For many years, law firms have been able to predict their revenue with a reasonable degree of confidence. They knew how many partners they had, how many associates they had, what utilisation looked like, and how much work was likely to come in. That model was not perfect, but it was familiar. AI makes that much less certain.

The question is no longer simply, "Can we use technology to do the work faster?" The better questions are: which parts of our revenue are most at risk, which parts are defensible, what do clients really need from us, and how do we build services that keep us relevant?

That matters because law firms are not only competing with other law firms anymore. They are competing with legal technology providers, AI platforms, alternative providers and, increasingly, clients' own internal capabilities. Those competitors often understand product development and sales better than law firms do. That is a real risk.

I think law firms need to be much more deliberate about where their future revenue is going to come from.

For a long time, many firms have been able to model the future by looking at the past. They could say, "This is what our partners billed last year, this is what our associates billed, this is our utilisation, and therefore next year should look broadly similar, plus a bit of growth." That has worked for a long time.

I am not convinced it will continue to work in the same way.

We may all be overestimating how quickly things will change. It may be that next year looks a lot like this year, except with much bigger external technology costs sitting in the IT budget. But the strategic uncertainty is real. Firms are spending serious money on tools such as Harvey and Legora, yet many are not properly measuring return on investment. At a breakfast we hosted, we asked a group of law firm leaders how many of them had Harvey or Legora. They all had one of them. We then asked how many were measuring ROI. No one said they were.

That is a problem. Obviously!

If firms are going to spend heavily on AI, they need to know what it is for. Is it to reduce cost? Is it to improve margin? Is it to create new services? Is it to protect existing relationships? Is it to sell something different? Or is it simply a defensive move because everyone else appears to be doing it?

The firms that do best will be the ones that stop treating this as just an IT project and start treating it as a strategic business question.

Products can be powerful, but they are much harder than lawyers think

At Simmons & Simmons, we had a number of legal products. One was Rocketeer, which we described as the world's first AI trademark lawyer. It could review word marks and assess the likelihood of confusion. Another, and certainly the most successful, was Navigator, a cross-border funds regulatory tool.

Navigator was powerful because it was not simply a database of law. The really valuable part was how the law was applied in practice. It dealt with questions such as what marketing activity you could undertake for different funds across different jurisdictions. That required a huge amount of effort. There were more than 100 jurisdictions involved, with local counsel updating a standard question set to keep the information current.

The important point is that Simmons had access to a network and to information that was not available elsewhere. It was not simply written down in a textbook or sitting in Lexis. The value came from combining legal knowledge, practical application, structure, updating and access.

That is what law firms should pay attention to.

AI will improve elements of that process, but the valuable thing is not just the technology. It is the knowledge, the structure, the network, the application and the trust.

There is a danger that lawyers say, "We should build a product," without really understanding what that means. Building products is hard. Product management is hard. Roadmaps are hard. Architecture is hard. Making product decisions is hard. Working out what clients will pay for is hard. Maintaining and improving the product is hard.

It is not enough to build a nice questionnaire or a marketing gimmick and call it a product. If clients are going to pay for it, it has to solve a real problem, and it has to be worth paying for.

Sticky services matter

One of the reasons legal products matter is that they can be sticky.

Legal work is often episodic. A client has a dispute, a deal, a regulatory issue, a transaction, a restructuring, a problem. The work comes in waves. Products and technology-enabled services can create a more continuous relationship. They can give the firm a reason to keep speaking to clients even when there is not a major piece of work underway.

That is valuable in two ways.

First, it helps deepen existing client relationships. When we were looking at products at Simmons, one of the early challenges was simply making sure that our own clients knew what existed. Some products were relevant only to certain types of client, but others had much wider relevance.

Second, products can create a reason to speak to clients who are not yet clients. That changes the nature of business development. Traditional law firm business development is often relationship-led. It is about who you know, what you are known for, and whether you are there at the right time. Product selling is different. It requires a pipeline, a targeted list, a clearer ideal customer profile, and a much more specific understanding of the problem being solved.

That is not necessarily how lawyers are used to selling. It is much closer to proper sales. I do not mean aggressive selling. I mean structured, disciplined, consultative selling with a clear proposition.

Law firms need to understand that because they are increasingly competing with organisations that are very good at selling products. Legal tech companies are already selling directly to legal departments. They will look at the amount of money clients spend on law firms and say, "If we can take 20 per cent of that, that is our market."

Law firms should not assume that client relationships alone will protect them.

Product revenue creates internal tensions

One of the things firms often underestimate is the internal politics of product revenue.

Who owns the product? Does it sit in its own profit and loss account? Does a partner own it? Does the client partner get the credit? Does the partner who contributed the expertise get the credit? What happens if another partner introduces it to a client? Who gets the revenue recognition? Who gets the points?

That may sound boring, but it matters because it can block progress. If partners do not understand how they will be rewarded, or if they think someone else will get the credit, they may not support it.

If firms want to build and sell productised legal services, they need to think about governance, incentives, attribution and revenue recognition from the beginning.

Lawyers are not always the right people to build the technology

Law firms absolutely can build products that clients want. I have seen that work. I ran a large P&L that proved clients will buy these things.

But that does not mean lawyers should build the technology themselves.

The legal expertise is crucial, but the product build requires different skills. The best developers are not usually going to law firms. In many firms, if you are not a lawyer, you are not seen as the person bringing in the money. You are not treated as the fighter pilot or the surgeon. That affects the kind of technical talent firms attract and how empowered that talent feels.

That is not a criticism of individuals. It is a structural point. Law firms have traditionally been built around lawyers. Product businesses are built differently.

If a firm wants to build technology-enabled services, it needs people who understand product development, project management, user experience, sales, client adoption and ongoing maintenance. It also needs lawyers who are willing to contribute their expertise in a structured way.

That is often the hard bit.

When I was looking at product ideas, I had a simple filter. If a partner suggested a product, I would send back a short questionnaire of about ten questions. Who is it for? What problem does it solve? Why do you think it is a good idea? Basic questions.

In a majority of cases, the questionnaire never came back.

That told me almost everything I needed to know. If someone could not answer those basic questions, or did not have the time or appetite to engage with them, then the product was unlikely to succeed. A product cannot rely on a partner having a passing burst of enthusiasm. It needs sustained attention.

The unique thing law firms have is what is in their lawyers' heads. I have been approached by tech companies who wanted access to that knowledge. They had the technology, but they needed the lawyers' brains. The challenge is getting that knowledge out of people's heads and into something structured, useful and commercial.

That is one of the reasons I am interested in voice-first agentic AI.

Getting knowledge out of people's heads

At Legal Engine, much of what we are building is voice-first agentic AI. The starting point is a simple observation. The most valuable knowledge in a law firm is almost never written down. It sits in lawyers' heads. It surfaces in conversations, on calls, in meetings, in the quick exchange after a client lunch. It includes the things partners know about clients, about deals, about how a piece of work actually went, about who is worth speaking to, about what really happened on the last matter. Almost none of it ends up in the firm's systems in any structured way.

That is the real exposure firms face from AI. It is not just that machines might do parts of the work faster. It is that AI exposes how badly firms have managed the tacit knowledge that was always supposed to be their differentiator. Generalisation is a feature of the models. Specialisation has to be a feature of the firms built on top of them. That specialisation lives, today, in people's heads, and most of it disappears the moment the conversation ends.

We think about knowledge in three layers. There is the long half-life material: credentials, client history, deal experience, the things firms have always tried to manage in systems and never quite managed well. There is the medium half-life material: regulatory updates, market context, the kind of thing that is often better pulled from external sources anyway. And there is the short half-life material: what happened on a call this morning, what a partner just learned about a client, what a lateral hire brings with them in the first weeks. The short half-life material is the most valuable and the hardest to capture. By the end of the day, most of it is gone.

Voice is the natural mechanism for capturing that material. People are much less self-censoring when they talk than when they type. The friction is lower. The information is richer. And it can be done in small repeated conversations rather than one painful workflow.

The model is not a lawyer sitting for half an hour talking to a tool. It is six-minute debriefs once a week. A short conversation after a matter closes. A quick check-in after a new business meeting. A focused exchange before a directory submission. The agent asks the questions the firm wishes someone were already asking and recording. With a good schema behind it, the answers feed straight into the firm's existing systems and processes.

We think about the agents themselves as colleagues you delegate responsibility to, not as tools you operate. A skill is what an agent can do. A responsibility is an outcome the agent is accountable for. That distinction matters because it changes how firms adopt this. They are not buying another piece of software. They are building out a team, just with a different kind of colleague.

The applications follow from the underlying observation. Business development. Knowledge management. Client listening. Matter reviews. Credentials and directory submissions. The point is the same in each case: capture what is already in people's heads, structure it, and route it back into the firm's workflows so it stops disappearing.

Client listening is a good example. Many firms know they should interview clients at the end of matters. In practice, it often does not happen. The partner does not want to do it. It feels uncomfortable. It is expensive to outsource. It ends up happening once a year, in a planned interview, with ten generic questions. An agentic approach allows many smaller conversations. A three-minute call asking, "How did that go?" If the client says something interesting, the agent follows up. The deep human interview still has its place where it is needed. But the volume of feedback the firm receives changes by an order of magnitude.

That matters for pricing, too. If you do not listen properly to clients, you will struggle to understand value.

And the framing matters. This is not about doing the same work with fewer people. It is about doing more with the same people. Firms that get this right will be in a position to take on more work, deepen more relationships, and find more opportunities, without having to expand their cost base in proportion. That is the growth case for AI in law firms. It is the case, I think, firms should be making to themselves.

The "premium work" defence is risky

One line I hear from firms is that they will focus on premium work and leave the lower-value work to others.

I understand the instinct, but I think there is a risk in that.

The danger is that the premium work gets smaller and smaller. Meanwhile, the firms or providers that find a way to do the cheaper, more routine work may end up owning the relationship. If a firm does all of your lower-level work efficiently and effectively, you may well go to that firm when the big matter comes along. Clients only want so many vendors on their list.

So firms need to look carefully at what revenue is truly defensible. What work is profitable? What is the cost of acquisition? What is the cost of sale? What work is most at risk? What do clients want to do themselves? Where can the firm get ahead of that rather than simply waiting for the work to disappear?

There will always be value in specialist legal advice. There is always a benefit in outsourcing some work to people who do it many times a year, across many clients, and who have collective experience. That will not disappear.

But the form of that value may change. The way it generates revenue may change. The way firms maintain client relationships may change.

That requires a proper strategic plan, not just a business plan written once and put in a drawer.

Checking clients' AI homework is a real opportunity

One very practical opportunity is helping clients check work they have created using AI.

Clients are already using AI. They will increasingly come to lawyers and say, "I have produced this contract," or "I have drafted these terms and conditions," or "I have created this policy. Can you check it?"

That is a very obvious fixed-fee service.

A firm could say, "If you have used AI to draft an employment contract, we have a price to review it, check it, advise on the risks and sign it off." The price may vary depending on scope and risk, but it is much better suited to fixed pricing than hourly billing.

There is value there because the lawyer is taking responsibility. The client is not just paying for time. They are paying for assurance, expertise, risk assessment and, in many cases, the comfort of the firm's insurance and professional judgment.

Over time, firms may use their own AI tools to support that review work. They may learn what client-generated documents tend to get wrong. They may build more efficient review processes. That could make the work more profitable.

But it needs to be designed properly. Firms will need to ask questions such as: what did the client put into the AI tool? What source material was used? Was confidential information uploaded? Was someone else's document copied? What risks are hidden in the prompt or the process, not just in the output?

This is a good example of how AI creates new legal work, but not necessarily in the old form.

Do not turn tokens into the new billable hour

I do not think firms can charge clients directly for token usage.

There may be a temptation to do it. Firms are spending large amounts on AI tools and will need to recover that cost somehow. But charging for tokens as a line item feels like trying to pass on the cost of a deal room, or postage and photocopying, as if it is separate from the service.

Clients are unlikely to welcome that.

Token usage is a cost of doing business. Firms may need to factor it into their pricing, just as they factor in rent, salaries, insurance, technology and other overheads. But I do not think clients will accept a bill that says, in effect, "Here is your legal advice, and here is the AI usage charge."

There is also a deeper problem. If one firm uses £5,000 of tokens to produce an output and another firm uses £1,000 because it is better at using the technology, should the first firm be paid more? That would just recreate the worst logic of the billable hour. The slowest horse would win again, only this time the horse is token consumption rather than recorded time.

The better answer is to price the outcome, the value, the responsibility and the service.

Liability may be the deciding issue

There is a lot of speculation about whether legal technology platforms or AI providers might become direct competitors to law firms. Could a platform become, in effect, a law firm? Could clients go directly to a tool rather than to a lawyer?

The key issue is liability.

If a provider is willing to take responsibility for the output, and if insurers can find a way to price that risk, then things become very interesting. At the moment, many organisations are still very reluctant to take responsibility. Law firms, barristers and professionals carry significant insurance because clients and other professionals need someone to stand behind the advice.

If AI providers with very large valuations and significant capital decide they can take that risk, that could change the market. Until then, law firms still have an important role because they provide judgment, responsibility, insurance and accountability.

But firms should not be complacent. The market is moving.

The practical message for law firm leaders

My advice to law firm leaders is to start with the business model, not the technology.

Ask where your revenue comes from. Ask which parts are most vulnerable. Ask which client relationships are truly defensible. Ask what clients are beginning to do for themselves. Ask where legal tech providers might disintermediate you. Ask where you have knowledge that could be structured, productised or used to create a more continuous relationship.

Then ask whether your firm has the capabilities to respond.

Do you understand product development? Do you have a sales function that can sell productised services? Do your incentives support collaboration? Do your partners know why they should contribute their knowledge? Do you have a way of getting expertise out of people's heads? Do you listen to clients properly? Do you have pricing models that reflect value rather than time?

This is not easy. It is genuinely hard. I think managing partners today are facing a bigger change than many of their predecessors had to manage. The old assumptions about leverage, utilisation, revenue and growth are under pressure at the same time as clients are becoming more sophisticated and technology providers are becoming more ambitious.

But there is also a real opportunity.

Law firms have expertise, trust, relationships, judgment and practical experience. Those things are valuable. The challenge is to package, price, communicate and deliver them in ways that make sense in an AI-enabled market.

The firms that do that well will not simply be faster versions of their old selves. They will be different kinds of businesses.

WORDS WITH THE WISE

CHANTAL MCNAUGHT

Introduction

Chantal McNaught is a legal technology and AI specialist, currently Director of Ethics and AI Practices at 43° Below. She is also completing a PhD in Law at Bond University on how lawyers navigate the conflict between "law as a profession" and "law as a business."

Core Advice from Chantal McNaught

My starting point is that the conflict between law as a profession and law as a business is not new.

I am actively researching and writing my PhD thesis on how lawyers navigate that conflict. AI has become a huge catalyst for that discussion, but the underlying dilemma is very old. Lawyers have always had to balance duties to the court, duties to the client, duties to the administration of justice, duties to the business and duties to themselves.

That is why AI feels so unsettling. Generative AI produces content that looks and sounds legalistic. It can generate words in the format that lawyers have traditionally produced. That immediately raises the question: if a machine can produce something that looks like legal work, what is left for the lawyer to do?

That is not just a technical question. It is an identity question.

For many lawyers, what we do is bound up with who we are. We are trained into a professional identity. We are taught that we have duties beyond the client. We are not simply mouthpieces. We are not mercantile agents. We are officers of the court. We are part of a system that protects the rule of law and the functioning of civilised society.

When AI produces something that sounds like us, lawyers can feel as though they are looking into a black mirror. It sounds like me, but it is not me. That can feel threatening. But the threat often comes from misunderstanding what clients actually buy from lawyers.

Clients are not buying the paperwork.

That is one of the most important points I would make. No one buys the paperwork. The paperwork itself is not the value. The contract, the form, the pleading, the letter, the advice note – those are often the artefacts of the work, but they are not the whole of the work.

Clients are buying assistance with reality.

They are buying the conversation in which the lawyer helps them understand what has happened, what matters, what the risks are, what choices they have, and what the consequences may be. They are buying the ability to say, "Walk me through what you think you have agreed," and then to help both sides express that agreement in terms they can live with and are less likely to dispute.

A client with a family law problem is not really buying a document. They may be frightened, distressed, confused or angry. A client in a shareholder dispute may not understand why a former business partner is acting in a particular way. A client in a transaction may not understand what still needs to happen before completion. The value is not merely in text generation. The value is in helping that client navigate the problem.

That is why the pricing conversation has to change.

Legal services are "credence goods" – a term used by economists to explain the challenge with describing value when there is a knowledge asymmetry between the lawyer and the client. The lawyer understands the components of the work better than the client. That is not unique to law. A computer repair shop is also selling a credence good. If your laptop breaks and the repair shop quotes you more than the cost of the laptop, you may struggle to understand why. The repair shop knows what is involved. You do not.

Legal services work in a similar way. The client often cannot see the value because they cannot see the knowledge, experience and judgment required in the production of the service. That is one reason time-based billing has stuck for so long in professional services. Time became a proxy. It was a way of saying: this is how much effort went into the work.

But time is not the same thing as value.

I do not like recording my time. I am not a machine. Professionals are not factory machines. We are not simply feeding raw material into a process, never getting tired, bored, hungry, angry, or lonely. We are more like the engineer who knows where to strike the machine. The value is not the physical act of striking it. The value is knowing where to strike.

That is the same with lawyers. The value is not merely the hours. It is the experience, judgment, training, emotional labour, risk assessment and professional responsibility that sit behind the work.

This matters when we talk about fixed fees, value-based pricing or any alternative to hourly billing. Lawyers often worry about risk. Litigators, in particular, may say that fixed fees only benefit the service provider because there is too much uncertainty. They may say that hourly billing is fairer because the client takes the risk of how long the work takes.

I understand that concern. Some legal work is speculative. Situations change. The other side may behave unpredictably. The law may shift. The client's circumstances may change. But that does not remove the need for better conversations and a better understanding of the value of the legal service being hired.

The real issue is not whether every matter can be priced perfectly at the start. The real issue is whether lawyers are willing to have honest, practical conversations about the client's budget, the next stage of the work, the risks, the options and what can realistically be achieved.

Instead of saying, "This matter might cost between £2,000 and £200,000," and thinking that the professional obligation has been satisfied, lawyers need to ask better questions. What is the client trying to achieve? What can they afford? What is the next sensible step? What can be done from A to B? What choices does the client have?

That is where pricing becomes ethical as well as commercial.

There is a difference between complying with a rule and acting in the spirit of the rule. If the purpose of a cost estimate is to manage expectations and avoid bill shock, then a technically compliant but practically useless estimate does not really solve the problem. The estimate should be part of a conversation. It should help the client understand what is happening and what choices they have.

Budget conversations should be brought forward. They should not be left until the client is already anxious, committed or shocked by the bill. If the client has £5,000, the lawyer should be able to say, "This is what we can sensibly do for £5,000." That is a much more useful conversation than pretending that a broad range has solved the issue.

There is also an important point about what lawyers are prepared to lose.

In my research, I am interested in how lawyers navigate competing values. There is rarely one perfect answer. The question I pose is rather: what value can be tolerated to be lost in this situation?

That may sound abstract, but it is very practical.

If a lawyer takes on work at a price the client cannot afford, the lawyer may be creating a future conflict. If a law firm agrees to do work it does not have the capacity to do, it may be selling tomorrow for what it can get today. If a lawyer avoids a difficult conversation about fees, the result may be a worse problem later.

The same applies to pro bono or low-fee work. There will be situations where professional obligations are engaged, and a lawyer cannot simply walk away. But there will also be situations where the hard truth is that the firm does not have the capacity to take on the work. That does not make the lawyer uncaring. It means the lawyer has to balance professional duty, business sustainability, client need and the firm's ability to keep serving clients tomorrow.

Pricing is part of that ethical balancing exercise.

AI adds another layer to this. It is not enough to say, "We have an AI policy." Policies may be beautifully drafted and still fail in practice. If lawyers use AI without sufficient supervision, without understanding its limits and without taking responsibility for the output, then the problem is not just technological. It is professional.

Generative AI is dangerously compelling because it can sound confident. Human beings tend to associate confidence with competence. That creates danger. A junior lawyer, or someone at the beginning of their learning journey, may be more susceptible to accepting AI-generated material because they do not yet have the subject matter expertise to spot what is wrong.

That is why lawyers remain so important. In matters of law, lawyers are "BS" detectors.

The fear that AI will simply take lawyers' jobs often comes from misunderstanding why people buy lawyers in the first place. They are not buying legal-looking words. They are buying the ability to test those words, challenge them, understand them and apply them responsibly to a real situation. They are looking for specialised problem solvers.

This is also why the profession should be worried about experienced lawyers leaving. If good middle-career lawyers leave the law because they feel trapped in the "paper prison" or because they think AI has made their work meaningless, the profession loses something: its future leaders, mentors, and those with the judgment to spot when something is wrong.

That creates a risk. If more junior people are using AI and are more likely to accept hallucinated material, but the experienced lawyers who could supervise, challenge and train them are leaving, then we have a much bigger problem.

Thus, my advice to law firm leaders is this: do not make AI only about efficiency. Do not make pricing only about recovery. Do not make ethics only about compliance. These are all connected questions.

Ask what clients are really buying.

Ask what your lawyers are really providing.

Ask what risks you are asking the client to carry.

Ask what risks the firm is willing to carry.

Ask what values you are prepared to lose, and which ones you must protect.

The firms that do this well will not simply bolt AI onto old habits. They will use this moment to rethink the relationship between professional judgment, client value, pricing, and ethical responsibility.

The firms that do it badly will remain trapped in the paperwork, thinking the document is the product. They will think compliance is the same as ethics. They will think a policy is the same as supervision, and they will think a time record is the same as value.

Of course, these things are not true.

The future of pricing legal services requires lawyers to understand the human value of their work. The real value remains in the judgment, context, professional responsibility and the ability to help through difficult situations, not just generating the paperwork faster.

That is what lawyers need to price. It is an error to conflate productivity with value.

WORDS WITH THE WISE

MITCH KOWALSKI

Introduction

Mitch Kowalski is the author of *Avoiding Extinction: Reimagining Legal Services for the 21st Century* and has long been one of the clearest voices arguing that the legal profession needs to rethink how it delivers, prices and communicates its value.

Mitch brings a particularly valuable perspective because he comes to this conversation as in-house counsel working inside a technology company. He is not looking at AI, pricing and legal services from the outside. He is living with these questions every day as a buyer of legal services, a user of legal technology and someone who has to decide when work should stay in-house and when it is genuinely worth paying external lawyers to do it.

His central message is uncomfortable but important. Law firms need to understand what clients are really buying. It is not paper. It is not drafting. It is not hours. It is not knowledge on its own. Increasingly, clients can access many of those things themselves. What they will pay for is judgment, commerciality and the ability to help them make better decisions when the matter is important enough to justify external help.

Core Advice from Mitch Kowalski

I come at this from an in-house perspective, and also from inside a technology company. The internal in-house conversation is very different from the traditional law firm conversation.

In our world, the question is not, "How do we preserve the existing legal services model?" The question is, "How do we get the work done properly, manage risk, and use technology so that we do not have to keep spending so much money externally?"

At the moment, the money spent on external counsel is significantly higher than the money spent on the internal legal team. The goal is to invert that. Not by hiring hundreds of additional lawyers, but by using technology properly, building internal capability and using external lawyers only when they are truly needed.

That is the direction I think many in-house teams will eventually move in. Some will move slowly, because fear is still a big factor. But the direction of travel is clear. Clients are going to become much more disciplined about what they send out, why they send it out and what they are prepared to pay for.

The starting point for law firms is to ask a simple question: what are clients really buying from you?

From where I sit, we can do a lot ourselves. We can draft. We can review. We can summarise. We can use technology to help us understand documents, compare clauses, translate material, prepare first drafts and identify issues. Knowledge itself is not enough. Drafting itself is not enough. The paper is not the value.

The value is judgment and commerciality.

That is the sweet spot for external lawyers. If my internal team does not have the judgment, the commercial experience or the confidence to make the call, then there may be a reason to go outside. If the matter is complex enough, valuable enough or risky enough, then there may be a reason to involve external counsel. But that is a much narrower category of work than many law firms would like to believe.

For example, we may handle acquisitions and divestitures internally up to a significant level. A $50 million transaction may not need to go outside. A billion-dollar deal probably would. There is a threshold of complexity, value and risk that drives the decision. But the days when work was automatically sent to a large law firm simply because that was the safe thing to do are being challenged.

That does not mean every in-house team is already there. Many are not. There are still in-house lawyers who send work out because they are afraid. They worry that if something goes wrong, their job will be on the line. If they use a big brand firm and something goes wrong, at least they can say they chose the safe option. It is the old "nobody ever got fired for buying IBM" mentality.

That fear will not disappear overnight. It requires leadership from the general counsel or chief legal officer. Someone has to say, "Make the calls. Use the tools. Manage the risk. Of course, mistakes may happen, but make sure they are not really big mistakes." Without that leadership, the old habits will continue.

But as internal legal teams become more confident, law firms need to understand the consequences. If in-house teams take back the ordinary, run-of-the-mill work, large law firms have a problem. A lot of what they currently sell is not "bet the farm" work. If clients decide they can do that work themselves, accept the risk and avoid paying a premium, then the traditional model becomes much harder to defend.

That is why pricing has to change.

I do not like the billable hour. The whole concept of charging for the inputs into what you are creating drives me mad. In-house counsel do not want to review bills line by line. We have better things to do than work out whether a firm has duplicated effort, put too many people on a call or charged us for work that was not really valuable.

I would much rather agree a price for a phase of work and then move on. If we agree that a piece of work is $20,000, then that is the price. We are adults. We are professionals. I do not need to know how long it took you. I do not want to micromanage how you did it. I care whether the output is what I expected and whether it delivers value to me.

Shadow billing does not help. I do not care. If we have agreed the price, I do not need a second conversation about how long it took.

That becomes even more important with AI. If technology allows work to be done faster, then pricing by time becomes even more absurd. You cannot say, "This used to take two hours, but now it takes thirty minutes, so I am still going to charge you for two hours." That is dishonest. You cannot have it both ways. If you want to charge by the hour, then charge for the time actually spent. If that does not work commercially for you, then change the pricing model.

What I find strange is that some lawyers still seem to be trying to use the billable hour to justify value pricing. I was on a panel where someone suggested that AI would not get rid of the billable hour. Instead, rates would simply go up to compensate for the fact that the work takes less time. So you end up with lawyers charging $2,000 an hour because they can do something in fifteen minutes.

That will create sticker shock. Buyers are going to look at that and say, "What are you talking about?" In reality, that lawyer is almost admitting the work has a particular value. They just cannot bring themselves to price it that way, so they are trying to force a value-based calculation through an hourly rate. Lawyers are very tied to the idea that pricing is scientific. It is not. At some point, firms need to stop pretending and price differently.

AI also changes the conversation about what should be charged to clients. To me, AI is overhead. It is the cost of doing business. It is like electricity, telephones, rent, technology systems or the tools you need to do your job. I do not want to see a separate line item for tokens. If a law firm sent me a bill with an AI token charge on it, I would go crazy. I would ask, "What are you even talking about?"

The firm should manage its pricing to cover its costs. That is what businesses do. But breaking out artificial little charges for technology usage is not helpful. It creates friction, invites challenge and makes clients wonder whether the firm is simply trying to recover its investment in a way that has nothing to do with value.

There is also a danger that token charging recreates the slowest horse problem. If one lawyer is poor at using the technology and uses more tokens, does the client pay more? That cannot be right. The client should not be penalised because the lawyer is inefficient with the tool.

The better answer is to agree the price based on the value, scope and risk of the work, and then let the firm decide how best to deliver it.

On the communication side, I do not necessarily care whether my external lawyers are using AI, provided the output is right and they are not trying to charge me in a dishonest way. I would hope they are using it where it helps. In one matter, a firm told us that a summary had been prepared using AI. I was impressed by the openness. It was a Scottish lease, and they had prepared a helpful summary of the main clauses. We had already agreed a price, so I did not care that AI was used. In fact, it made sense.

The key point is not whether AI was used. The key point is whether the lawyers remain responsible for the output. If they use AI and then fail to check the work, that is a serious problem. We are still seeing lawyers relying on hallucinated cases. I find that astonishing. If you are walking into court and relying on authorities, how can you not have read them? That is such a foreign concept to me.

AI is exposing poor lawyering. It is showing us who is lazy, who is careless and who is not doing the basic work. The same applies to billing. If a lawyer does something quickly using AI and then grosses up the time, that exposes a different kind of problem. It is not an AI problem. It is an honesty problem.

AI should also force the profession to rethink training. People worry about how young lawyers will be trained if AI does more of the first-draft and document-review work. But let us be honest: the profession has not always trained young lawyers properly in the first place. Giving someone a pile of documents to read does not automatically make them a better lawyer. Sending back a redline that eviscerates their draft does not train them either.

Training requires structure, discipline and explanation. A senior lawyer has to say, "This is why I changed this. This is why that clause bothered me. This is what the client told us. This is the commercial issue you missed." That is how judgment is developed.

AI could help us do that better. We can give a junior lawyer a document, show them what the AI produced, and ask: what is missing? What instructions would you give the AI to improve the output? What else should we be thinking about? Why does this clause matter? What would the client care about?

That kind of exercise trains lawyers to be better editors, better reviewers and better instructors. It also trains them to give better instructions to people generally, which is something many lawyers are not very good at.

In the future, lawyers may become less like authors and more like editors. That does not mean their role becomes less important. It means their value lies in knowing what to accept, what to challenge, what to improve and what does not feel right. A good lawyer will look at a clause and say, "Something about this bothers me." Then they will use the tools to test alternatives, refine the wording and make the document commercially stronger.

That is judgment. That is where value sits.

For law firms, the practical message is clear. Stop assuming that everything you currently sell will continue to be valued by clients. Stop assuming that clients want to pay for process. Stop assuming that time is a proxy for value. And stop assuming that AI can simply be bolted onto the old model.

Clients do not want to buy your hours. They do not want to pay for your technology as a separate disbursement. They do not want to review bills line by line. They do not want three lawyers on a call when one will do. They want judgment, commerciality, clarity, responsibility and a result that helps them make better decisions.

If law firms can provide that, there is still a strong role for them. If they cannot, clients will increasingly work out how to do more for themselves.

WORDS WITH THE WISE

AKU SORAINEN

Introduction

Aku Sorainen is the founder and Senior Partner of Sorainen, one of the leading law firms in the Baltics. He brings a particularly useful perspective to the debate about AI, pricing and the future of legal services because he is not observing change from the sidelines. He is actively engaging with it.

His message is both practical and challenging. AI will not simply make lawyers faster. It will force law firms to understand their own data, rethink how they price work, measure what matters, and build a culture in which knowledge is shared rather than trapped inside individual partners' heads.

For law firm leaders, Aku's warning is clear. Technology is developing quickly, but the real issue may not be the technology at all. It may be the culture, incentives and leadership of the firm.

Core Advice from Aku Sorainen

I see two lines of development in relation to AI.

The first is the use of existing AI tools to help lawyers do the legal work. These tools, such as Legora, Harvey or Saga, can assist with document drafting, data room review and other tasks that lawyers have traditionally spent many hours completing.

The second line is, in some ways, even more important. It is about using AI to understand the law firm itself, such as the "soft" operational data that often doesn't get recorded. At Sorainen, we are increasingly looking at how we can use the data inside the firm to understand how our marketing and business development efforts have generated work and how much work comes from other sources, how much time has historically been spent on different types of assignments, how work has been staffed and whether the right people were involved in the assignment, how offers and matters have performed, how much profit we made on the assignment, and how we might better price and budget similar work in the future. A holistic practice management tool such as Crespect is invaluable.

That matters enormously for pricing.

If you want to price properly, you still need to understand your cost base and your likely input. Value pricing does not mean guessing. It does not mean throwing away all management information. You need to know, at least as a bottom line, how much time and resource a particular type of matter is likely to require. Then you can decide how to price it.

One of the big opportunities with AI is that it can help us avoid loss-making matters. If you can see from your data that certain types of work have been profitable and others have not, you can make better decisions. You can budget better. You can price better. You can also ask better questions before you take on the work.

At the moment, around half of our work is done on fixed fees and around half on hourly rates. Some firms may already be further along the fixed-fee path, but we are moving in that direction. However, fixed fees create their own challenge. When lawyers work on a fixed fee, some of them stop recording time carefully because they think it no longer matters. Sometimes, younger lawyers may stop recording time, because they might feel ashamed for having spent too much time on doing something.

That is a mistake.

Even if time is not used as the basis of the bill to the client, it still has value as management information. If you stop recording input, you lose the ability to learn. You lose the ability to understand whether the work was profitable. You lose the ability to improve budgeting. You lose the ability to see who contributed to the work and how.

There is a lot of discussion about measuring only output and results. Of course, output matters. But output is affected by many things you cannot directly control. The economy may be growing or declining. A matter may become more complicated than expected. Internal projects may take longer than planned. There are always variables you cannot know at the beginning.

That is why I do not think law firms should skip measuring input.

I am in favour of measuring inputs because they assist with budgeting properly for the future. If you record input and measure it consistently, you get better. Your tools get better. Your systems get better. Your processes get better. Your future estimates become more accurate even if the AI tools change your working processes.

This does not mean that everyone must account for every minute of an eight-hour day. That is not our approach. But we do expect meaningful, value-creating entries to be recorded. That might be client work, but it might also be mentoring, knowledge work, training, appraisal, business development or other contributions to the firm.

These softer contributions matter. But how do you know who is mentoring, who is supporting others, who is helping build the institution, unless you capture that input somewhere?

This links directly to culture.

AI is developing very quickly, but law firm culture often develops much more slowly. In many firms, there is a divide. You have the enthusiasts who attend conferences, network, experiment with tools and speak publicly about innovation. Then you have the majority, who may be far behind in adopting the technology.

The reason is often not the technology itself. It is how partners are measured and rewarded.

In many law firms, partner appraisal is still focused on financials: personal billing, personal origination, supervision of work and similar measures. Those things may matter, but they do not necessarily encourage technology adoption, knowledge sharing or data discipline.

If you reward only individual financial performance, you should not be surprised if partners focus on their own financial performance. If you want collaboration, innovation and knowledge sharing, you need to measure and reward those things too.

This is becoming critical because AI depends on data.

Many lawyers using AI tools will upload their favourite precedents, the ones they use every day, and ask the tool to help them draft or analyse. That is useful, but it is not enough. Anyone can do that, and what is the purpose of working together with others if individual practitioners now have access to the same tools and LLMs. The big issue is whether the firm has organised and structured its knowledge properly, so that lawyers are starting from the best available know-how across the firm. That institutional know-how might be one of the key competitive advantages of a law firm. It's not a coincidence that in May 2026, Kirkland & Ellis announced that they decided to invest USD 500M into developing their own AI platform. They have know-how and institutional data they want to utilise better and guard from competitors.

Every law firm has huge volumes of documents. At Sorainen, we have millions of documents in our document management system. But not all of that material is valuable. The challenge is to identify the valuable part, organise it, and make it available so that AI can help us use it.

That is not just a technology problem. It is a problem with data hygiene.

If partners are encouraged to compete with each other, they will keep knowledge in their own heads, and the firm will struggle to become data-centric. If partners are encouraged to collaborate, share know-how and think institutionally, the firm has a much better starting point.

At Sorainen, we have been building a collaborative culture for more than 20 years. We did not originally do that because of AI. But now it is clear that collaboration has a direct impact on data quality and knowledge sharing. Even so, collaboration is not enough. You also need discipline. You need data hygiene. It is a great starting point that people agree to share information for the mutual benefit of all, but you need policies, processes and technology to ensure your systems don't get polluted with unnecessary data.

Looking ahead, I believe one of the biggest issues for law firms will be how they become genuinely data-centric. Much of the most valuable knowledge in a law firm still sits in partners' heads, and that is not news; it has always sat there since the early dawn of the legal profession. For decades, people have tried to figure out how to institutionalise that knowledge. The AI just brings this issue to the table with loud colours and big letters. If you look beyond legal documents and emails and look at the business development entries, debriefings, leads and other operational soft data, now lawyers don't necessarily need to write perfect essays for the system. One of the useful things about AI is that you can give it hints. You can point it in the right direction. AI can update and complement your given hints. AI can say that old information is no longer valid and new information should be used instead. But if you give the system no hints and no direction at all, the benefits of the AI are much more limited.

Another point I feel strongly about is leadership. I am surprised that so few senior law firm leaders attend legal technology conferences. You often see heads of IT and innovation people there, but not enough senior partners, managing partners or CEOs.

That is a problem because senior leadership sets the direction of the firm.

Technology is moving so quickly, and there are now so many legal tech companies, that it is very difficult for heads of IT alone to navigate the whole environment. Their natural responsibility is to keep the systems safe, manage risk and avoid unnecessary disruption. That is important, but it can also mean they become the brakes on innovation.

Senior leadership must not simply delegate the technology to the IT department, as that may mean they delegate a large element of the future of the firm.

The senior leaders need to understand what is happening in the technology environment. They need to decide what the firm should try, what risks it is prepared to take, what direction it wants to move in, and what responsibility leadership will accept. Innovation cannot just be an IT project. It has to be a leadership issue.

At the same time, many lawyers are still making enough money in the old way. That is one of the reasons change is difficult. The house is not burning enough yet. When firms are still profitable, it is hard to persuade partners that the business model needs to change.

But that comfort is dangerous.

The future will require firms to be more collaborative, more disciplined with data, more thoughtful about pricing and more serious about leadership. AI will not reward firms that simply add new tools on top of old habits. It will reward firms that understand their own knowledge, organise it properly, measure what matters, and use technology to improve the way they serve clients.

WORDS WITH THE WISE

NOO JONES

Introduction

Noo Jones is a Business Psychologist, learning expert and the founder of Athena Professional. She works with professionals and professional service firms to help them think more seriously about capability, learning, leadership and development.

Her perspective matters because the legal profession is facing a moment where simply teaching lawyers to use new tools will not be enough. AI, client expectations, pricing pressure and changing business models are all forcing firms to ask a bigger question: what capabilities will lawyers need in the future, and how do firms create the conditions for those capabilities to develop?

Noo's central message is clear. Law firms should stop thinking about "training" as a series of events, courses or technical updates. She much prefers the idea of continuous learning. In an AI world, that distinction matters.

Core Advice from Noo Jones

The future of legal services will not be shaped only by technology. It will be shaped by how well law firms learn.

AI is already changing the relationship between lawyers and clients. It is changing what clients expect, what they are willing to pay for, and how they judge whether a lawyer is adding value. Some firms are responding with curiosity and urgency. Others are still acting as though AI is not relevant to their work or their clients.

That is dangerous.

For me, the starting point is not the technology itself. It is purpose. Before a firm asks, "What AI tools should we buy?" or "What skills do our lawyers need?", it should first ask, "What kind of firm are we trying to become?" and "What kind of value are we here to provide?"

Without that strategic clarity, learning becomes fragmented. People attend sessions, receive updates, download guidance, perhaps experiment with tools, but the firm does not really change. In a world where AI is altering the work, the economics and the client relationship, that is not enough.

I have a real dislike of the word "training" when it is used too narrowly. Continuous learning is a better description.

Training can sound like something that is done to people. It can sound like a course, a webinar, a box to tick, or a way of making people complete tasks faster. Of course, there will always be technical knowledge that lawyers need to acquire. But the bigger issue now is continuous learning.

Law firms need to build learning into the way they operate. That means helping people develop judgment, adaptability, commercial awareness, critical thinking, client understanding and confidence with digital practice. It also means helping lawyers understand risk, value, pricing and the commercial context in which their clients operate.

Those capabilities do not appear because someone attended a one-hour session. They develop when a firm has a clear purpose, a coherent strategy and managers who support learning through everyday conversations.

In my view, firms should begin with the foundations. What is our purpose? What are our values? What do we want our lawyers to be capable of doing? How do we want clients to experience working with us? What does good judgment look like here? What does responsible AI use look like here?

Only then should the firm design the learning.

The mistake is to rush straight to the tool. AI is important, but it is not the whole conversation. Some firms are already scanning the horizon, thinking about solutions and asking how technology will change their service model. Others are still treating AI as something peripheral, or assuming it will not affect their area of practice. That is particularly risky in areas where process-heavy work, such as conveyancing or contract work, may be vulnerable to automation or client challenge.

Clients are becoming more informed. Some are already asking why they should pay lawyers for work that AI could help produce. That changes the pricing conversation. It also changes the lawyer's role. If the machine can help generate the first draft, summary or analysis, then the value of the lawyer lies elsewhere: in judgment, responsibility, context, ethics, risk assessment, client understanding and the ability to help the client make a better decision.

But firms should not respond to this by pretending that AI removes the need for lawyers. It does not. It changes what lawyers must be good at.

One of the most important human capabilities is the ability to understand what the client really needs. Lawyers often think they are listening, but in reality, they may simply be waiting for the client to finish speaking so they can give advice. That is not the same thing. Proper client understanding requires curiosity, patience and the ability to hold a purposeful conversation.

A client may ask for a document, a contract, a letter or an answer. But the real need may be deeper. They may want certainty, protection, confidence, speed, reassurance, a commercial route through a problem, or help navigating a difficult decision. If the lawyer only responds to the surface request, they may miss the value.

There is also a significant internal communication challenge. Many lawyers are anxious about AI. Some fear that it will replace them. Others worry about making mistakes. Some may feel embarrassed that they do not understand the technology. Junior lawyers may feel pressure from all directions: to produce work quickly, to learn new tools, to avoid errors, to meet expectations and to build relationships in a profession that is changing around them.

That is why psychological safety matters. People need to feel able to speak up, ask questions, admit uncertainty and learn from mistakes. If a firm creates a culture where people hide errors or pretend to understand things they do not understand, AI will make that more dangerous, not less.

The profession also needs to be honest about risk. There have already been examples where lawyers have relied on AI-generated material without proper checking. That is not an AI problem alone. It is a supervision, judgment and learning problem. The answer is not panic. The answer is to build capability carefully and deliberately.

Firms need clear expectations about responsible AI use. They need to explain those expectations internally and externally. Internally, lawyers need to know what is permitted, what is not, when human checking is required, and where accountability sits. Externally, clients need reassurance that the firm is using technology responsibly, not cutting corners, hiding processes or passing off machine output as professional judgment.

Communication with clients should be open, confident and grounded in purpose. The message should not be, "We are using AI because everyone else is." It should be, "We are using appropriate tools to improve the quality, consistency and efficiency of our service, while preserving the judgment, responsibility and client understanding that you come to us for."

That is a very different message.

I also think law firms need to stop relying on serendipity as their main learning model. Too much professional development has historically depended on who you sit near, which partner you work for, what kind of matter happens to land on your desk, or whether someone has time to explain things properly. That is not enough in a rapidly changing environment.

The SQE process in England and Wales, with its focus on practical learning and outcomes, reflects a broader point. Lawyers need to be able to evidence and reflect on what they are learning, not simply attend sessions. Firms should be helping people build capability through structured pathways, meaningful feedback, manager support and regular development conversations.

Managers are central to this. A firm-wide learning strategy will not work if managers do not support it. People need routine check-ins. They need help connecting their development to the firm's strategy and to client value. They need to understand not only what they are learning, but why it matters.

The firms that do this well will not try to implement twenty initiatives at once. They will build carefully. They will start with purpose, then capability, then learning pathways, then support structures. They will help people take reasoned decisions and calculated risks. They will create the conditions in which lawyers can grow.

The human side of legal practice is not disappearing. In many ways, it is becoming more important. Trust, judgment, empathy, conversation, commercial understanding and the ability to help clients make sense of complexity will matter more, not less.

AI can help with many things. It can support drafting, research, analysis, process and knowledge work. But it does not replace the lawyer's responsibility to understand the client, exercise judgment and provide a service that is genuinely valuable.

That is the opportunity for law firms. Not just to become faster. Not just to become more efficient. But to become better at learning, better at listening, better at explaining value and better at helping clients achieve the outcomes that matter to them.

The firms that thrive in an AI world will not simply be the firms that buy the best technology. They will be the firms that learn best.

They will understand their purpose. They will develop their people deliberately. They will create cultures where lawyers feel safe to grow, question, experiment and improve. They will help clients understand the value of human judgment in a world where technology can do more and more of the task-based work.

For lawyers, the challenge is not just to learn how to use AI. It is to learn how to become more valuable because AI exists.

That means becoming better listeners, better thinkers, better advisers and better learners.

WORDS WITH THE WISE

FELIX RILEY

Introduction

Felix Riley is a keynote speaker, business strategist, writer and adviser on "Brilliant Thinking". His career has taken him from BBC comedy writing to the City, entrepreneurship, corporate leadership, business turnarounds and thriller writing.

That gloriously un-lawyerly background is exactly why his perspective is useful. Felix is not trying to teach lawyers the law. He is asking whether lawyers are thinking boldly enough about AI, pricing, client value and the future of their own profession.

Core Advice from Felix Riley

I am not anti-AI.

Let me start there.

I use it. I like it. I can see where it is useful. If you want to summarise something, repackage something, transcribe something, produce a first draft, interrogate a long document, or organise your thinking, it can be bloody brilliant.

But I do think the legal profession needs to take a breath.

Because AI is being sold to lawyers with a very large dose of fear.

Law is an obvious target for the AI industry. It is a huge global market. It is rules-based. It is document-heavy. It has precedent, process, regulation, complexity and margin. If you were designing a sector for AI vendors to go after, law would be close to perfect.

So, I understand why the noise is so loud.

But noise is not strategy.

My concern is not that law firms will use AI. Of course they will. My concern is that some firms will over-believe the hype, rush into adoption without thinking properly about return, hollow out their junior ranks, become dependent on a small number of dominant AI providers, and then discover that they have given away the very thing clients actually value.

That thing is not process.

It is judgment.

It is wisdom.

It is the ability to look at a situation and say, "Yes, you might be able to do that, but I would not."

That is the bit clients really pay for.

If a client comes to a lawyer and says, "I want to take my neighbour to court because the fence is too high," the valuable answer is not always a technical answer about the law of boundaries, planning, nuisance or rights of light. The valuable answer may be:

"You may win. Don't do it."

That is what impresses me.

Not the ability to produce more words. Not the ability to produce a longer answer. Not the ability to generate a 40-page legal-looking document. Clients can already do that with ChatGPT. In fact, lawyers are already seeing clients arrive with huge AI-generated documents and asking them to "cast an eye over it". The lawyer then has to explain that reviewing the client's 40 pages may cost more than simply giving the right advice in the first place.

That is the point.

The client does not know what matters.

The client does not know what is irrelevant.

The client does not know which question to ask.

The lawyer does.

Or at least, the good lawyer does.

That is why I think AI should force law firms to ask a much better question: what do we actually bring that the machine cannot?

If the answer is process, you have a problem.

If the answer is drafting, you have a problem.

If the answer is "we can produce a lot of documents", you have a problem.

But if the answer is judgment, creativity, perspective, commercial instinct, human understanding and the ability to get to the real issue, then you still have something valuable. In fact, you may have something more valuable than ever.

Because the more AI does the routine work, the more exposed the lawyer becomes.

There is nowhere to hide.

If the machine can produce the first draft, the lawyer has to produce the wisdom.

If the machine can summarise the law, the lawyer has to know what to do with it.

If the machine can generate options, the lawyer has to help the client choose.

That is where the value is.

This is why I am sceptical of the idea that every law firm needs to be seen as being at the absolute cutting edge of AI. I am not saying ignore it. I am saying do not be stampeded. Take the obvious quick wins. Use the tools where they help. But do not confuse adoption with strategy.

There is no glory in buying technology if you cannot show the return.

There is no intelligence in copying another firm just because FOMO has taken over the partnership.

There is no long-term strategy in using AI to remove the work that used to train young lawyers, unless you have thought very carefully about how those young lawyers are now going to learn.

That, for me, is one of the biggest issues.

Where are the future partners coming from?

Where are the culture carriers coming from?

Where are the people who will learn the instincts, the judgment, the feel, the wisdom?

If you take away too much of the junior work, then you must replace it with something else. You cannot simply say, "AI will do that now," and imagine the next generation will somehow become wise by magic.

They will not.

Judgment is not downloaded.

It is developed.

It comes from exposure, mistakes, supervision, reflection, experience and watching people who know what they are doing. If firms strip that out, they may improve the short-term economics but damage the long-term profession.

That is not transformation.

That is asset-stripping.

I also think lawyers have a particular cultural challenge with AI because lawyers are trained not to make mistakes. That is necessary. It is part of the discipline. It is why clients trust them with serious problems. But everything is double-edged.

The same training that makes lawyers careful can also make them risk-averse, defensive and unimaginative.

Lawyers are very good at defending positions. That is their job. But it also means they can become attached to bad ideas. They can justify them. They can anchor too early. They can be too quick to say why something will not work.

That is dangerous in a moment like this.

Because AI is not just a technology issue. It is a thinking issue.

Law firms need to learn how to think better together.

They need to create rooms where people are allowed to have bad ideas. That sounds odd, but it is vital. If every idea has to be safe, polished and defensible before it is spoken, you will never get to the interesting stuff.

You need play.

You need permission.

You need people to say the thing that may be wrong so that someone else can build on it and get to the thing that is right.

You do not need ten brilliant ideas.

You may only need one.

But you often have to go through a lot of bad ideas to find it.

That is hard for lawyers, because bad ideas feel unsafe. But if law firms want to respond properly to AI, pricing and the future of legal services, they have to get past that. They have to permit experimentation. They have to stop treating every conversation as if it were a cross-examination.

This is where I think Shaun's 8-P Point Plan is interesting

For me, this is clearly part of **P#1 Paradigm**. The profession has to shift from process thinking to outcome thinking. Lawyers cannot define themselves by the production of work if the production of work is increasingly automated. They have to define themselves by the quality of the decision they help the client make.

It is also part of **P#3 Plan**. AI adoption cannot just be procurement. It cannot be "buy the shiny thing and hope". Firms need to plan how AI will be used, where it creates value, how it affects training, how it affects pricing, how it affects risk, how it affects supervision and how it affects the client experience.

It is also part of **P#5 Permit**. Lawyers need permission to experiment, to play, to test, to fail, to learn and to think beyond the obvious. Without that permission, the firm will simply bolt new technology onto old habits.

And it is definitely part of **P#7 Persevere**. This is not an email from the managing partner saying, "From Monday, we are doing AI." This is cultural work. It takes time.

My view is that, when the dust settles, a lot of AI tools will become fairly standard. They will be useful. They will be normal. They will be expected. But they will not, by themselves, be much of a differentiator.

AI may become like Excel for accountants.

Useful? Absolutely.

Important? Of course.

A reason to choose one accountant over another? Not really.

You do not choose the accountant because they have Excel. You choose the accountant because they know what the numbers mean.

The same will be true of lawyers.

Clients will not choose a lawyer merely because the lawyer has access to AI. Everyone will have access to AI. Clients will choose the lawyer who knows what to do with it.

The lawyer who can challenge it. Improve it. Reject it. Apply it. Explain it. Translate it into a better decision.

That is the future value of the lawyer.

Not typing.

Not process.

Not volume.

Not time.

Judgment.

And that is why law firms need to be very careful not to price the wrong thing.

If AI reduces the time taken to produce the work, and the firm still prices as though time is the value, then the firm has walked straight into the trap.

The value is not the time saved.

The value is the outcome achieved.

The value is the risk avoided.

The value is the decision made.

The value is the dispute not started.

The value is the relationship preserved.

The value is the phone call made at the right moment instead of the aggressive letter sent at the wrong one.

So, my advice to law firms is simple.

Use AI, but do not worship it.

Take the quick wins, but do not believe every pitch.

Automate the process but protect the judgment.

Train your young lawyers, or you will damage your own future.

Create space for better thinking, or you will become a process business with a law firm logo.

And above all, remember that the most valuable legal question may still be the simplest one:

"Why?"

Why do you want to do this?

Why does this matter?

Why now?

What are you really trying to achieve?

Because when a lawyer asks that question properly, the whole matter can change.

That is not AI.

That is acumen.

That is wisdom.

That is what clients should pay for.

WORDS WITH THE WISE

BEN WEINBERGER

Introduction

Ben Weinberger is a lawyer, technologist and legal industry strategist with a sharp eye for where the profession is heading next. He is the author of *The Death of Big Law*, a provocative look at how technology, client pressure and new delivery models are challenging the traditional law firm machine.

Ben brings a practical, commercially minded perspective to the future of legal services, asking the questions many firms would rather avoid: what happens when the old model stops working, and who is brave enough to build something better?

Core Advice from Ben Weinberger

The conflict between AI and the billable hour is not new. Law firms have been buying technology for years that makes work more efficient, while still billing on a model that rewards time spent.

I saw this as a consultant advising on document management systems in the 1990s. We would help firms select systems using ROI calculations that showed large efficiency savings. But under the billable hour, that created a strange result. The firm ended up spending money on technology that made work faster, but by making that work faster, the firm lost money on time that would otherwise have been billable.

That same issue now appears with AI.

If the firm is billing by the hour, and AI reduces the time needed to do the work, then the billable hour model becomes a problem. The firm may become more efficient, but it may also reduce the amount it can charge. Firms are spending money to lose money. Again.

Clients are now driving this change. Some clients have already said they will not pay for work that AI could do. Clients also have access to AI tools themselves, and in some situations, they are getting a "good enough" answer without paying law firm rates.

That does not mean clients no longer need lawyers. It means law firms need to be clearer about what they are selling.

Clients do not care how many hours something takes. They care about the answer, the outcome, the turnaround time, the price, and the level of service.

The paradigm shift is that firms cannot simply add AI to the old hourly model and assume everything still works. AI changes the economics of the work.

There is a real place for alternative pricing. I like the idea of fixed quarterly retainers for defined work. A client pays, for example, a fixed amount each quarter for an agreed scope. If something extraordinary happens, that can be dealt with separately.

That sort of model means the firm must understand its costs, its efficiency, and the risk it is taking. Both sides need to understand who is taking the risk. Shadow billing, which became a common practice when fixed fees first gained popularity, undermines that because, if both sides keep checking the hours, they have not really moved away from the hourly model.

A firm needs to understand the work, the cost, and the scope before changing the pricing model. Fixed fees and retainers only work properly if the firm knows what it is agreeing to deliver.

When looking for AI use cases, firms should start with the work nobody wants to do. The junk work. The procedural work. The formatting work. The tasks that waste time and frustrate people.

AI can help create a first draft. It can help overcome writer's block. It can help with the work that gets in the way of more valuable work. But it still needs review. AI can behave like an overenthusiastic first-year associate. It may produce something useful, but some of it may be wrong.

Making sensible decisions about where to use AI is only part of the challenge. The other part is getting people to adopt it successfully. Understanding people and knowing how to navigate a firm is crucial.

Change management matters. It relies on people. You need to know who the real influencers are in the firm. You cannot just assume they are the people with the biggest titles.

Sometimes the influencer is a secretary who has been there for 30 years and knows how everything really works. Sometimes it is a long-serving partner in the corner office. These people can become your biggest supporters if you bring them with you properly.

You also need to be careful about training groups. Do not put partners in a room with everyone else and expect honest learning. Partners behave differently when they are with associates or secretaries. They may pretend they understand, or they may rip the idea apart. That can kill the project.

Train people in the right groups. Understand the politics. Understand the personalities.

Communication needs to be short, clear, and attention-grabbing. You cannot really over-communicate before, during, or after a project, but the communication has to be readable.

There will be detractors. The people who say, "That will never work", need to be handled carefully. There is no single answer. It depends on the person and the situation.

But do not put obvious detractors into the pioneer group. If a senior partner gives the sideways glance that says the project is nonsense, an associate is unlikely to go against them.

The project needs support from the top. If the people at the top are not amenable to change, implementation becomes much harder.

One final real challenge firms will have to address is associate development. If AI removes the work junior lawyers used to do to learn, firms need to think about how those lawyers will develop. I do not pretend to have fully solved that problem, but it is a serious one.

WORDS WITH THE WISE

HEATHER SUTTIE

Introduction

Heather Suttie is a legal market strategy and management consultant who has advised law firms and legal service providers since 1998.

Based in Toronto and working internationally, she helps firms – from global law firms to boutiques and NewLaw businesses – sharpen their strategy, strengthen their market position, improve client relationships and build sustainable competitive advantage.

Core Advice from Heather Suttie

AI and pricing are two sides of the same coin.

AI is an efficiency enabler. It helps work get done faster. That creates a direct problem for the billable hour. If a firm is still charging by time, and AI reduces the time, then the pricing model is under pressure.

The billable hour's days are numbered.

Some Australian firms are already moving away from target hours and towards output, productivity and value. The point is not how many hours were recorded; the point is what value was delivered to the client.

Clients are asking harder questions. They want to know whether AI is being used. They want transparency. They want to understand whether efficiency gains are being passed on. If firms do not talk openly about AI, clients may ask: what else are they not telling us?

The better approach is to explain AI's use clearly. For example, "We have this piece of technology. It helps us do our work. It gets you a better result. It is beneficial for everybody."

The structure of many law firms is under pressure. The traditional pyramid model depends on junior lawyers doing work at the bottom of the pyramid, with that work supporting the economics of the firm. If AI removes or reduces that work, the structure becomes difficult to sustain.

That also creates a partnership problem. Younger lawyers may ask who will buy them out in 20 years if the junior ranks have been reduced and the traditional model no longer works.

So, AI and pricing are not only technology issues; they impact structure.

Leadership matters. Many law firm leaders are not equipped to drive this kind of transformation. Many are elected because of seniority, not because they have business acumen or strategic vision.

Some leaders also avoid difficult conversations because they need to keep partners onside. That makes leading change even harder.

Firms need leaders who are willing to make difficult decisions about the business model, not just the technology.

Value-based pricing needs to be practical. It can be done through small, medium and large options. Those options can work for individual lawyers, teams, practice groups, industry groups and larger firms as a whole.

The barrier is often not technical. It is psychological. Lawyers are still trapped in six-minute increment thinking. They need to move from time-based thinking to scope-based thinking. What is included? What is excluded? What assumptions are being made? What are the stages? What value is being delivered?

When a firm completes a mandate under budget, the answer is not to hand money back but instead to add value. Tell the client that there is room in the price and offer something more that the client will consider valuable. This action builds trust if done honestly and transparently.

The real opportunity is not only to practice innovation. Using AI for legal research, document review and drafting is now table stakes. The bigger question is business innovation. Many firms appoint innovation leaders who focus on practice innovation, but the real issue is that the business model itself is changing. Transforming the model requires business expertise, not legal expertise.

Firms need to become more focused. From the outside, many firms look the same. They are beige and grey as porridge. The future will demand industry focus. Firms need legal expertise, but also proven, hands-on industry knowledge and business experience. Clients expect more than a legal answer, which they can get from other lawyers, if not AI. Clients expect advisors to provide forward motion, future vision and commercial judgment.

Private equity is changing the market actively. Lawyers may find it frightening, but private equity involvement removes waste, deadwood and poor performance. If firms cannot reform themselves fast, external capital may do it for them.

Leadership will have to make difficult decisions about which work to keep, which work to commoditise, and which work to stop doing. This will impact the people the firm employs. Law firms are not private members clubs; they are lean businesses that must be bottom-line driven to survive.

Heather's practical advice

Do not treat AI as a side issue.

It affects pricing.

It affects structure.

It affects leadership.

It affects the future shape of the firm.

Move away from six-minute thinking.

Build small, medium and large pricing options, and let clients choose.

Scope properly.

Be transparent with clients.

Sell all technology through to clients, including explaining how AI benefits the work product and outcome.

Focus on value, output, productivity and outcome by better managing client expectations.

And recognise that by 2030, the legal services environment will look and behave very differently from how it does today.

WORDS WITH THE WISE

KAROLINA ŠILINGIENĖ

Introduction

Karolina is co-founder and Chief Customer Success Officer at Crespect, where she helps law firms rethink legal practice management through AI-driven technology. Her work focuses on making law firm operations more connected, practical and intelligent by bringing together areas such as CRM, workflow automation, compliance, billing, reporting and data-driven insight.

Karolina's central message is a practical one: AI will not magically improve a law firm if the firm's own operational knowledge is scattered, outdated, hidden in people's heads or trapped in systems nobody uses properly.

Core Advice from Karolina Šilingienė

When I speak with law firms about technology and AI, I often see the same issue. Everyone hopes AI will be the silver bullet, but AI can only work with the information it can access. If a firm's operational data is sitting in old, clunky, on-premise systems, or in separate spreadsheets, Outlook folders, practice management systems and people's heads, then the AI does not have much useful intelligence to work with.

That is why I think law firms need to put their house in order. Before AI can properly help you, the firm needs to structure the information it already has. There is a lot of attention on AI tools that help lawyers draft faster, review documents faster or prepare legal advice faster. Those tools are important, but I am also interested in the back end of the law firm: the way the firm actually operates.

There are so many patterns sitting inside a law firm. Write-offs. Invoice corrections. Discounts. Old habits. The same people being staffed on the same types of work. The same teams being formed in the same way, even when there may be a more efficient way of doing the work. The data is there, but often nobody is analysing it properly.

That matters for pricing. If you do not know where you are discounting, writing off, correcting invoices or repeating inefficient behaviours, how can you price with confidence? How can you understand whether a client is profitable? How can you decide whether a piece of work should be priced differently next time?

A law firm's operational data can show where it is inefficient. It can show where processes are too complicated. It can show where work is being handled in ways that do not make business sense. Used properly, that information can free lawyers from administration and allow them to spend more time being lawyers.

One of the biggest issues is that law firms often do not really know their clients as a firm. A partner may know one part of the relationship, but the wider firm does not have the full picture. In a larger firm, the real estate partner may only know the real estate work. They may go into a client meeting without knowing that the litigation team has recently defended the same client in a business-critical dispute, or that an IP consultant has worked on a brand registration, or that there are compliance issues handled by someone else in the firm.

That makes the firm look less joined-up than it should. It also weakens the claim that the firm is a trusted adviser. How can you be the trusted legal adviser if you are not even aware of what is happening with that client in another department?

Knowing which sports team your client's key contact supports is extra, but let's think about knowing the legal and business relationship between the client and the firm. Has the client had payment issues? Are there ongoing disputes? Have they complained about a particular way of working? Have they given feedback in a debrief meeting? Have they bought only one type of service from the firm when there are other areas where the firm could help? Have they attended the firm's webinars on specific topics or joined a reception?

That knowledge should not live only in one person's head. If the relationship partner leaves, retires, becomes ill or simply moves on, what happens to the client relationship? Does it stay with the firm, or does it disappear with that individual?

This is why operative knowledge must be shared. It is not enough for one partner to know the client. The team needs to know the client.

There is a very simple analogy. If you pick up your phone and say, "Call my wife," the first time Siri may ask, "Who is your wife?" You have to give the system some information before it can help you. Once it has that information, it can respond more intelligently and save you time. It is the same with law firm systems and AI. If the tools are empty, or full of old and outdated information, they will not be helpful.

The future I see is one where AI becomes like a seasoned executive assistant. It can tell you that a client's revenue is dropping. It can remind you that you have not spoken to them in six months. It can point out that they have just closed a dispute and there may be a follow-up opportunity. It can help you prepare for a meeting by summarising the relationship health, the work done, the unpaid invoices, the white-space opportunities and the sensible speaking points.

But it can only do that if the firm has captured the information in the first place.

That means lawyers need to change the way they think about entering data. It should not be seen as entering data for the sake of entering data. It should be seen as enabling the smart assistants that will help them become better relationship managers.

I do not say "better lawyers" because many lawyers are already excellent lawyers. They have the education and technical skill. But in the legal business, they also need to be account managers and caretakers of client relationships. They need to follow up. They need to spot opportunities. They need to understand the client lifecycle. They need to make sure the relationship is viable and loyal.

Too often, lawyers see practice management systems or CRM systems as a dumping ground for non-billable time. They feel they are being measured, monitored, rewarded or punished. They do not see the system as a personal support mechanism. That is a cultural issue as much as a technology issue.

Sometimes the tools are old and poor. Sometimes the tools are good, but the firm does not have a data-centric culture. Sometimes users have not been educated about the potential. There are many layers to the problem.

But when the tool is there, the knowledge is there and the data-centric culture is appreciated and properly rewarded in the law firm, opportunities are unlocked. Lawyers can become better relationship managers. They can generate more work from existing clients rather than spending all their energy on new client acquisition, which is usually much more expensive.

The value is often already in the client portfolio. The question is whether the firm can see it.

A good example is a new partner joining a firm. Perhaps they have a target to grow revenue in transfer pricing or another specialist area. If the firm has clear client penetration data, the new partner can see which existing clients have not bought that service before. They can see the sectors in which those clients operate. They can ask for introductions from colleagues who already have trusted relationships established with those clients.

That is much faster than starting from nothing with a completely new client. The service agreement may already be in place. The relationship may already exist. The firm simply needs to join the dots.

This is where collaboration becomes critical. If the firm has an "eat what you kill" culture, people may not want to share information. They may not want other partners to benefit from their knowledge. But if they do not enter that information, they will not benefit from the AI system being able to find it and advise them either.

So this comes back to culture and even to partnership appraisal. What does the firm reward? Is it only billable hours? Is it individual profit? Or does the firm reward cross-referrals, collaboration, shared supervision and the wider value created for the firm?

If a law firm says it believes in collaboration and transparency, its systems, behaviours and rewards need to support that. Otherwise, the firm may have collaborative features in its software, but nobody will use them.

Client feedback is another important example. In my own experience in business development, annual client interviews could be very revealing. Clients would open up and say what was working and what was not. Sometimes they were tired of giving the same feedback again and again. The firm might take notes, and people might appear to take it seriously, but a year later, the same mistakes were still happening.

That is because the knowledge was not institutionalised. It stayed only with the people who attended the feedback session. If a different department later worked with the same client, they might not know what the client had already said.

Those touchpoints need to be captured. If a CEO says, "Always copy me in; I want to be involved," that is not a small detail. It is useful relationship knowledge. If that CEO later moves to another company that also becomes a client, the firm should still know that preference. Imagine being able to say, "We know you like to stay closely involved, so we will make sure you are copied in." That shows the client that the firm remembers and cares.

This is what good can look like. Before a client meeting, the lawyer can ask the AI assistant for a meeting brief. What work have we done for this client? Who has met them? What did they say last time? Are there unpaid invoices? What service lines have they not used? What opportunities are there? Are there recent public developments affecting their business? What should I ask them about?

Instead of going to four different places, checking financials, CRM notes, asking about matter history and lessons learnt in the firm's corridors and also public news, the assistant can bring that intelligence together. It gives the lawyer a more complete view of the client history and relationship with the firm. It helps the lawyer have a more valuable conversation.

That is also relevant to pricing. If you understand the client's context, history, relationship, needs and risks, you are better placed to price the value of your advice. The client is not only paying for a document or a task. They are paying for the safety net the firm provides. They are paying for lawyers who already know the legal issues and the context, and who can get to the point more quickly because they do not have to educate themselves from scratch.

There is an old anecdote about paying the engineer with a hammer because he knows where to hit. I think there is a similar point for trusted lawyers. Clients aren't paying for the time something takes; they pay for knowledge, judgment and context. But the firm can only price that properly if the knowledge is captured and available, rather than living only in one person's head.

Financial hygiene is also essential. Law firms should be looking at their client lists and asking which clients are profitable, which are not, where the tail should be cut, where prices should be increased and where the firm is holding on to work for the wrong reasons.

Lawyers are often very focused on the legal aspects: the deal, the dispute, the technical challenge. But the business also needs to understand client health, client lifecycle, lifetime value and profitability. These are basic business concepts, but they are still too often neglected in law firms.

There may be good reasons to keep an unprofitable client. Perhaps it is a blue-chip name or strategically important. But not every unprofitable client is worth keeping. "Any pound is a good pound" is not a good business strategy.

Law firms also need to be honest about the type of work they take on. Sometimes lawyers want to do a matter because it is interesting, unique or a first precedent in the market. That may be a legitimate reason in some cases, but it is not automatically good for the business. Leadership has to ask why the firm is doing the work and whether it fits the strategy.

My wider warning is that technology will not fix a firm that does not want to be transparent, collaborative or data-driven. AI can be powerful, but it needs good information. If the data is poor, hidden or not entered at all, the opportunity is lost.

The firms that will benefit most are those that treat operational knowledge as an asset. They will capture it, structure it, share it and use it. They will understand that the knowledge sitting inside the firm is not administration. It is part of the value the firm can bring to clients.

WORDS WITH THE WISE

MARK BARRETT

Introduction

Mark Barrett is the founder of Automation Outcomes Ltd, an AI-enabled automation, training and governance business that works with professional services firms and regulated organisations. His work focuses on helping non-technical professionals use AI and automation safely, productively and practically.

Mark's perspective is especially useful because he is not approaching AI as a shiny technology exercise. He is looking at how work actually gets done, where the bottlenecks sit, how people behave, what governance requires and how firms can turn AI from a vague promise into a properly managed business capability.

Core Advice from Mark Barrett

My central message to law firms is this: AI is not just another piece of software for the IT budget. It is a change in how work is done. That means it has to be treated as a business issue, a governance issue, a training issue, a pricing issue and a client communication issue.

Many firms have already deployed AI tools, or are about to. Some have invested in expensive legal AI platforms. Others have Microsoft Copilot sitting inside their existing environment and are not yet using it properly. In both cases, the risk is similar. Firms either assume the tool will solve the problem, or they assume their lawyers will instinctively know how to use it because they already know how to review documents, summarise matters, draft advice or conduct research.

That is a dangerous assumption.

AI changes the mechanics of the work. It changes the speed of production. It changes the review process. It changes where risk appears. It changes what junior lawyers need to learn and what senior lawyers need to supervise. It also changes the conversation with clients, because clients will increasingly want to know how AI is being used, whether it is safe, whether it improves the work and why they are being charged what they are being charged.

For law firm leaders, the question is no longer, "Should we use AI?" AI is already here. When even the Pope is talking about AI, it is difficult to pretend this is still niche, experimental or something that can be safely ignored. It has entered the mainstream, and law firms now need to decide how they will use it, govern it, explain it and price the work that flows from it.

The better question is, "What value are we trying to get from it, how do we use it safely, and how do we build that into the way we train, govern, price and explain our work?"

The first thing I would say to law firm leaders is this: stop assuming that AI is right for every use case.

Quite often, the thing a lawyer wants AI to do can already be done inside an existing system. It may be a native capability in Word. It may be available inside the case management system. It may already sit inside a practice management platform. In many cases, using the native capability will be more reliable, more controlled and easier to govern than trying to force an AI tool to do the same thing.

AI has created an expectation that we can simply tell a system, in natural language, to do something, and it will do it. That is powerful, but it also creates a problem. It tempts people to bypass the people who understand systems, process, security and governance. It creates the impression that lawyers do not need to talk to IT, operations, risk or compliance. In a regulated legal environment, that is not a sensible starting point.

The traditional approach to technology was more structured. You started with strategy. You asked what you were trying to achieve. You identified your requirements. You thought about governance, controls and security. You tested the system. You trained people. You communicated properly. Then you deployed.

AI has disrupted that sequence. In many organisations, people already have AI, or they have access to consumer tools. Firms then feel under pressure to deploy an approved work tool quickly, partly because they are worried about shadow AI. That is understandable, but it means many firms are now trying to catch up on governance, training and communication after deployment has already happened.

That is why I describe the AI journey less as a straight line and more as a circle. Strategy, governance, training, enablement, communication, pricing and go-to-market all sit on the same circle, but different firms are starting at different points. Some have started with deployment. Some have started with training. Some have started with policy. Some have started because a competitor bought a tool, and they felt they needed to do the same.

Wherever you are on that circle, you need to work out what is missing.

If you have already deployed AI, the next logical step is to train and enable people properly. At the same time, you need to build compliance into the process. Not as a heavy, clunky overlay that slows everyone down, but as something as frictionless as possible. Good governance should not sit outside the work. It should be baked into the way the work is done.

That means building in human oversight and review points. It means making sure the information, the updates, the checks and the audit trail are part of the workflow. The more you can engineer those things into the process, the less you are relying on busy people remembering to do the right thing at the end. Removing friction is a key principle.

One of the biggest mistakes I see is firms giving lawyers an AI tool and assuming that, because those lawyers already know how to review a document, conduct research or produce a matter summary, they will know how to do those tasks with AI. They will not necessarily know. It is a different way of working.

AI is a probability engine. It gives probabilistic responses. It may give a slightly different answer each time. So lawyers need to learn how to instruct it, how to give it context, how to define the output they want and how to challenge what comes back.

The organisation also needs to think about how it configures AI so that the output gets closer to the consistent, declarative result the firm needs. That means baking in the firm's process, its intellectual property, its quality standards, its experience and its domain knowledge. That is where the firm's real value sits.

This is not simply a matter of asking AI a better question. It is about embedding the firm's way of working into the tool, and then using the tool in a way that reflects the firm's risk profile, client obligations and professional standards.

One of the most important disciplines lawyers need to develop is an adversarial approach to AI output. They must not treat the first answer as the final answer. They need to challenge it, test it, ask where it may be wrong, and do so proportionately to the importance and risk of the task.

That does not mean every output needs to be checked in the same way. A low-risk internal summary is not the same as work going to court or advice being sent to a client. But the principle matters. AI should not remove judgment. It should require better judgment.

This also creates a new bottleneck.

AI can produce a lot of work very quickly. A task that might previously have taken four hours, or even two or three days, may now be done in half an hour or a couple of hours. That is not automatically a complete benefit. If you increase throughput fourfold or fivefold, the review burden moves somewhere else. The bottleneck becomes supervision, checking and quality assurance.

Legal work is regulated work. Firms cannot simply say, "AI produced it, so that is fine." There has to be review. But if the instruction set is better, the AI configuration is better, the checkpoints are built in, and the adversarial challenge is part of the process, then the human review can become faster and more effective.

That is where training, governance and configuration come together.

This is also where pricing comes in.

Some people assume that if AI allows a task to be done more quickly, the work must automatically become cheaper. I do not think that is the right way to look at it. Yes, AI may reduce the time spent on a particular activity, but there is a lot of work that sits behind safe and effective AI use.

There is the cost of the tools. There is the cost of training. There is the cost of governance. There is the cost of compliance. There is the cost of configuring the systems. There is the cost of senior people designing, reviewing and supervising the process. There is the cost of building and maintaining the firm's knowledge and intellectual property inside the workflow. There is the cost of constant improvement.

That has to be recognised in the commercial model.

AI is not free magic. It may look like magic to the client when something happens quickly and elegantly, but the reason it works is because someone has designed the process, trained the people, built the controls and applied years of experience. A good illusionist may make the trick look effortless, but people are not paying only for the five minutes on stage. They are paying for the years of preparation, design, practice and expertise that make the five minutes possible.

The same principle applies to AI-enabled legal services.

The value is not just in the speed. The value is in the outcome, the reliability, the reduced risk, the broader scope of review, the better use of knowledge, the ability to process more information, and the professional judgment wrapped around the tool.

That is why AI should not simply be treated as a line in the IT budget. It is a business cost and a business investment. It is transforming how the firm works. It should be considered by leadership, not just technology. A firm of any reasonable size should have an AI steering group or similar structure. Technology should be represented, but so should HR, partners, risk, compliance and the legal teams whose work will be affected.

Different areas of law will be affected differently. What AI means for conveyancing will not be exactly the same as what it means for commercial contracts, litigation, intellectual property, private client or regulatory work. Firms need people from different parts of the business involved in the conversation.

The steering group should not meet once, produce a policy and disappear. AI is changing too quickly for that. The group should keep asking: how are we using it, what is working, what is not working, what has changed, where are the risks, where are the bottlenecks, and what do we need to do next?

That ongoing review is essential because the tools change constantly. Interfaces change. Capabilities change. Models change. Vendor terms change. New features appear. Something that worked one month may need to be adapted the next. Firms need a constant improvement mindset, not a one-off implementation mindset.

The firms that do this well will not be the ones that simply buy the most impressive tool. They will be the ones that connect strategy, governance, training, communication, workflow and pricing.

One of the simplest examples is training.

When I train people on tools such as Copilot or Claude, I do not start by assuming everyone in the room is at the same level. I ask people to assess themselves. One might be "curious". Five might be "expert practitioner". Often, people come into the session thinking they are a three or a four. Then, as we go through the real functionality, the structure, the risks and the safe ways of working, they realise they had gaps in the fundamentals regardless of months or years of experience using generative AI.

That is not a failure. It is progress. They may feel they have taken one step back in their self-assessment, but they have taken two steps forward in their ability to use the tool safely and productively.

The important point is that training has to be tailored. An intellectual property team dealing with trade mark disputes and renewals will need different examples from a conveyancing team, a litigation team or a corporate team. The use cases need to be relevant to the room. The firm's systems, matter processes, bottlenecks and compliance requirements all matter.

A generic demonstration is not enough.

Another example is client intake in conveyancing. I have seen firms still sending out Word documents that clients print, complete by hand and return. In one discovery session, we were able to take that kind of document and use AI to help turn it into a form that could capture information in a machine-readable way. That opens the door to automation, checks against data sources, conflict checks, anti-money laundering steps, KYC processes and other compliance activity.

That is not glamorous AI. It is practical AI. It removes friction. It makes the process more reliable. It improves the work before you even get to the heavier legal drafting or review tasks.

In contract review and due diligence, AI can also change the scale of what is possible. Instead of reviewing only a sample of documents, firms may be able to conduct a first-pass review across a much larger body of material. AI can help extract relevant clauses, identify missing information, populate tables and highlight issues. That does not remove the need for lawyers. It changes where lawyers add value. It allows them to spend more time on judgment, challenge and decision-making.

There are also firms creating their own internal tools. Harbottle & Lewis, for example, created Harbot, an internal chatbot engine trained on their information. More generally, I have seen firms building chatbot-style agents, transcription capabilities and AI-enabled workflows to make themselves more productive. Many smaller and medium-sized firms may not need to start with the biggest specialist legal AI platform. A great deal can already be done with the core vendor tools they have, particularly Microsoft Copilot, if those tools are configured and governed properly.

That does not mean Copilot is perfect. It can feel clunky. But if you configure it well and train people properly, the gap narrows. For many firms, particularly those already living in the Microsoft environment, the compliance and data governance advantages are significant.

5 Warnings

My first warning is not to confuse deployment with adoption.

A firm may say it has rolled out AI, but that does not mean people are using it effectively. I have heard of large firms where effective adoption is very low. Sometimes deployment becomes a box-ticking exercise: we have the tool, therefore we are moving forward. But if people only use a small fraction of the capability, and have not been trained to understand what the tool can really do, the firm is not getting the value.

My second warning is not to measure success by the wrong activity. Telling people to log into Copilot and ask it for a recipe may increase a usage statistic, but it does not create meaningful adoption. It sets the wrong expectation. A better approach is to give people a proper work-related prompt or use case that shows them, immediately, how the tool can help them do something useful.

My third warning is about hallucinations and misplaced trust. Lawyers are used to working with legal research platforms where they expect the material to come from a validated legal library. AI changes that. Even when AI is integrated into legal tools, it remains capable of probabilistic output, error and hallucination. Human oversight remains essential.

My fourth warning is about client visibility. Firms need to be clear about how they use AI, particularly where data, confidentiality, retention, jurisdiction and client terms are concerned. If a tool processes information in a way that is inconsistent with client obligations, that is a serious issue. Firms need to understand what is happening to the information, where it is processed, how long it is retained and whether client terms permit that use.

This has to feed into engagement letters and client communication. Clients should not be left guessing. If firms do not explain how AI is being used, a credibility gap opens up. Clients may wonder whether they are being charged properly, whether their confidential information is safe, and whether the firm is using AI responsibly.

My fifth warning is that legal may be making more noise about AI than it is making structured progress. In my experience, financial services organisations are often more proactive. They are investing in training, enablement, governance and ongoing review. They understand that regulated work needs structure. Legal should pay attention to that.

Software development is another useful comparison. Developers are already using AI extensively. They are producing more code, but they are also investing more in quality assurance and testing because AI creates bottlenecks somewhere else. Legal is moving in a similar direction. In some ways, legal is becoming more like a software development industry. The work is becoming digitised, and firms will need stronger process thinking, testing, quality assurance and governance.

AI is here. It is not a passing experiment. But the firms that benefit most will not be the firms that simply buy the newest platform or make the loudest announcement. They will be the firms that understand that AI is a business transformation tool. It needs strategy, governance, training, communication and pricing all working together.

For law firms, the opportunity is significant. AI can remove friction, improve productivity, widen the scope of review, support better decision-making and help firms build more valuable services. But it will only do that if firms stop treating it as free magic.

The magic is not in the tool. The magic is in the way the firm designs the work, trains its people, protects its clients, applies its expertise and explains its value.

That is what clients should be paying for.

WORDS WITH THE WISE

ABBY WINKWORTH

Introduction

Abby Winkworth is a legal sector consultant and adviser who works with law firm leaders on strategy, operations, transformation, growth and client experience. She is Principal Consultant at Ambire Advisory, co-founder of The COOL Network, and Chair of the Law Society's Leadership and Management Section.

She is interested in what law firms are really for, how they create social as well as commercial value, how they remain relevant to clients, and how they build sustainable futures in a world that is changing quickly.

Core Advice from Abby Winkworth

I think AI is currently at a point where it is less about money than it is about time.

That is quite an odd thing to say in a book about pricing, but in a market where people don't really understand the value of the service they are buying, a lot of the time, what they are looking for is things to happen faster. So, for instance, when clients are buying or selling their house, what they care about most is how quickly they can move from where they are to where they want to be. They want progress. They want certainty about how long it is going to take. They want the thing to happen. They take for granted that it will all go according to plan, so speed is their measure.

So, although the industry is a little obsessed with whether AI can make service delivery cheaper to produce, for the client it is about whether we can remove delay, get things started sooner, speed up institutions and processes that have historically relied on slow, non-technological answers, and create a better experience.

That is why I think the most interesting use cases of AI are not the ones that make lawyers faster. They are the ones that help firms understand what is driving client behaviour and serve them better.

In one project I am involved with, the ambition is to create an end-to-end response to what we see clients needing. The end result is to connect the client journey from marketing, through client management, billing, case management and pricing management, so that everything joins up. With one source of truth, you can start to mine data properly, understand patterns, predict behaviour and respond rapidly to what they may want or need next.

As someone whose career has been built on "following the money", that, to me, is where the opportunity lies.

Efficiency is not enough

For most of the projects I see in law firms, the starting position is still: "How can we use AI to save internal time and make our people more efficient?"

That is understandable, but I do find it a bit frustrating.

The more you badge AI predominantly as a time-saving tool, the more difficult it becomes to price that saving to the client. Making the business more efficient is something clients expect firms to be doing anyway. Amazon increasingly gives away 24 hours or even same-day delivery as standard. Fast delivery simply becomes what is expected.

Law firms need to think about AI in the same way because investing in efficiency gains has become the price of staying in the game.

The question should not only be, "How do we become more efficient?" It should also be, "How do we create more value?"

That is where I do not yet see enough firms focusing. With some noticeable exceptions, AI is not being designed, used, or valued within firms as a tool to grow revenue, create new opportunities, improve client satisfaction or fundamentally improve the client experience. Those are the areas that interest me most.

You cannot grow a law firm through efficiency and cost savings. At some point, you must create value that clients can see, feel and are prepared to pay for.

Use AI to understand the client journey

Law firms still do not understand the client experience well enough.

They will happily map a legal workflow, but as soon as you mention client journey mapping, people look at you as though you are trying to spend their money for no reason.

My experience outside of the legal industry makes me very wary of putting client experience in the slow lane.

If you do not understand the client journey, how can you build better services? How can you price properly? How can you know what the client values? How can you know where the friction is? How can you know what makes the client anxious, confused, reassured or delighted?

At this point, in mid-2026, we have all heard of laypeople using public LLMs to "have a go" at their legal problem to save time, money and the trepidation of explaining (two or three times) to a not always sympathetic stranger what their issue is. How bad must their experience be of legal pricing and delivery to decide to put their trust in AI before contacting a lawyer?

AI can help firms get underneath the client experience. It can help identify pinch points, areas of concern and moments that lawyers might regard as insignificant but which, in the client's mind, are phenomenally significant.

That matters because lawyers and clients often see the same process very differently. A lawyer may think, "That is a small administrative step." The client may think, "That is the point at which I lost confidence," or "That is the point at which I felt no one was listening."

When AI is used alongside behavioural analytics, client journey mapping and proper client listening, it can help firms get ahead of client needs. It can help firms spot triggers and risks earlier. It can help firms support individuals at important life stages. In the business market, it can help firms act as a de-risker, looking at what clients are doing, prompting lawyers to address what is driving behaviour, second-guessing decisions and feeding useful information to them before they get into difficulty.

That is something a firm can sell alongside its legal expertise. Or, at the very least, it is something that justifies more premium pricing for the service.

De-risk for the client, not just for the lawyer

One of the problems with traditional legal pricing is that too often the price is used to de-risk the lawyer's work, rather than to de-risk the client's situation.

A client may come to a lawyer needing a practical answer. The lawyer responds with caveats, options, uncertainty and a very high price because they are protecting themselves. Of course, legal risk must be managed properly, but clients do not simply want a list of theoretical possibilities. They want educated choice.

They want someone willing to say, "On the basis of what we know, this is likely to happen," or "This is the option I would recommend, and this is why."

Clients come to a lawyer because they do not know what path to take, or because they want to travel down a path in the company of a trusted advisor.

They want an informed, educated choice. They want good, independent judgment. They want guidance. They want somebody who can help them understand probability, risk and consequence.

That is where lawyers will continue to have enormous value.

AI can help with analysis, drafting, sorting, scanning, summarising and process. But the real value is in helping clients avoid the cliff edge before they are sleepwalking towards it. It is in helping them make better decisions. It is in de-risking their world, not just de-risking the lawyer's file.

The junior lawyer problem is real

There is another issue that firms need to confront honestly: what happens to junior lawyers?

For years, junior lawyers spent time doing tasks that technology has already reduced or removed. I can remember my junior colleagues hovering over photocopiers, removing staples, putting them back in again, collating documents, checking bundles and being paid for it. Enormous chunks of time disappeared into that sort of work, and now it has just gone.

I admit that I do get a bit fed up with the way chargeable hours are used to manage junior lawyers: "You should be recording seven or eight chargeable hours a day," we say, while taking away many of the tasks that used to fill their time. They are supposed to replace that time with more meaningful work, but their partners are not always giving them that meaningful work.

There is a simple solution: Give them more client management responsibility. It's a win-win. We know that clients expect to spend more time with junior lawyers and, in any event, do not want to pay for a senior lawyer or partner on simple work, but they find junior lawyers lack commerciality and the skills of curiosity and listening.

And why is that? It is because we do not teach it to them. They are often trying to work out how to make a difference to their firm and their client without the leadership, skills, knowledge and recognition that make such ambition achievable.

As AI removes routine work, firms need to think much more carefully about training, supervision, work allocation, commercial education and the development of judgment. It doesn't help the firm, the individual or the industry to say, "AI will make everyone more efficient," and leave juniors to work out how to navigate the empty space.

Human beings are still the point

My view is simple: humans are very good at being human. AI is getting better at being AI.

If we do not start focusing properly on the human side of legal services, we will end up in an AI sludge of our own making.

Our clients are humans first, and our people are humans first.

Clients are not merely files, matters, data points or workflows. They are people trying to move house, protect a family, resolve a dispute, grow a business, avoid risk, build something or get through a difficult moment. They have fears, ambitions, pressures and blind spots.

Our people are not just units of production either. They need to learn, develop, think, grow, ask questions, build confidence and understand how to use technology well.

If we allow AI to strip out work and do not replace that work with better training, better client understanding and better commercial education, then how will the profession find its successors, how will clients find answers?

Leadership needs curiosity, governance and a willingness to learn

The successful AI and transformation projects I see are led by people who are comfortable to admit that they do not have all the answers.

They tend to be people with a growth mindset, curiosity and a willingness to invest time in understanding what is possible.

As a leader, I do not think you need to have the complete picture in your head from day one. In fact, that may now be impossible. But curiosity is a human's superpower. If you are willing to explore the art of the possible and surround yourself with people who can help you, then you can turn curiosity into action.

That may mean having a COO or a Chief Transformation Officer, Chief Technology Officer or Chief AI Officer who can explore ideas, build proper business cases, make projects measurable, manage delivery and review return on investment.

The IT team grew up – they have become change managers. They have energy and often vast amounts of resource and knowledge, but they also need guardrails and governance. They need measurable business cases. They need people who can start, middle, complete and finish projects. They need review. They need discipline.

The firms that do well will be the ones that can start with a grand plan or vision, accept that they do not know everything, learn from mistakes and put the right structures in place.

The future is moving under our feet

One of the difficult things about now is that the future is accelerating towards us so quickly.

If you remember BBC's Tomorrow's World back in the 1990s, they tried to predict what life would be like in 10 or 15 years' time, and of course, in retrospect, they often got it hilariously wrong. But that is because you can only see the future horizon from the hill you are standing on right now.

Today, it feels like the hill itself is moving under our feet.

It is racing towards the future faster than we can keep up. At any moment, a new mountain may materialise in front of us, and our whole perspective will change again – and all our predictions will suffer the fate of "Tomorrow's World".

So, I guess I mean that it is unrealistic to walk into AI projects thinking you have a fixed, perfect view of the end result. You need a picture of where you are trying to get to, but you must be willing to redraw that picture as things change.

I like the Bain model of the beach, the sponge and the spine. In simple terms, you need a picture of the beach you are heading for, and the spine to hold yourself together, but you also need to understand the ability of you and your firm to absorb all that change. Today, you may be able to picture the beach, the cabana, the palm trees and the coconuts in perfect detail. Tomorrow, part of that picture may have changed completely, and you will have to change with it.

That is the reality of the moment we are in.

Law firms are becoming much more agile in how they think, decide and respond. That is not easy, because lawyers are not always naturally good at change. But we are not just facing a change in technology. We are facing a change in business model, pricing model, training model and client expectation.

We need to rethink legal education and lawyer identity

One thing that worries me is legal education.

I have a child studying law at university, and I do not think he is being taught the things that will be most useful to him when he enters the job market.

Our future lawyers need more than pure legal knowledge. They need to be taught how to be commercial, curious and entrepreneurial, how to show their genuine interest and concern for the people they are working with. They need to know how to help people find solutions.

The law is a tool they can use. It is not all they are.

That may be a fundamental change. I was speaking recently to a Law firm leader and lawyer about how he identified himself as a law firm leader. He said, "No, I am an entrepreneur. I just happen to be a law firm leader." I thought that was exactly the mindset we need more of.

I fear but am equally energised by the sense that the legal world is not going to stand still long enough for people to define themselves only as lawyers.

AI has the power to be democratising if we decide to use it well. We are already seeing people carve themselves out of larger firms and start boutiques. That may continue. It may not simply be the death of big law. It may be the rise of a post-industrial legal industry, structured in a very different way.

Some firms may struggle to survive

I think there is a large part of the legal market, particularly from the bottom of the mid-market down, for whom AI still feels like something happening "over there".

They may not feel able to get near it. They may not think they can afford it. They may not have the bandwidth to deal with it. Some of those firms may ultimately struggle to survive.

Someone will find a way to harness AI and make it work better. We are already seeing very low-cost legal products, membership models and minimum-fee services. Some will fail. Some will be poor. But eventually, parts of that market will work. After just a few years, the big vendors of legal AI are finding themselves in disrupted markets – the incredibly expensive Big Law products may be superseded by the next wave of AI. One that is more accessible to the 85% of UK Law firms that are small or micro firms.

That will have knock-on effects, including on the courts and the wider legal system.

At the other end, many firms are experimenting with Copilot, ChatGPT, Claude and other tools. That is fine. It can help with communication, marketing and some internal work. But firms need to be clear about what they are trying to achieve.

My advice is simple: stop for a minute.

Put all your projects on the table. Work out what is adding value and what is not. Then concentrate on the things that are.

There are too many shiny objects. There are too many products. There are too many vendors. They are not all going to survive. The market will consolidate. It reminds me of Betamax and VHS. Betamax may have been better, but everyone went with VHS. In legal technology, two or three brands may rise to the surface, and a lot will disappear or be absorbed.

That consolidation may not be driven only by AI, but it will certainly be enabled by AI. More importantly, it will be driven by clients' rising expectations of what they should get for their money.

Communication with clients matters

Clients are already asking questions about AI, even if they do not always ask them directly.

They want to know whether firms are using it. They want to know whether they are being charged fairly. They want to know whether savings are being passed on. They want to know whether work has been done properly. They want to know whether there is risk.

Some in-house teams may suspect firms are not being honest about AI use. In some cases, the truth may be that firms themselves do not know how to measure it properly. But that is not a good enough long-term answer.

Law firms need to communicate clearly and honestly. They need to explain how they are using AI, why they are using it, what safeguards are in place, how human judgment remains involved, and how the client benefits.

They also need to be careful. Using AI badly can damage a brand quickly. Clients will not be reassured by a firm that appears to be experimenting carelessly with their work.

Internal communication matters too. It affects their work, training, confidence, value, pricing and future careers. If firms do not communicate that properly, they will create anxiety, resistance and confusion. On the other hand, when done well (and I do see it done well), it is a shot in the arm, a cause for collaboration and exploration. A leveller – where the AI natives (and the rest of us) get to use the tools they dreamed of using.

The opportunity is bigger than efficiency

For me, the big themes are these.

First, the focus on efficiency is too narrow. You cannot grow your way into the future through cost savings.

Second, the role of junior staff and their education needs serious attention. Everyone is thinking about it, but not enough firms are doing enough about it.

Third, client experience has to become central. Firms need to understand what clients value now and what they will value in the future.

Fourth, firms need to create revenue opportunities outside the simple promise of efficiency.

Law is very good at sticking its feet firmly in the ground and refusing to move. But it is getting harder and harder to do that now.

I am glad to be working in the legal industry while this is happening.

It is a more exciting place to work now than it has been for much of my career, because people are finally asking the big questions.

What is law for?

How do we create value?

How do we sustain a future in this industry?

Those are much more interesting questions than, "How do we make the same old work happen a bit faster?"

That is where law firms should be putting their energy.

WORDS WITH THE WISE

WENDY JEPHSON

Introduction

Wendy Jephson is the CEO and co-founder of Let's Think. She is a dual-qualified lawyer, business psychologist and technology entrepreneur.

Wendy began her career as a lawyer, training in London before moving in-house, first to Xerox and then to Eli Lilly, where she spent much of her legal career. Her work as an in-house lawyer gave her a deep interest in decision-making, judgment and risk in real-world legal practice.

Through Let's Think, Wendy is now applying behavioural science and AI to one of the biggest challenges facing law firms: how to help younger lawyers learn from older, wiser lawyers when the old model of learning by osmosis is being disrupted.

Core Advice from Wendy Jephson

My central message is that AI should not simply be used to make legal work faster. If law firms only use AI for automation, they risk removing some of the very experiences through which lawyers learn judgment, develop expertise and understand risk.

Used well, AI can do something much more valuable. It can help lawyers reveal the thinking that usually stays hidden. It can help experienced lawyers unpack what they notice, why they act, how they make decisions, and what they are predicting might happen next. That thinking can then be shared with junior lawyers, used to brief teams, improve supervision, create better records and explain value more clearly to clients.

That matters because the future of legal pricing will not only depend on whether firms can produce documents more efficiently. It will depend on whether they can explain the value of the thinking behind those documents.

In an AI world, lawyers will increasingly be asked: "What am I paying for?" My answer is that clients are paying for judgment, experience, risk assessment, commercial understanding and the ability to guide them towards the right outcome. But lawyers will need to become much better at showing that work.

For centuries, lawyers have learned by osmosis. They sat beside more experienced lawyers, listened to them, watched them in client meetings, saw how they handled risk, and gradually picked up the craft.

That model was never perfect. Some supervisors were excellent. Others were less so. But there was something valuable in learning alongside someone in the moment. A junior lawyer could ask, "What were you noticing there?" or "Why did you do that?" and, if the senior lawyer was willing and able to explain, some of that tacit expertise could be passed on.

The problem is that this model has now been disrupted. Hybrid working has changed how people spend time together. Technology has changed how work is done. AI is now changing what tasks junior lawyers actually get to do.

So my concern is simple: let's not throw the baby out with the bathwater.

The old learning model had good things in it. The challenge is to preserve and improve those good things in a new working environment. That is what we are trying to do with Let's Think.

The most valuable knowledge in a law firm is often the knowledge that is hardest to write down. It is the knowledge sitting inside experienced lawyers' heads. It is what they notice on a client call. It is why they pause before answering a question. It is the risk they see before anyone else sees it. It is the sense that something is missing, or that a particular line of enquiry matters, or that a client's real problem is not quite the problem they first described.

Experts often struggle to explain this because they just do it. They know what to do, but they may not immediately know how they know. You have to slow them down a little so they can unpack their own thinking.

That is where technology can help.

The technology we have built is designed as a thinking partner. It asks questions. It prompts lawyers to reflect. It helps them dig into their own thinking for their own benefit first, but in doing so, it captures something valuable. It captures the reasoning, the decisions, the cues, the predictions and the judgment that would otherwise never be written down.

That captured thinking can then be turned into useful learning scenarios.

For example, a partner working on a matter can use the technology to think aloud about what has happened so far, what they are paying attention to, what they are considering next and why. That can then be packaged for a junior lawyer. The junior can be given the scenario, asked what they think should happen next, choose an option, and then see the partner's decision and reasoning.

That is powerful because the junior has to think first. They are not simply being given the answer. They are being invited to exercise their own judgment, compare it with the expert's reasoning, and learn from the difference.

This is not just abstract training. It can happen on live matters. It can also be used to create a rich record of work that happened months or years earlier. That record can then help a lawyer joining a team or moving into a new seat understand how work really happens in that department.

One area we are particularly focused on is investigations, especially white-collar crime investigations. In that kind of work, lawyers often need to keep a record of the decisions they made and the reasoning behind them. Later, someone may ask: Why did you make that decision then? What was your reasoning? Do you have a contemporaneous record?

That record can be painful to create. But if the lawyer can quickly reflect on what has happened during the day, what they decided, what they were thinking and what they plan to do next, the technology can help create that record as the matter progresses. That record is useful for the matter itself, but it also becomes a rich learning resource.

A junior lawyer can then see how an investigation unfolded. They can see the context, the decisions, the reasoning and the messy reality of the work. They do not have to wait years to build up every experience in real time. They can start to see what experienced lawyers were seeing.

That is how firms can help younger lawyers get their eye in.

Expertise develops through exposure to many examples. In any domain, experts learn what to look for. They see the signal in the noise. A tennis player may not just watch the ball; they may watch the opponent's body movement because that tells them where the ball is likely to go. Lawyers do something similar. In a risky conversation, an experienced lawyer is tuned into certain cues. They hear what is being said, but they also hear what is not being said.

A trainee may be in the same meeting, desperately taking notes, but not yet know what to listen for. That is not because they are not intelligent. It is because they have not yet built the mental models that help them notice what matters.

The opportunity is to use technology to capture those expert mental models and make them available to juniors. Not as a substitute for supervision, but as a way of making supervision better.

Mentoring in law firms can be hit and miss. Senior lawyers are busy. Mentoring is often non-chargeable. People are not always rewarded for doing it well. A junior may be told to "go away and think about it," but without enough scaffolding to know how to think about it.

If the junior can first see how the partner is thinking, they can come back with a better question. They can say, "I can see why you were thinking about this. I got stuck here. Would this work?" That is a much better conversation than simply asking, "What should I do?"

Everyone likes it when someone jumps off their own thinking.

This also links directly to pricing and client communication.

For years, lawyers have not had to explain their thinking. The client saw the document, the contract, the advice note, the mark-up, or the email. That was the tangible thing. The thinking behind it remained invisible.

AI changes that. If a client believes a document can be produced more quickly by technology, they are more likely to ask what they are really paying for. That is not just a pricing problem. It is a communication problem.

Lawyers now need to show their workings.

When a client asks, "What am I paying for?", they are really asking the lawyer to explain how they are thinking and why that thinking matters. They are asking to see the judgment, the strategy, the risk assessment, the commercial understanding and the experience that sits behind the output.

As an in-house lawyer, that was what I paid for. I would call the external partner because I wanted their pragmatic judgment. I wanted them to tell me how to navigate the issue. Some of that was law, of course, but much of it was commercial know-how, industry understanding and experience of how things actually work.

Clients are not buying knowledge in the abstract. They are not buying time for its own sake. They want their problem solved. They want an outcome. The lawyer uses knowledge, expertise, experience and time to help them get there.

In an AI world, that distinction becomes crucial.

It may be possible to use AI for some parts of a task. But not everything can be handed to technology. Some parts of the work may be AI-assisted. Some may be human-owned. Some may involve judgment, client handling, negotiation, strategic thinking or managing the concerns of the other side.

The problem is that, unless you show this, the client may think everything can be given to technology.

That is why it is useful to break work down into its component parts. Firms can show where AI can assist, where human judgment is required, where strategic thinking takes place, and where the lawyer is managing risk, people and outcomes. You can give the elephant shape.

This can also help with pricing. If a firm is quoting £100,000 for a matter and the client says, "Surely this should be cheaper now you are using AI," the firm needs to be able to explain what is actually involved. It needs to show that the value is not just in the production of documents, but in the thinking, the strategy, the judgment and the ability to respond when new information comes in.

New information can change everything. A lawyer may have to throw the whole picture up in the air again and think carefully about what the new information means. That thinking time is valuable, but it is often invisible and hard to explain.

So the question for law firms is not simply, "How much time did we save?" The easier question to measure is whether AI has made something faster. The more important question is: what has changed as a result?

What learning opportunity has been lost?

What conversation no longer happens?

What judgment is no longer being developed?

What value is still being created but not explained?

What does the client now need to understand?

There are also internal communication challenges. Law firms need to explain to their own people how AI is to be used and where human thinking still matters. Junior lawyers should not fear AI, but they should understand it. They need to know how the tools work, when to use them, where the edge is and what the limitations are.

AI can look very convincing. That is one of the dangers. A junior lawyer must still be able to ask: What would an expert notice here? What would they challenge? What has the tool missed because it did not ask the right question, or because the right information was not provided?

The future lawyer still needs to think for themselves. They still need to build their own judgment. They still need to develop the neural muscles required to answer hard questions. Technology can help them get there faster, but only if it is designed and used in a way that supports thinking rather than replacing it.

That is why I do not think success in AI adoption will simply belong to the fastest firms. It will belong to the firms that expand their cognitive capability.

The firms that stand out will be the ones that use AI not only to speed up work, but to deepen expertise. They will capture what experienced lawyers know. They will help junior lawyers learn faster and better. They will make supervision more effective. They will create better records. They will explain value more clearly to clients. They will show the difference between what technology can do and what expert human judgment contributes.

We sometimes say it is not just know-how. It is knowing what, when, why, who and how. That is what expert advice really involves.

Those firms will also be better at client relationships. Even where a client does not get the ideal outcome, the client may still come back if they trusted the lawyer, understood the journey and believed the lawyer's expertise gave them the best possible chance. Clients return because they trust the judgment, not because every matter is perfect.

That is the future challenge for law firms.

AI will change legal work. It will change learning. It will change pricing conversations. It will change what clients expect. But the answer is not to pretend that legal work is only about efficiency.

The answer is to make the thinking visible.

Show the reasoning.

Show the judgment.

Show the workings.

Because in the end, that is what clients are paying for.

WORDS WITH THE WISE

ANDREW ALLEN

Introduction

Andrew is a partner and head of the legal sector team at PKF Francis Clark, where he advises law firms across the UK on strategy, profit improvement, tax, structuring, audit and accounting. He has advised law firms for nearly 30 years and works regularly with firms in and around the UK Top 200. He is also vice chair of the Law Society Leadership and Management Section, past chair of the ICAEW Solicitors' Special Interest Group, an author of financial benchmarking reports for law firms, and co-author of *The Law Society's Solicitors and the Accounts Rules.*

Andrew Allen brings a particularly valuable perspective to the debate about AI, pricing and the future economics of law firms because he sees the numbers behind the rhetoric.

Core Advice from Andrew Allen

The clearest increase I am seeing in law firm profit and loss accounts is IT spend. That is being driven by AI licences and, in some firms, practice management system costs.

The issue is cost recovery.

Firms are spending money on AI. People are doing fewer hours on some jobs. Fewer hours are being charged to clients. The client gets the benefit of the time saving, while the firm carries the AI overhead.

Most firms are still using AI for administrative work. Around 80% are using it for internal or matter administration. Only about one in five are using it in legal advice, and even then, the use is fairly soft touch.

Some firms have bought AI products, done some basic training and treated the job as done. It is not done. They still need policies, training protocols, claims risk thinking and pricing strategies.

AI is not just an IT project. It has pricing consequences.

If a firm charges by the hour and AI reduces the time spent, the bill reduces. If the firm charges a fixed fee, it may keep the benefit of the saved time, but it still needs to understand the cost of the AI and whether the fixed fee was right.

There may be attempts to add AI as a separate bill line item. IT costs may now be too large simply to hide inside charge-out rates. But clients may challenge those charges, particularly if they think AI should have made the work cheaper.

The firm therefore needs to explain where the value sits: supervision, judgment, responsibility and risk.

Value pricing is still not embedded in most firms. Some firms mention it. Some teams use it occasionally. Very few appear to apply it consistently across all teams.

Firms also need to know their costs. Time recording still matters because it gives a baseline. Even if the client is not charged by the hour, the firm still needs to know what the work costs.

Many firms do not train people properly on time recording. They train people on AML, confidentiality and compliance, but not on how to record time or understand the economics of the work.

AI also raises a training issue. If AI removes junior tasks such as bundles, chronologies and first drafts, firms need to think about how junior lawyers will develop experience and judgment.

My warning is simple.

Do not buy AI and assume the pricing will sort itself out.

Ask what AI costs, where it saves time, who gets the benefit of that saving, and how the firm recovers its investment.

Otherwise, the firm spends more, records fewer hours, charges less, and leaks margin.

WORDS WITH THE WISE

JOANNA GAUDOIN

Introduction

Joanna brings a practical, people-centred perspective to the debate about AI, pricing and the future of legal services.

Through ClientWise, she helps law firms strengthen business development, client relationships and the human skills lawyers need to build trust.

Her point is simple: AI does not make those skills less important. It makes them more important.

Core Advice from Joanna Gaudoin

I think AI is both a massive opportunity and a threat. It is an opportunity if firms use it properly. It can release time. It can remove some of the mundane tasks, the administrative work and some of the lower-value legal tasks. That should give lawyers more time to focus on clients, relationships and higher-value work.

But it is also a threat if firms rush into it without thinking. Some firms are panic-buying AI tools without asking what they are trying to achieve. Others are doing very little at all. Both positions are dangerous in different ways.

The first question should not be, "What AI should we buy?" It should be, "What are we trying to achieve?" Sometimes the answer may not even be full AI. It may be a simpler piece of automation. The danger is that firms spend a lot of money on technology, people do not use it properly, or it ends up taking more time rather than less.

The firms that will stand out are the ones that use AI to free up human time and then use that time well. That means spending more time understanding clients, developing relationships and finding higher-value work. Clients will not continue to pay premium prices for basic legal work if they believe the firm is simply putting it through AI, or if they think they can do something similar themselves.

So, for me, the issue is not just AI. It is what AI makes more important.

Technical knowledge still matters, of course, but it is no longer enough on its own. Every law firm says it has good technical lawyers. Many firms also say they have great client service. But the question is: how is that actually demonstrated?

The real differentiator will be how lawyers apply their knowledge to the client's specific situation. That requires judgment. It requires commercial understanding. It requires the ability to listen properly, ask better questions and build trust.

This is why I think law firms need to take soft skills much more seriously. I know "soft skills" can sound vague, but I do not mean anything fluffy. I mean the practical skills lawyers need to build rapport, develop existing clients, work with introducers, network properly, collaborate across departments and become more useful to clients.

I would start early. Do not leave the juniors out. The younger you can start with lawyers, the better. Even at a junior level, individuals can be building their profile and their network and considering how they interact with current clients, as well as supporting senior lawyers with business development tasks such as researching potential events and identifying relevant introducers.

I have worked with senior associates who were twelve years qualified and had received no proper non-technical training. They were great technically and with how they engage with existing clients on a matter-by-matter basis, but struggled with how to bring in more work, including developing relationships further with existing clients. Only delving into these skills so far into their careers meant it was a steep learning curve to start seeing their professional lives through a different lens.

Firms should not wait until someone is nearly a partner before helping them understand business development, client relationships and commercial conversations. If this happens, it means new partners can't start strongly in their new role. They lack confidence and can't fully do what they need to for the firm.

A good place to start is to ask what lawyers should be doing at different levels. When should they begin engaging with clients? When should they be developing introducer relationships? When should they be thinking about new clients? When should they be having strategic conversations with colleagues in other departments?

Then ask what skills they need to do those things well. Where are their skills now? What is the gap? How will the firm/individual close it?

I have written business development competency frameworks for firms before. The value of that sort of framework is that it makes the expectations visible. It gives people a structure. It helps the firm say, "At this level, this is what we expect, this is what we will support you with, and this is how we will help you improve." Alongside this, it is pivotal that lawyers understand why they need to contribute to business development beyond it being a stated competency.

There are some generic skills that everybody needs. Building rapport is one example. Lawyers need that internally and externally. But there are also situation-specific skills. How do you network at an event? How do you develop an existing client relationship? How do you have a conversation with a colleague in another department about cross-referrals? How do you start becoming a trusted adviser rather than just the person who does a transaction?

Lawyers need to understand why they are being asked to do something, what they need to do and how to do it. If lawyers do not know how to tackle something, they often stay away from it. That is not necessarily because they are unwilling. It is often because lawyers hate not knowing.

That is why one-off training is not enough. A firm cannot send people to a ninety-minute session, tick the box and expect behaviour to change. People may enjoy the session, go back to their desks and then do absolutely nothing with it.

Training needs follow-up. It needs to be embedded into the firm's processes and systems. If someone's performance review says they need to build better relationships with existing clients, the firm should ask what support it has given that person to do it, and how improvement will be measured.

Existing clients matter hugely. In a world where AI changes the economics of delivery, firms need to become more embedded with the clients who already know them. That does not mean taking those clients for granted. It means investing in the relationship properly.

When I work with firms on business development, one of the first questions I ask is: what services do we really want to do proactive business development around, and who are they for? That affects the business development strategy and plan, the pricing and the way the firm thinks about its market, to ultimately achieve its objectives.

If a firm says it works with SMEs, for example, it needs to think about the SME lifecycle. You may work with a business when it is a start-up, but you want to know it well enough that when it needs something more sophisticated – a franchise agreement, a licensing agreement or another significant piece of work – it does not go somewhere else. You want that client to see you as the lawyer supporting the business, not simply the firm that handled one transaction or created one document.

I also think lawyers need to understand politics, with a small "p". Politics is everywhere. It does not have to be negative. It simply means people have different values, assumptions and beliefs.

Internally, that means understanding colleagues, partners and other departments. Other departments may not have the same priorities. They may see clients differently. They may worry that someone is stepping on their toes. There can be fiefdoms in law firms, with people holding on to "their" clients. That is not helpful. Eventually, the client may sense it and become frustrated.

Externally, politics matters too. If you are working with a corporate client, you should not know only one person. If your whole relationship is with the GC and that person leaves, the relationship may weaken quickly. If you are a private client lawyer working with a wealthy family, the main client today may not be there in twenty years. You need the skills to build appropriate relationships with the next generation as well.

Law firms also need to be honest about CRM and systems. In many firms, the information is still in partners' heads, in Outlook or scattered around the business. A CRM can be valuable, but it has to be set up properly, and people need to be clear how to use it – easily and simply.

I would rather a firm worked out what business development looks like first and then chose the right system, rather than buying a system and trying to retrofit the strategy around it. Like AI, if the system is overcomplicated, people will not engage with it.

Good client service is not just about doing the legal task. I sometimes ask lawyers to think about a service they have bought recently. It could be getting a car serviced, having a bike repaired or buying some other service. What was good? What was bad? Would they recommend that provider? Why?

Very often, the answer is not about price. It is about how the service was delivered. The car was ready early. Someone called with an update. They remembered that timing mattered. They made the client feel understood.

That is the point lawyers need to absorb. It is not just the matter. It is the "how". It is the communication, the understanding and the feeling that the client matters.

That connects directly to pricing. Before you can price around value, you need to understand what the client values. In a conveyancing matter, for example, the value may not simply be "complete the transaction". The real value may be that the family needs to be in the new home before the children start school in September. That changes the conversation. It changes the service. It can change the options you offer.

I am not a pricing specialist, but I do see how much pricing depends on understanding the client properly. If you do not understand what matters to the client, it is very hard to explain the value of what you are offering.

So my advice is this: do not assume AI removes the need for human skill. It increases the need for it. The future lawyer needs more than technical expertise. The future lawyer needs to understand clients, build trust, communicate well, use technology intelligently and focus human effort where it really makes a difference.

WORDS WITH THE WISE

KERRY JACK

Introduction

Kerry Jack is Chief Executive Officer of Black Letter Communications, a specialist legal PR and communications agency. She has worked in legal PR and communications for over 30 years and advises law firms, corporates and individuals on strategic communications, reputation, media strategy and crisis handling.

Kerry Jack's central message is simple: law firms cannot treat AI as a technology story alone. It is a communications story, a client confidence story and, increasingly, a pricing story.

Core Advice from Kerry Jack

I think law firms need to start by understanding that AI is not just something they buy and put into the business. It changes the way they talk about themselves, the way clients see them and the way they explain their value.

In my world, the same thing has happened in communications. Thirty years ago, I might have walked into a client's office with a big book of press cuttings and said, "Look at all this coverage we've got you." That was the proof of value. Now, clients are much more interested in whether the coverage was seen by the right people and whether it made those people act in the right way. It is less about volume and more about outcomes.

That feels very similar to what is happening in law. It is no longer enough to say, "We reviewed 20,000 documents." The client wants to know what that achieved. What problem did it solve? What outcome did it deliver? What risk did it reduce? What decision did it help them make?

That is where law firms need to move their thinking.

One of the examples I always remember is a large London law firm that was at the vanguard of AI and created a spin-out business that was going to help clients reduce their reliance on law firms. At the time, that was brave. It was saying to clients, "We are going to help you do your job better. We are going to build something with you that solves your problem." The important point was that they built it with clients. The client's view was in it. The lawyer's experience was in it. It was not just a law firm building a product in isolation and then trying to sell it.

That approach changed the relationship. Clients used the product, but they also saw the firm differently. They still went to the lawyers for the big-ticket work, because that was where the lawyers really added value.

That is a lesson for law firms now. AI should not simply be about using fewer people, cutting costs or making more margin. There is a danger of what I would call leadership hallucination. Some leaders may assume that AI means they can get rid of lawyers, use cheaper people and make more money. That is the wrong way to look at it. The real question is: where does the value move?

If AI takes some of the process away, then the law firm needs to explain what remains. In my view, what remains is judgement, confidence and reassurance. Clients are buying confidence. They want to know that the lawyer will get them where they need to get to. They are buying judgement. They are buying reassurance.

That is why education is so important. Law firms need to educate clients about how AI can help, but they also need to demonstrate where the lawyers add value. The firms that are best able to explain why human judgement matters will be the ones that come out of this well.

I have not yet seen many firms do that properly. I have seen firms talk about being tech-savvy. I have seen them talk about innovation. I have seen the usual AI washing. But I have not seen many firms really take the bull by the horns and explain their AI story in a way that makes clients feel more confident, rather than just making clients think the work should be cheaper.

The messaging needs to move away from cost. It should be about how AI helps the firm be better. How it helps the client get more out of the relationship. How it improves the quality of the work, the experience and the outcome.

Investment is a key part of that message. Firms should be saying, "We have invested in this so that we can help you better." AI is not the whole team. It is another member of the team. It is something the firm is developing and using, but it is not the be-all and end-all. The lawyer still matters.

That has to be communicated internally as well as externally. Every firm needs a narrative about its use of AI, but that narrative should not sit in a separate box marked "AI". It should become part of the firm's overall story. Good firms have strong corporate narratives. They know what they stand for and what they say to the market. AI needs to be added into that story.

The internal piece is just as important as the external piece. If a client asks five partners about the firm's approach to AI and gets five different answers, that is a problem. If one partner says the firm does not really use AI, another says they use it all the time, another gives a discount, and another cannot explain the policy at all, the firm has lost control of the message.

Law firms need one hymn sheet. They need to know what they say to clients. They need to know what they say to their own people. They need to know how AI fits with their pricing, their risk management, their client service and their values.

There is also a real opportunity here for firms that are prepared to communicate honestly. I am tired of law firms telling people they are innovative and that they really care about client service. I have been hearing that for 30 years. My advice is the same now as it was then: do not tell me, show me.

If more than 9,000 law firms in England and Wales are all saying the same thing, how can any of them stand out? AI could be a genuine differentiator for some firms, but only if they are brave and bold enough to explain what they are doing in a meaningful way.

That does not mean pretending everything is perfect. In fact, I think there is power in being a little vulnerable. I would love to see a law firm talk openly and honestly about its AI journey, including what it has learned and where it has made mistakes. As a potential client, I would find that refreshing. It would show me a firm that genuinely wants to learn and do better for its clients.

There is also a crisis communications point here. When something goes wrong with AI, and we are starting to see more high-profile examples of this, a law firm cannot assume that one statement will fix it. Clients will ask serious questions. Was AI used on my matter? Was the work checked properly? Were the right safeguards in place? Who was supervising it? What else might have gone wrong?

Those are not just PR questions. They are trust questions.

On pricing, I think the same issue comes back again and again. Lawyers need to stop thinking only about inputs. They need to think about outcomes. In PR, we try to get lawyers to stop thinking like lawyers and start thinking like journalists. Journalists want stories. They want outcomes. They want problems and solutions. That way of thinking would help lawyers talk about value more clearly.

If an immigration lawyer says they are selling a form that grants a client access to the UK, that is not the real value. The client is buying the right to start a new life. The client is buying the chance to bring their family over, to marry, to work, to live differently. Lawyers need to think about the value they bring in that wider sense.

I think this should be taught much earlier. Wouldn't it be amazing if, when lawyers were training, they were taught how to value what they deliver? Not just how many hours they recorded or which forms they completed, but what result they helped create for the client.

When we won a pitch earlier this year, we asked the law firm why they had chosen us. They said that, after speaking to us, they thought, "They'll get shit done." What they were really saying was that they believed we would get the right outcomes for them. They were not buying our internal processes. They were buying confidence that we had understood them, thought about where they wanted to get to and could help them get there.

That is the mindset law firms need. Start at the end of the relationship and work backwards. What does the client want to walk away with? What ambition are you helping them achieve? What future are you helping them create?

That is a very different conversation from, "Here is how many hours it will take."

WORDS WITH THE WISE

ROBERT HANNA

Introduction

Robert Hanna brings a slightly different perspective to the pricing debate. He is not running a law firm, and he is not claiming to have all the answers on value-based pricing. What he does have is a rare vantage point.

Through the Legally Speaking Podcast, his work with KC Partners, his events and his constant conversations across the legal world, Robert has spoken with hundreds of lawyers, law firm leaders, legal technologists, entrepreneurs, recruiters, founders and professional bodies.

Core Advice from Robert Hanna

I come at this from the conversations I have had across the legal sector. I have interviewed a lot of people. I have been in the rooms, at the events, on the podcasts, with the founders, the law firm leaders, the legal technologists and the people trying to build something better. When you hear enough of those conversations, some themes start to become very clear.

The first thing I would say to law firms is this: do the internal audit before you go shopping.

A lot of firms are spending serious money on technology. Some of that money will be well spent. Some of it will not. The question is not simply, "Have we bought AI?" The question is, "Have we bought the right thing, for the right reason, to solve the right problem?"

I think this is where a lot of people go wrong. They have not looked properly at what they already have. They have not asked whether existing systems are being used properly. I am guilty of this myself. I probably do not know 80 per cent of what some existing tools can already do. There are powerful things already sitting inside firms that are not being used.

Then along comes a legal tech company with a very polished sales process, and firms buy something new because it sounds exciting. That is not innovation. That is procurement with a dopamine hit.

The firms that are doing this well are not just implementing technology to do what they already do. They are using technology to move themselves forward.

Think of the legal technology stack as a car. You can have the fancy lights, the nice seats, the extra features, but if the engine does not work, the car is not going anywhere. Clio is interesting because, in my view, it is becoming part of the engine.

What I find significant is the movement from a system of record to a system of action. Historically, a case management system might have stored information. It kept the file. It recorded what had happened. Useful, yes, but largely passive.

The shift now is towards systems that do something. They can help produce first drafts. They can pick out key information. They can connect intake with workflow. They can help lawyers get to the point of judgment faster.

That matters because the lawyer should not be starting from scratch every time. If a first draft has been created, if relevant material has been surfaced, if the system can point the lawyer to verifiable information, then the lawyer's time is better spent reviewing, refining, challenging and applying judgment.

That is the important point. The best technology should not remove the lawyer's judgment. It should create more space for it.

Another example I see is around client intake. I have seen a system which is a client voice AI receptionist. The interesting point is not simply that it can take an enquiry and create a form. That is useful, but it is not the whole story.

The smarter point is that it can have a natural, empathetic conversation with the prospective client, ask questions, qualify the issue and route the matter more intelligently. So instead of saying, "Here is another divorce enquiry, who wants it?", the system can identify the more specific issue and direct it towards the lawyer with the relevant experience.

That is much more powerful. It is not just intake. It is action. It is attorney matching. It is helping the firm avoid waste and helping the client get to the right person more quickly.

This is where I think the real innovators are going. They are solving real-world problems. They are improving speed, quality, efficiency and client experience. They are freeing lawyers up to use their brains on the things that actually matter.

Otherwise, what are we doing? We are still just doing the same old work and charging for it in the same old way.

The second point is about judgment.

Law firms can go out and buy all the AI tools they want, but they still have to ask: what is in the heads of our experienced lawyers, and how is that being transferred?

That judgment, wisdom and knowledge is incredibly valuable. It is also vulnerable. What happens if one of your rainmaker partners is tapped on the shoulder, gets a big offer and leaves? Their cognitive thinking walks out of the door with them.

Firms need to think seriously about how they capture and protect that cognitive capital. How do they train the next generation? How do they make sure juniors still develop judgment in an AI world where the nature of their training will be very different? How do they avoid losing the very thing clients are actually prepared to pay for?

That is not a soft issue. It is a business issue. It is a pricing issue. It is a risk issue.

If AI does more of the repeatable work, then the value of the lawyer moves even more clearly towards judgment, interpretation, communication, advocacy, trust and decision-making. Firms that cannot explain, develop and price those things will struggle.

The third point is transparency.

One of the messages I heard from conversations around London International Disputes Week was very straightforward: tell your clients when you are using AI. Do not be afraid of it. Be transparent.

Clients do not want mystery. They want to know what is being used, why it is being used, how it helps them and what benefit is being passed on. If AI helps you work faster, improves quality, reduces duplication or gives the client a better experience, say so. Explain it.

The danger is secrecy. If clients think their law firms are using AI but not telling them, suspicion creeps in. They start wondering whether they are being charged for work that technology has already done. That becomes a trust problem.

So my advice is: communicate. Tell clients what you are doing. Tell them how it is supervised. Tell them where the lawyer remains responsible. Tell them how it benefits them. Do not hide from the conversation.

The fourth point is that lawyers need to invest in the human skills that AI will not replace.

One of the most popular and interesting podcast episodes we did was about voice. The question was whether your voice might be sabotaging your legal career. That might sound like a side issue, but it is not.

In an AI world, the way lawyers communicate becomes even more important. Your pace, tone, volume, vocal variety and ability to build trust all matter. They matter on client calls. They matter when speaking to prospective clients. They matter on stage, in advocacy, in networking and in leadership.

If everyone has access to AI, what makes the difference? It may be the person who communicates better, builds trust faster, listens properly and gives the client confidence.

That is why personal development is not some optional extra. It is part of the future skillset. Lawyers should be asking themselves: what can I sharpen that cannot simply be automated?

The fifth point is business model change.

I am seeing more interest in different structures. Employee ownership of firms in England and Wales is one example. I spoke with Jonathan Wearing at Ison Harrison, and I think more firms should at least look seriously at that type of model if they can. It may not be right for everyone, but the potential benefits around growth, culture and retention are worth understanding.

I also think the dispersed law firm model will continue to grow. We have had conversations with people from firms such as Taylor Rose and gunnercooke, and these models are not going away. They offer flexibility. They attract lawyers who do not want the traditional structure. They allow lawyers to build their own practices with support around them.

But there is a warning here. If lawyers are going to price their own work, they need to be good at it. If a firm recruits lots of consultants who are poor at pricing, poor at scoping and poor at client management, that creates a different problem. Flexibility is not enough. The model still needs discipline, support, training and quality control.

I also see the rise of fractional legal careers continuing. More general counsel and senior lawyers are taking on work in a fractional capacity across different businesses and sectors. Law firms need to understand that trend and keep those relationships alive. The client ecosystem is changing, and the people who influence buying decisions may not sit in the same neat boxes they used to.

The sixth point is leadership.

Leadership means very little if it is not followed by action. You can say all the right things about innovation, culture and values, but people watch what you actually do.

I heard William Peake, the Global Managing Partner of Harneys, one of the world's leading offshore law firms, make a point that stayed with me. One of the best questions you can ask is: when was a time you lost trust in your current employer, and what did they do to win it back?

That is a great question because every organisation gets things wrong. Every leader makes mistakes. The issue is not whether trust is ever dented. The issue is whether you notice, own it and rebuild it.

In law firms, this matters enormously. If leaders talk about change but avoid difficult conversations, fail to call out behaviour that contradicts the firm's values or refuse to act when the model needs to change, people notice. Trust leaks away.

The leaders who will do well in this next phase are the ones who are curious, visible, prepared to learn and willing to act. They will not just sit behind the desk. They will go to events, listen, network, shape conversations and bring ideas back into the firm.

The people I see cutting through are the ones who are out there. They are at conferences. They are at Legal Tech events. They are listening to founders, clients, technologists and other law firm leaders. They are not waiting for the future to arrive in an email.

My overall advice to law firms is this: you cannot sit still. The people who are innovating are solving real problems. They are not just talking about AI. They are using it to improve speed, quality, access, communication and client experience.

But do not start with the tool. Start with the problem. Audit what you already have. Be honest about what your firm is good at. Protect and transfer judgment. Communicate openly with clients. Develop the human skills that matter. Look carefully at your business model. Lead with action.

And then ask the pricing question.

Because once work is faster, more automated and more intelligently routed, the old model starts to look very exposed. If you are still trying to price everything by time, you may find yourself charging less for the work that technology has improved, while failing to capture the value of the judgment, trust and expertise clients actually need.

That is the opportunity. Not just to use AI, but to rethink what legal value really is.

APPENDIX 1: INTRODUCTION TO THE JUDGMENT AND BUSINESS ACUMEN AND PRICING CANVAS EXAMPLES

Before we go any further, I want to pause to address something that may sound obvious but which isn't.

If I say to lawyers, "In an AI-enabled world, you must price your judgment and business acumen," some will nod sagely, write it down and agree with me. Then, ten minutes later, some of them will quietly ask themselves: "What does that actually mean?"

That is not a stupid question. In fact, it is an important one.

For years, many lawyers have been trained to describe their work by reference to activity. They researched the point, drafted the clause, reviewed the contract, prepared the bundle, wrote the advice, attended the hearing, dealt with the correspondence, and recorded the time.

All of that may be true. But it does not necessarily explain the value.

In an AI-enabled legal market, that distinction matters enormously. If AI can assist with research, drafting, summarising, comparing, checking, reviewing and producing first-pass analysis, then lawyers will need to become much better at explaining what they bring that AI does not. That is where judgment and business acumen come in.

The examples in this section have been included because many lawyers will need help naming the value they already create. They may exercise judgment every day, but they do not always describe it as judgment. They may use business acumen every day, but they may not call it acumen. They may help clients avoid disastrous decisions, calm emotional disputes, spot hidden risks, assess commercial consequences, choose between imperfect options, and understand what really matters, but then they still send a bill that makes it seem as though the value was the time taken to do the task.

That has to change.

The examples cover a wide range of practice areas, including family law, residential conveyancing, commercial property, employment, company and commercial law, disputes, wills and probate, immigration, criminal law, IP, tax, regulatory, data protection and others. They show that judgment is not one mysterious grand concept reserved for silks, senior partners, or people who like speaking at conferences. It appears in everyday legal work, across every practice area.

Judgment is knowing when the client's fight is really about emotion rather than law. It is knowing when a title defect is merely legal noise and when it is genuinely dangerous. It is knowing when the client should settle, when they should wait, when they should walk away, when they should hold the line and when they should stop themselves from sending the email that will become Exhibit A in the tribunal bundle.

Business acumen is understanding what is really going on underneath the legal issue. It is seeing the commercial purpose behind the contract, the family dynamics behind the will, the management failure behind the employment dispute, the operational risk behind the data breach, the reputation issue behind the regulatory investigation, or the cash-flow problem behind the legal question.

Put simply, acumen asks: "What is really happening here?"

Judgment asks: "So, what should we do about it?"

That is the value.

AI may produce the ingredients. The lawyer still has to decide what meal should be served, whether the guests can eat it, whether the kitchen is on fire, and whether the client should be told that the dish they asked for is a very bad idea.

These examples are therefore not included as decoration. They are here to help lawyers see, name, explain, package and price the value they bring. They are also here to help firms train junior lawyers differently, because if AI removes some of the old task-based learning, firms will need to be far more deliberate about teaching judgment, context, client understanding and commercial sense.

CONTENTS

1. Family law
2. Residential conveyancing
3. Commercial property work
4. Employment law
5. Company and commercial law
6. Dispute resolution
7. Wills, trusts and probate
8. Immigration law
9. Criminal law
10. Intellectual property law
11. Agricultural law
12. Tax law
13. Personal injury and clinical negligence
14. Regulatory and professional discipline

15. Data protection and privacy
16. Banking and finance
17. Insolvency and restructuring
18. Planning law
19. Environmental law
20. Education law
21. Public law and judicial review
22. Charity and not-for-profit law

1. FAMILY LAW

Judgment elements

1. Assessing whether the client wants justice, revenge, safety, closure, financial stability or emotional validation.
2. Distinguishing between a legal fight that matters and a personal fight that will destroy value.
3. Judging whether negotiation, mediation, collaborative law, arbitration or court proceedings are most likely to produce the best outcome.
4. Assessing whether one party is using money, children or procedure as a weapon.
5. Identifying safeguarding concerns that may not be obvious from the documents.
6. Judging whether a client is emotionally ready to make a binding financial decision.
7. Forecasting how a judge is likely to view conduct, disclosure failures, needs, earning capacity and child arrangements.
8. Deciding when to take a firm stance and when to lower the temperature.
9. Assessing whether a proposed settlement is merely mathematically acceptable or actually workable for the family.
10. Spotting hidden financial complexity: company structures, trusts, pensions, crypto, overseas assets or lifestyle inconsistencies.
11. Knowing when a client's non-negotiable position is really a grief response.
12. Helping the client understand that winning in family law may mean protecting children, preserving dignity and avoiding years of conflict.

Five examples of good judgment

1. Knowing when the fight is really about emotion, not law: the client says they want justice, but the experienced lawyer recognises hurt, anger and punishment. Good judgment is helping the client avoid spending £30,000 fighting over £5,000 of furniture.
2. Assessing whether a settlement is workable in real life: AI may calculate a financial split. The lawyer judges whether the arrangement actually allows both households to function and children to be housed.
3. Spotting coercive control behind polite instructions: a client may say, 'I am happy to agree.' The lawyer notices hesitation, fear, inconsistent instructions or excessive concern about the other party's reaction.
4. Knowing when to cool the temperature: the lawyer decides not to send the aggressive letter the client wants because it will inflame the dispute and damage co-parenting.
5. Forecasting how a judge will see the parties: a client may think their conduct is justified. The lawyer judges that a court may see it as unreasonable, controlling or child-focused in words only.

AI Pricing Canvas example

Canvas question	Example answer
What problem is the client solving?	Client needs to resolve financial arrangements after separation without destroying the family, the children's stability or their own financial future.
What outcome does the client need?	A workable, court-realistic settlement that protects housing, income, pensions and future family arrangements.
What can AI assist with?	Chronology, asset schedule, document summary, first-pass comparison of disclosure and draft settlement scenarios.
What requires lawyer judgment?	Whether the settlement is realistic, whether the client is being driven by grief or revenge, and how a judge is likely to view needs, conduct and disclosure.
What acumen is required?	Understanding family dynamics, emotional pressure, housing needs, cash flow, pensions and the practical reality of running two households.
What risk does the firm carry?	Advice may shape long-term financial security, child arrangements and whether the client avoids years of destructive litigation.
What supervision and checking are needed?	Review of AI-generated asset summaries, pension calculations, disclosure gaps and draft consent order wording.
What value does the client receive?	Clarity, protection, reduced conflict, a realistic settlement strategy and a route away from litigation.
What pricing options could be offered?	Essential settlement advice / Negotiated settlement package / Full court-ready strategy and representation.
AI discount answer	AI helps organise the material, but the fee reflects judgment about risk, fairness, family reality and the outcome the client can actually live with.

2. RESIDENTIAL CONVEYANCING

Judgment elements

1. Assessing whether a title defect is technical, insurable, negotiable or genuinely dangerous.
2. Judging whether a search result is routine or a warning sign.
3. Deciding whether a restrictive covenant is likely to matter in practice.
4. Assessing whether indemnity insurance is good enough or whether the client needs the underlying problem resolved.
5. Judging whether pressure from estate agents, brokers or the chain is creating unacceptable risk.
6. Spotting when standard leasehold wording creates a long-term resale or mortgageability problem.
7. Assessing whether service charge, ground rent, cladding, estate rent charge or management company issues are tolerable.
8. Knowing when to tell the client: 'You can buy this property, but you need to understand exactly what you are buying.'
9. Prioritising the issues that matter to a first-time buyer, downsizer, investor or separating couple.
10. Anticipating lender concerns before they derail completion.
11. Judging whether replies to enquiries are evasive, incomplete or commercially acceptable.
12. Managing completion risk in a chain where one weak link can damage everyone.

Five examples of good judgment

1. Knowing whether a title defect is real danger or legal noise: AI can flag a restrictive covenant. The lawyer judges whether it affects intended use, resale value or mortgageability.
2. Resisting pressure from the chain: estate agents, brokers and clients may all be shouting 'exchange today'. Good judgment is saying: 'Not until this issue is answered.'
3. Explaining leasehold risk in plain English: AI can summarise ground rent clauses. The lawyer judges whether the clause creates future saleability problems or lender concerns.
4. Knowing when indemnity insurance is not enough: a policy may satisfy the lender but not solve the client's practical problem, such as inability to build, extend, park or access the property.

5. Protecting the client from their own excitement: the client has fallen in love with the house. The lawyer slows them down and explains flood risk, boundary issues, rent charge or planning concerns before commitment.

AI Pricing Canvas example

Canvas question	Example answer
What problem is the client solving?	Client wants to buy a leasehold flat but needs to know whether the property is safe to buy, mortgageable and resaleable.
What outcome does the client need?	Exchange and completion only when the material risks are understood, explained and either resolved or consciously accepted.
What can AI assist with?	Search summaries, lease clause extraction, title review checklist, enquiry tracking and report-on-title first draft.
What requires lawyer judgment?	Whether ground rent, service charge, cladding, management company or lease wording creates a real future problem.
What acumen is required?	Understanding lender expectations, first-time buyer anxiety, resale risk, affordability and the pressure of the chain.
What risk does the firm carry?	The client may rely on the advice for the largest purchase of their life. A missed issue may affect value, mortgageability or resale.
What supervision and checking are needed?	Lawyer review of title, lease, searches, replies to enquiries, lender requirements and AI-generated summaries.
What value does the client receive?	Confidence that they understand what they are buying before they commit.
What pricing options could be offered?	Standard purchase / Enhanced leasehold risk report / Premium chain-management and lender-risk package.
AI discount answer	AI can help process documents faster, but the value lies in knowing which risks matter and stopping the client buying a problem.

3. COMMERCIAL PROPERTY WORK

Judgment elements

1. Assessing whether the property supports the client's business plan, not just whether the title is technically acceptable.
2. Judging the commercial significance of lease terms: break rights, alienation, repair, rent review, service charge and reinstatement.
3. Identifying when a minor planning issue could threaten funding, occupation, development or exit.
4. Assessing whether the client should accept title insurance, seek a price reduction or walk away.
5. Forecasting how a landlord, tenant, funder, developer or local authority may behave.

6. Judging whether a timetable is realistic given searches, surveys, board approvals, planning or lender requirements.
7. Knowing when to escalate an issue to surveyors, tax advisers, planners, environmental consultants or funders.
8. Assessing whether the lease allocates risk fairly or quietly dumps future cost on the client.
9. Judging the real value of a break clause by asking whether the client can actually comply with the conditions.
10. Spotting when a property deal is being driven by optimism rather than evidence.
11. Deciding which points are worth negotiating and which will simply irritate the other side.
12. Helping the client understand the long-term consequences of signing a bad lease for short-term convenience.

Five examples of good judgment

1. Reading the lease against the business plan: AI can summarise lease terms. The lawyer asks whether the client can actually trade, grow, assign, sublet, alter and exit under this lease.
2. Spotting a break clause that is almost useless: the lease contains a break right, but the lawyer judges that the conditions are so strict that the client may never exercise it safely.
3. Knowing when a planning issue is deal-critical: a minor planning irregularity may not matter for one buyer but may destroy value for a developer, lender or occupier.
4. Balancing speed against future exposure: the client wants to complete quickly. The lawyer judges whether speed is worth accepting environmental, title, repair or service charge risk.
5. Understanding the hidden economics of the deal: the rent looks acceptable, but service charge, reinstatement, dilapidations and rent review make the deal much more expensive than the headline figure suggests.

AI Pricing Canvas example

Canvas question	Example answer
What problem is the client solving?	Client needs premises that support its business plan without incurring hidden future costs or operational restrictions.
What outcome does the client need?	A lease that allows trading, growth, exit, assignment, alteration and financial predictability.
What can AI assist with?	Lease summary, clause comparison, due diligence checklist, search summary and first draft of lease report.

What requires lawyer judgment?	Whether break conditions, repair obligations, service charge, reinstatement and rent review make the lease commercially dangerous.
What acumen is required?	Understanding the client's business model, cash flow, expansion plans, funding, exit strategy and operational needs.
What risk does the firm carry?	A poor lease may trap the client in expensive premises and damage profitability for years.
What supervision and checking are needed?	Review of AI lease analysis, title issues, planning risks, environmental reports and negotiation points.
What value does the client receive?	A commercially usable lease, not just a legally completed transaction.
What pricing options could be offered?	Lease essentials / Commercial risk report / Negotiation and strategic occupancy package.
AI discount answer	AI may summarise the lease, but it cannot decide whether the lease supports the business. That is the value.

4. EMPLOYMENT LAW

Judgment elements

1. Assessing whether the employer has a legal problem, a management problem, a culture problem or all three.
2. Judging whether dismissal, settlement, performance management, mediation or investigation is the right route.
3. Forecasting tribunal risk by evaluating evidence, witnesses, documents, timing and credibility.
4. Assessing whether the client's desired action is legally defensible but commercially foolish.
5. Judging how an employee, union, regulator, press or workforce may react.
6. Identifying discrimination, whistleblowing, victimisation or protected disclosure issues buried inside ordinary workplace language.
7. Knowing when to advise restraint: 'Do not send that email.'
8. Assessing whether a grievance is genuine, tactical, retaliatory or a warning signal of systemic failure.
9. Helping employers make decisions that are fair, documented and human.
10. Helping employees understand whether a claim is worth pursuing emotionally, financially and evidentially.
11. Evaluating whether settlement terms protect confidentiality, tax position, references, announcements and future risk.
12. Advising on the reputational consequences of winning an employment dispute in the wrong way.

Five examples of good judgment

1. Knowing when the legal problem is really a management failure: the employer asks, 'Can we dismiss?' The lawyer judges that the better question is why nobody has managed the person properly for two years.
2. Spotting discrimination risk hidden in ordinary language: a manager says the employee is 'not a good cultural fit'. The lawyer hears potential age, race, sex, disability or maternity risk depending on context.
3. Advising restraint before the damaging email is sent: good judgment is saying, 'Do not send that. It will become Exhibit A in the tribunal bundle.'
4. Assessing witness credibility early: the documents look good, but the lawyer judges that the key manager will perform poorly under cross-examination, and that settlement may be wiser.
5. Knowing when to settle even if the employer is technically right: the claim may be defensible, but cost, distraction, reputational risk and morale make settlement the better commercial decision.

AI Pricing Canvas example

Canvas question	Example answer
What problem is the client solving?	Employer needs to manage a difficult senior exit without creating tribunal, reputation or workforce risk.
What outcome does the client need?	A fair, documented and commercially sensible exit strategy.
What can AI assist with?	Document review, chronology, draft scripts, draft settlement agreement, risk matrix and policy comparison.
What requires lawyer judgment?	Whether dismissal, performance management, mediation, investigation or settlement is the right route.
What acumen is required?	Understanding workplace politics, culture, management failure, employee leverage and likely internal reaction.
What risk does the firm carry?	Wrong advice may lead to unfair dismissal, discrimination, whistleblowing, breaches of confidentiality, or reputational exposure.
What supervision and checking are needed?	Review of evidence, witness credibility, privileged communications and AI-generated draft documents.
What value does the client receive?	A managed route through a sensitive people issue before it becomes Exhibit A in the tribunal bundle.
What pricing options could be offered?	Risk assessment / Managed exit plan / Full negotiation and settlement package.
AI discount answer	AI can help prepare documents, but the value is in knowing what the employer should do, when, and how to avoid making it worse.

5. COMPANY AND COMMERCIAL LAW

Judgment elements

1. Understanding the commercial purpose behind the contract, not just the words in it.
2. Judging which risk allocation points genuinely matter to the client's business model.
3. Assessing whether a liability cap is commercially sensible, insurable and enforceable.
4. Knowing when to concede a clause to preserve the relationship.
5. Knowing when to hold the line because the clause goes to existential risk.
6. Forecasting how the contract will operate when things go wrong, not when everyone is friendly.
7. Spotting internal client misalignment between finance, sales, operations, legal and the board.
8. Judging whether a proposed governance structure will work in practice.
9. Assessing shareholder dynamics: deadlock, control, exit, minority protection and future funding.
10. Identifying when the other side's drafting reveals a hidden commercial agenda.
11. Translating legal risk into business language: margin, control, cash flow, supply continuity, data, brand and exit value.
12. Helping clients decide whether to sign, renegotiate, delay or walk away.

Five examples of good judgment

1. Knowing which clause actually matters: AI may redline fifty points. The lawyer judges that only three matter commercially: liability, termination and payment risk.
2. Seeing the business problem behind the contract: the client asks for a supply agreement. The lawyer realises the real issue is dependency on one supplier with no realistic alternative.
3. Knowing when to concede: good judgment is accepting a point that does not materially hurt the client in order to win the point that really matters.
4. Spotting internal misalignment: sales wants the deal signed, finance hates the payment terms, and operations cannot deliver the service levels. The lawyer sees the business disagreement.
5. Judging whether the relationship can survive the drafting: the lawyer knows that an over-lawyered contract may damage a strategic relationship before it starts.

AI Pricing Canvas example

Canvas question	Example answer
What problem is the client solving?	A growth company needs to sign a major customer contract without accepting risk that damages margin, cash flow or control.
What outcome does the client need?	A contract position that protects revenue, limits liability and remains commercially acceptable.
What can AI assist with?	Clause extraction, contract summary, deviation report, risk flagging and comparison against preferred positions.
What requires lawyer judgment?	Which risks are genuinely material, which points are worth negotiating and which concessions are commercially acceptable.
What acumen is required?	Understanding sales pressure, revenue targets, customer importance, operational capability and bargaining power.
What risk does the firm carry?	The advice may affect liability, revenue recognition, delivery obligations and future disputes.
What supervision and checking are needed?	Lawyer review of AI clause analysis, exclusions, indemnities, service levels, termination and payment provisions.
What value does the client receive?	A deal the client can sign with eyes open, rather than a contract that quietly imports future pain.
What pricing options could be offered?	Red flag review / Negotiation-ready mark-up / Strategic deal-support package.
AI discount answer	AI may identify clauses quickly, but the fee reflects commercial judgment about what matters in this deal.

6. DISPUTE RESOLUTION

Judgment elements

1. Assessing merits, evidence, credibility, cost, delay, enforceability and opponent behaviour.
2. Judging whether the client wants vindication, money, precedent, confidentiality, deterrence or closure.
3. Forecasting litigation risk, including how a judge may react to the facts.
4. Assessing whether an opponent is rational, emotional, tactical, underfunded or using litigation as leverage.
5. Deciding when to issue, defend, mediate, make an offer, disclose, apply or settle.
6. Judging whether a Part 36 offer is pitched correctly.
7. Identifying the difference between a strong legal argument and a winnable case.
8. Assessing witness reliability before the client falls in love with its own story.
9. Knowing when a point is good law but bad advocacy.

10. Helping clients price risk rather than chase certainty.
11. Stress-testing the case from the opponent's perspective.
12. Advising when settlement is not weakness but intelligent risk control.

Five examples of good judgment

1. Knowing whether to fight or settle: the client has a good legal argument, but the lawyer judges that evidential risk, cost, delay and opponent behaviour make settlement better.
2. Testing the client's story before the opponent does: good judgment is asking awkward questions early, before cross-examination, disclosure, or mediation exposes the weakness.
3. Pitching the settlement offer properly: a good lawyer judges timing, amount, tone, pressure, litigation risk and how the offer will look later to a judge.
4. Knowing when winning is not winning: a client may win liability but spend more than the claim is worth, damage a relationship or create bad publicity.
5. Reading the opponent: the lawyer judges whether the opponent is rational, emotional, tactical, broke, insured, reputationally exposed, or simply trying to delay.

AI Pricing Canvas example

Canvas question	Example answer
What problem is the client solving?	Client needs to know whether to pursue, defend, settle or walk away from a commercial dispute.
What outcome does the client need?	A realistic litigation strategy based on merits, evidence, cost, risk, leverage and commercial objective.
What can AI assist with?	Document chronology, issue list, case law summary, pleadings first draft and evidence map.
What requires lawyer judgment?	Whether the claim is worth fighting, whether witnesses will withstand scrutiny and when settlement is better than being right.
What acumen is required?	Understanding reputation, cash flow, commercial relationships, management distraction and appetite for risk.
What risk does the firm carry?	Poor advice may lead to unnecessary litigation, excessive cost or missed settlement opportunities.
What supervision and checking are needed?	Review of AI-generated chronologies, legal authorities, evidence summaries and pleadings.
What value does the client receive?	A route to resolution, not simply a beautifully organised fight.
What pricing options could be offered?	Early merits assessment / Settlement strategy / Full litigation roadmap and representation.
AI discount answer	AI can organise the battlefield, but judgment decides whether the client should fight, settle or stop.

7. WILLS, TRUSTS AND PROBATE

Judgment elements

1. Assessing capacity, undue influence and vulnerability.
2. Judging whether the client's instructions are settled, pressured or reactive.
3. Identifying likely family conflicts before they turn into litigation.
4. Balancing tax efficiency with simplicity, control and family harmony.
5. Advising whether a trust is genuinely useful or creates unnecessary complexity.
6. Assessing whether equal treatment is fair treatment.
7. Helping clients understand the emotional consequences of excluding or favouring beneficiaries.
8. Spotting disappointed beneficiary risk.
9. Judging whether lifetime gifting creates care fee, tax, control or dependency problems.
10. Advising executors when to be firm, neutral, transparent or conciliatory.
11. Assessing when probate delay is administrative and when it signals deeper conflict.
12. Helping families make decisions when grief is impairing judgment.

Five examples of good judgment

1. Spotting capacity and undue influence concerns: AI can draft a will. The lawyer judges whether the client is giving free, capable and independent instructions.
2. Seeing the future family dispute: the client says, 'They will understand.' The lawyer knows they probably will not and records reasons carefully.
3. Balancing tax efficiency against family harmony: the most tax-efficient structure may create complexity, resentment or practical difficulty.
4. Knowing when equal is not fair: one child has worked in the family business for 30 years; another has had substantial lifetime gifts. The lawyer helps the client think beyond mathematical equality.
5. Guiding executors through grief and conflict: executors need judgment on communication, timing, neutrality and how to avoid turning probate into family warfare.

AI Pricing Canvas example

Canvas question	Example answer
What problem is the client solving?	Client wants to provide for a spouse, children from an earlier relationship and future inheritance wishes without creating family conflict.
What outcome does the client need?	A clear, tax-aware, family-sensitive estate plan that is legally robust and practically workable.
What can AI assist with?	Asset summary, draft will clauses, checklist of issues, inheritance tax prompts and letter of wishes first draft.
What requires lawyer judgment?	Whether the structure actually reflects family dynamics, dependency risks, fairness, capacity and future dispute risk.
What acumen is required?	Understanding family relationships, wealth preservation, tax exposure, vulnerability and emotional consequences.
What risk does the firm carry?	Poor advice may lead to invalid documents, tax problems, disappointed beneficiaries and litigation after death.
What supervision and checking are needed?	Review of capacity, instructions, tax assumptions, trust wording and AI-generated drafts.
What value does the client receive?	Peace of mind that their wishes are clear, defensible and less likely to cause a family war.
What pricing options could be offered?	Essential will / Blended family estate plan / Full succession and trust planning package.
AI discount answer	AI can draft words, but it cannot understand the family, spot the dispute waiting to happen or take responsibility for the plan.

8. IMMIGRATION LAW

Judgment elements

1. Assessing whether the client's objective is realistic under the relevant route.
2. Identifying evidential weaknesses before submission.
3. Judging whether a discrepancy is harmless, explainable or fatal.
4. Forecasting how a Home Office caseworker may view credibility, documents and chronology.
5. Advising whether to apply now, wait, gather more evidence or choose a different route.
6. Assessing the human impact of refusal, delay, removal, separation or loss of work rights.
7. Spotting safeguarding, trafficking, asylum or human rights issues that the client may not initially disclose.
8. Judging when an appeal, administrative review, fresh application or judicial review is the right path.

9. Helping corporate clients balance recruitment urgency with sponsorship compliance.
10. Assessing whether sponsor licence systems are robust enough to survive audit.
11. Translating complex rules into clear life choices.
12. Managing client expectations where the law offers hope but not certainty.

Five examples of good judgment

1. Judging whether the evidence tells a believable story: the documents may tick boxes, but the lawyer sees that the chronology looks inconsistent or artificial.
2. Choosing the right route, not just an available route: AI may list visa options. The lawyer judges which route best fits the client's long-term family, work, settlement or business plans.
3. Knowing when to wait: the client wants to apply immediately. The lawyer judges that a stronger application in six weeks is better than a weak application today.
4. Spotting hidden vulnerability: a client may present a simple visa problem. The lawyer identifies trafficking, domestic abuse, asylum, exploitation or safeguarding issues.
5. Advising a corporate sponsor on practical compliance: the rules may be understood. The lawyer assesses whether the client's HR systems are sufficient to withstand a Home Office audit.

AI Pricing Canvas example

Canvas question	Example answer
What problem is the client solving?	Employer needs to recruit or retain a key worker without breaching sponsor duties or delaying the hire.
What outcome does the client need?	A compliant, timely visa application with reduced refusal and sponsor compliance risk.
What can AI assist with?	Document checklist, first draft forms, eligibility summary, timeline and compliance reminders.
What requires lawyer judgment?	Whether the role, salary, sponsorship facts, and supporting documents meet the real requirements.
What acumen is required?	Understanding recruitment pressure, workforce planning, business continuity and Home Office risk appetite.
What risk does the firm carry?	Refusal may affect the worker, the employer's sponsor licence and the business need behind the hire.
What supervision and checking are needed?	Lawyer review of eligibility, documents, application answers, sponsor duties and AI-generated checklists.
What value does the client receive?	A safer route to getting the right person in the role at the right time.

What pricing options could be offered?	Eligibility review / Application preparation / Full sponsor compliance and visa support package.
AI discount answer	AI can help organise the application, but the value lies in avoiding refusals, delays, and sponsor risk.

9. CRIMINAL LAW

Judgment elements

1. Assessing the strength of prosecution evidence beyond the charge sheet.
2. Judging whether silence, comment, prepared statement or full interview participation is appropriate.
3. Evaluating disclosure failures and investigative gaps.
4. Assessing witness credibility, forensic evidence and police procedure.
5. Advising whether to plead, contest, seek discontinuance or negotiate basis of plea.
6. Forecasting sentencing risk.
7. Understanding how a conviction affects employment, travel, family, regulation or immigration status.
8. Judging whether the client is vulnerable, intoxicated, frightened, suggestible or not understanding the process.
9. Knowing when to challenge aggressively and when to preserve credibility.
10. Identifying whether there is a mental health, coercion, exploitation or safeguarding dimension.
11. Assessing whether a technically available defence is tactically wise.
12. Helping clients make decisions when panic may overwhelm reason.

Five examples of good judgment

1. Deciding what to do in an interview: good judgment is deciding whether the client should answer questions, provide a prepared statement, remain silent or challenge assumptions in disclosure.
2. Assessing the real strength of the prosecution case: AI can summarise the charge. The lawyer judges witness credibility, disclosure gaps, forensic weaknesses and procedural errors.
3. Knowing when a guilty plea is the best protection: the client wants to fight. The lawyer judges that an early plea may materially reduce the sentence and protect the client.

4. Seeing vulnerability in the client: the lawyer identifies mental health, learning difficulty, addiction, coercion or exploitation that changes how the case should be handled.
5. Understanding consequences beyond the sentence: good judgment includes advising on employment, travel, professional discipline, family consequences, immigration and reputation.

AI Pricing Canvas example

Canvas question	Example answer
What problem is the client solving?	Client faces investigation and needs immediate protection, clear advice and a strategy before making decisions that cannot be undone.
What outcome does the client need?	Proper advice on interview, evidence, risk, bail, reputation and next steps.
What can AI assist with?	Timeline, document summary, offence overview and preparation checklist.
What requires lawyer judgment?	Whether to answer questions, go no comment, make a prepared statement or challenge the basis of the investigation.
What acumen is required?	Understanding police approach, client vulnerability, evidential gaps, reputational consequences and family or employment impact.
What risk does the firm carry?	Early decisions may shape the entire case and the client's liberty, reputation and livelihood.
What supervision and checking are needed?	Lawyer review of facts, disclosure, interview strategy and any AI-generated legal summaries.
What value does the client receive?	Protection at the point of maximum pressure.
What pricing options could be offered?	Initial advice / Police station attendance / Full early defence strategy package.
AI discount answer	AI can summarise law, but it cannot sit with a frightened client and exercise judgment when liberty is at stake.

10. INTELLECTUAL PROPERTY LAW

Judgment elements

1. Assessing whether IP protection supports the client's actual business model.
2. Judging whether to register, enforce, license, sell, challenge or tolerate.
3. Evaluating whether infringement is legally arguable and commercially worth pursuing.
4. Forecasting how enforcement action may affect brand, customers, investors or partners.
5. Deciding whether the client needs speed, deterrence, damages, takedown, confidentiality or market positioning.

6. Assessing whether a design, brand, invention or work is core value or peripheral.
7. Judging whether litigation will increase the value of the IP or simply burn cash.
8. Identifying ownership problems created by founders, freelancers, employees or collaborators.
9. Advising on the trade-off between secrecy and registration.
10. Helping clients avoid over-lawyering early-stage ideas.
11. Spotting when 'we own the IP' is not supported by the paper trail.
12. Translating legal rights into business advantage.

Five examples of good judgment

1. Knowing whether enforcement is commercially wise: the client can send a threatening letter. The lawyer judges whether doing so will provoke a validity challenge, bad publicity or an unaffordable fight.
2. Deciding what IP is actually valuable: not every logo, design, process or idea deserves expensive protection. Good judgment is knowing what supports the client's business model.
3. Spotting ownership gaps: the client assumes it owns the IP. The lawyer checks founders, consultants, employees, agencies and collaboration agreements and spots the missing assignment.
4. Balancing secrecy and registration: the lawyer judges whether the client is better protected by patenting, copyright, confidentiality, trade secrets or speed to market.
5. Seeing IP as leverage, not just rights: good judgment is using IP to support investment, licensing, brand protection, market entry, negotiation or exit value.

AI Pricing Canvas example

Canvas question	Example answer
What problem is the client solving?	Business needs to protect a new brand before launch and avoid wasting money on a name it cannot own or defend.
What outcome does the client need?	A clear filing and protection strategy that supports growth, investment and market positioning.
What can AI assist with?	Initial clearance searches, similarity checks, class suggestions, watch reports and draft filing descriptions.
What requires lawyer judgment?	Whether conflict risk is tolerable, whether the mark is distinctive and how aggressively to protect it.
What acumen is required?	Understanding product roadmap, territories, competitor behaviour, investor expectations and brand value.
What risk does the firm carry?	Poor advice may lead to infringement, rebranding costs, opposition, weak protection, or lost market value.

What supervision and checking are needed?	Review of AI search outputs, classification, prior rights, filing strategy and enforcement recommendations.
What value does the client receive?	A protectable brand strategy, not just a trademark application.
What pricing options could be offered?	Clearance snapshot / Filing package / Brand protection and monitoring package.
AI discount answer	AI can search and compare, but the value is in judging whether the brand can safely carry the business.

11. AGRICULTURAL LAW

Judgment elements

1. Understanding that the farm may be a business, a home, a family identity and a legacy.
2. Assessing succession risk where family expectations are unclear or unspoken.
3. Judging the interaction between land ownership, occupation, partnership, tenancies and inheritance.
4. Identifying whether a farming arrangement is legally documented or merely assumed.
5. Assessing development, diversification, renewable energy, subsidy, environmental and planning opportunities.
6. Balancing tax efficiency against family fairness and operational control.
7. Judging whether a proposed structure will survive death, divorce, dispute or incapacity.
8. Spotting partnership property disputes before they become generational litigation.
9. Advising when to formalise arrangements that have operated informally for decades.
10. Assessing rural land rights: access, easements, sporting rights, mineral rights, water, boundaries and stewardship obligations.
11. Knowing when the emotional dynamics matter more than the legal drafting.
12. Helping families confront difficult conversations before crisis forces them.

Five examples of good judgment

1. Understanding that the farm is not just an asset: it is home, business, identity, inheritance and family history. Good judgment is advising with that reality in mind.

2. Spotting succession conflict before it erupts: one child works the farm, one does not, and both expect fairness. The lawyer sees the future dispute and forces clarity early.
3. Testing informal arrangements: farming families often rely on assumptions. The lawyer judges when 'we have always done it this way' is a litigation risk.
4. Balancing tax planning and family control: a structure may be tax efficient, but may leave the wrong person in control or create resentment.
5. Assessing diversification risk: the client wants renewables, tourism, development or environmental schemes. The lawyer judges planning, tenancy, tax, subsidy, access and long-term land value consequences.

AI Pricing Canvas example

Canvas question	Example answer
What problem is the client solving?	A farming family needs to plan succession, land use, and diversification without creating tax, ownership, or family conflicts.
What outcome does the client need?	A practical structure for land, business, family expectations and future income.
What can AI assist with?	Document summary, landholding schedule, planning checklist, tenancy review and draft option analysis.
What requires lawyer judgment?	Whether the proposed structure works for the family, the farm, the tax position and the next generation.
What acumen is required?	Understanding family dynamics, rural business economics, land value, subsidies, diversification and long-term stewardship.
What risk does the firm carry?	Poor advice may fracture family relationships, damage tax planning or restrict future land use.
What supervision and checking are needed?	Review of title, tenancies, partnership documents, tax assumptions and AI-generated summaries.
What value does the client receive?	A joined-up plan for land, business and family reality.
What pricing options could be offered?	Succession review / Farm structure plan / Full family, land and diversification package.
AI discount answer	AI can list the documents, but judgment is needed to understand the farm, the family and the future.

12. TAX LAW

Judgment elements

1. Assessing whether a tax position is robust, arguable, aggressive or reckless.
2. Judging the difference between tax planning, tax avoidance and unacceptable risk.
3. Forecasting how HMRC may view the transaction.

4. Evaluating whether the documentation supports the claimed tax treatment.
5. Advising whether the tax saving justifies the complexity, disclosure risk and future challenges.
6. Identifying when the legal form and commercial substance are misaligned.
7. Assessing penalties, interest, enquiry risk and reputational consequences.
8. Helping clients decide whether to disclose, amend, defend, settle or litigate.
9. Judging when counsel's opinion is needed.
10. Translating technical tax risk into board-level decision language.
11. Balancing tax efficiency with family, corporate or transactional objectives.
12. Knowing when the right answer is: 'You can do this, but I would not recommend it.'

Five examples of good judgment

1. Knowing when clever becomes dangerous: the tax analysis may be arguable. The lawyer judges whether the planning is robust, aggressive or likely to attract challenge.
2. Assessing HMRC behaviour: good judgment includes forecasting how HMRC may view the facts, not just what the legislation says.
3. Balancing saving against risk: the client may save £100,000 but face years of enquiry, penalties, cost and uncertainty. The lawyer helps price that risk.
4. Spotting substance-over-form problems: the documents may say one thing. The commercial reality may say another. Good judgment is seeing the mismatch.
5. Knowing when to say no: sometimes the most valuable advice is, 'You can probably do this, but I would not recommend it.'

AI Pricing Canvas example

Canvas question	Example answer
What problem is the client solving?	Client wants to complete a transaction without unexpected tax costs, challenges, or structural inefficiencies.
What outcome does the client need?	A tax-aware structure that supports the commercial deal and can be defended.
What can AI assist with?	Legislative summary, case law notes, tax issue checklist and first-pass structure comparison.
What requires lawyer judgment?	Whether the proposed approach is robust, proportionate, explainable and aligned with commercial substance.
What acumen is required?	Understanding deal economics, cash flow, investor expectations, HMRC risk and timing pressures.
What risk does the firm carry?	Advice may affect transaction value, reporting, future challenge, penalties and professional exposure.

What supervision and checking are needed?	Technical review of AI outputs, legislation, guidance, assumptions and transaction documents.
What value does the client receive?	A structure that does not let the tax tail accidentally bite the commercial dog.
What pricing options could be offered?	Tax risk note / Transaction tax review / Full structuring and implementation package.
AI discount answer	AI can summarise tax material, but the price reflects responsibility for applying it safely to the client's transaction.

13. PERSONAL INJURY AND CLINICAL NEGLIGENCE

Judgment elements

1. Assessing causation, not just injury.
2. Judging whether expert evidence is strong, weak or incomplete.
3. Forecasting quantum, litigation risk and settlement range.
4. Understanding the client's care, rehabilitation, employment and family needs.
5. Knowing when interim payments matter more than final damages.
6. Assessing whether the client's presentation will be persuasive.
7. Judging whether to settle now or wait for the prognosis to stabilise.
8. Translating medical complexity into legal and practical choices.

Five examples of good judgment

1. Knowing whether causation is the real battleground: the injury is obvious. The lawyer judges whether the defendant's conduct actually caused it.
2. Choosing the right expert: good judgment is knowing which expert will help, which will overreach and which will collapse under challenge.
3. Waiting before settlement: the client wants closure. The lawyer judges that the prognosis is not stable and that settling now may undervalue the lifelong need.
4. Understanding the client's lived reality: damages are not just numbers. The lawyer sees care, housing, work, family strain, equipment and dignity.
5. Judging credibility and surveillance risk: the lawyer helps the client understand how social media activity, inconsistency or exaggeration may damage the claim.

AI Pricing Canvas example

Canvas question	Example answer
What problem is the client solving?	Injured client needs compensation, care, rehabilitation and financial security after life-changing harm.
What outcome does the client need?	A properly valued claim that secures evidence, rehabilitation, interim payments and long-term protection.

What can AI assist with?	Medical chronology, document summary, liability research, schedule preparation and evidence gaps.
What requires lawyer judgment?	Causation, credibility, litigation risk, settlement timing and whether expert evidence is strong enough.
What acumen is required?	Understanding care needs, family pressure, rehabilitation, insurance behaviour and long-term financial consequences.
What risk does the firm carry?	Undervaluing the claim may damage the client's life for decades.
What supervision and checking are needed?	Review of medical records, expert reports, damages calculations and AI-generated chronologies.
What value does the client receive?	A route to recovery, support and proper compensation, not merely a processed claim.
What pricing options could be offered?	Initial claim assessment / Liability and quantum strategy / Full serious injury claim management.
AI discount answer	AI can organise records, but the value is in judgment about causation, evidence, settlement and the client's future needs.

14. REGULATORY AND PROFESSIONAL DISCIPLINE

Judgment elements

1. Assessing whether the client faces legal, regulatory, reputational or livelihood risk.
2. Judging whether cooperation, challenge, remediation or silence is appropriate.
3. Forecasting how a regulator may interpret conduct.
4. Advising on tone: defensive, contrite, factual, explanatory or remedial.
5. Identifying systemic issues behind an individual complaint.
6. Helping clients preserve credibility.
7. Judging when to self-report.
8. Managing parallel civil, criminal, employment and regulatory risks.

Five examples of good judgment

1. Knowing when to be candid, not clever: the lawyer judges that an over-defensive response may make the regulator more suspicious.
2. Separating the original issue from the conduct risk: often the cover-up, delay or lack of candour is more damaging than the original breach.
3. Advising on self-reporting: good judgment is deciding whether, when and how to notify a regulator before the issue escalates.
4. Managing parallel risks: a regulatory issue may also create employment, criminal, civil, insurance and reputational consequences.

5. Building a remediation story: the lawyer helps the client show insight, learning, systems improvement and future protection.

AI Pricing Canvas example

Canvas question	Example answer
What problem is the client solving?	Professional or business faces investigation and needs to protect licence, reputation and future ability to practise or trade.
What outcome does the client need?	A credible response strategy that manages legal, regulatory, evidential and reputational risk.
What can AI assist with?	Document chronology, issue map, policy comparison, draft response and evidence bundle index.
What requires lawyer judgment?	Whether to cooperate, challenge, self-report, remediate or contest allegations.
What acumen is required?	Understanding regulator behaviour, public confidence, professional standards, board pressure and reputational exposure.
What risk does the firm carry?	Advice may affect livelihood, licence, sanctions and public trust.
What supervision and checking are needed?	Lawyer review of AI-generated summaries, privilege, evidence, correspondence and regulatory submissions.
What value does the client receive?	A controlled, credible and defensible response at a moment when panic is dangerous.
What pricing options could be offered?	Initial risk review / Investigation response plan / Full regulatory defence and remediation package.
AI discount answer	AI can help marshal evidence, but judgment decides the stance to take with the regulator.

15. DATA PROTECTION AND PRIVACY

Judgment elements

1. Assessing whether a data incident is minor, reportable or business-critical.
2. Judging whether to notify regulators, customers, insurers or contractual counterparties.
3. Evaluating real-world harm, not just technical breach categories.
4. Forecasting reputational and enforcement risk.
5. Advising on proportionate remediation.
6. Balancing transparency with legal privilege and litigation risk.
7. Understanding how data flows through the business in practice.
8. Helping clients avoid treating privacy as a paperwork exercise.

Five examples of good judgment

1. Judging whether a breach is reportable: AI can list reporting rules. The lawyer assesses real risk to individuals, timing, sensitivity and regulatory expectations.
2. Knowing what to say to affected people: good judgment is balancing clarity, reassurance, legal accuracy and reputational protection.
3. Avoiding panic over low-risk incidents: not every data issue is a crisis. The lawyer judges a proportionate response.
4. Spotting the real commercial risk: the legal breach may be small, but the damage to trust with customers, funders, or partners may be large.
5. Protecting privilege and evidence: the lawyer judges how to investigate without creating unnecessary, harmful documents.

AI Pricing Canvas example

Canvas question	Example answer
What problem is the client solving?	Client has suffered a data incident and needs to know whether to notify, contain, investigate and communicate.
What outcome does the client need?	A rapid, defensible breach response that manages regulatory, customer, operational and reputational risk.
What can AI assist with?	Incident timeline, document review, affected-data categorisation, draft notification and risk checklist.
What requires lawyer judgment?	Whether the breach is notifiable, how serious it is, what to say and how to preserve privilege.
What acumen is required?	Understanding operational impact, customer trust, cyber response, regulator expectations and business continuity.
What risk does the firm carry?	Wrong advice may lead to regulatory penalties, litigation, reputational harm and privilege problems.
What supervision and checking are needed?	Review of AI-generated incident summaries, legal thresholds, notification wording and technical reports.
What value does the client receive?	Calm, structured decision-making when speed and accuracy both matter.
What pricing options could be offered?	Breach triage / Notification and response package / Full incident management and remediation support.
AI discount answer	AI can help process facts quickly, but the value is in deciding what must be done and what must not be said.

16. BANKING AND FINANCE

Judgment elements

1. Assessing whether security is effective, enforceable and commercially adequate.
2. Judging whether default risk is legal, financial, operational or relationship-driven.
3. Understanding intercreditor dynamics.
4. Forecasting lender behaviour under stress.
5. Advising borrowers on covenant headroom and negotiation leverage.
6. Spotting hidden insolvency or priority risks.
7. Balancing speed of funding against documentary protection.
8. Judging whether a waiver, amendment, refinance or enforcement route is best.

Five examples of good judgment

1. Seeing whether the covenant package fits the business: the agreement may be standard. The lawyer judges whether the borrower can realistically comply.
2. Assessing security in practical terms: it is not enough that security exists. The lawyer judges whether it is enforceable, valuable and properly ranked.
3. Understanding lender psychology: the lawyer forecasts whether the lender is likely to waive, renegotiate, enforce or exit.
4. Spotting insolvency proximity: good judgment is recognising when finance advice is becoming restructuring advice.
5. Balancing the speed of funding with future restrictions: the client wants money quickly. The lawyer judges whether the terms will strangle future growth.

AI Pricing Canvas example

Canvas question	Example answer
What problem is the client solving?	Borrower needs funding but must understand covenant, security and restriction risks before signing.
What outcome does the client need?	Finance documents that deliver funding without unnecessarily restricting future growth.
What can AI assist with?	Facility summary, covenant extraction, security checklist, condition precedent tracker and comparison to market positions.
What requires lawyer judgment?	Whether the security is effective, the covenants are workable, and default risk is manageable.
What acumen is required?	Understanding lender psychology, cash flow, growth plans, headroom, leverage and stress scenarios.
What risk does the firm carry?	Poor advice may restrict the business, trigger default or weaken security/enforcement positions.

What supervision and checking are needed?	Review of AI summaries, security documents, intercreditor issues, covenants and priority risks.
What value does the client receive?	Funding with eyes open, not a loan agreement that quietly strangles the business.
What pricing options could be offered?	Key terms review / Covenant and security risk report / Full negotiation and completion package.
AI discount answer	AI can extract terms, but judgment is needed to decide whether those terms are commercially survivable.

17. INSOLVENCY AND RESTRUCTURING

Judgment elements

1. Assessing whether rescue, sale, administration, liquidation or informal compromise is realistic.
2. Judging director conduct and wrongful trading risk.
3. Forecasting creditor behaviour.
4. Identifying transactions at undervalue, preferences or antecedent transaction risks.
5. Balancing legal duties against commercial survival.
6. Advising when to stop trading.
7. Managing reputational and employee consequences.
8. Helping directors act decisively under pressure.

Five examples of good judgment

1. Knowing when the rescue story is no longer credible: the client wants one more month. The lawyer judges that continued trading may increase director exposure.
2. Assessing director duties under pressure: good judgment is helping directors understand when their focus must shift from shareholders to creditors.
3. Choosing the right process: administration, liquidation, CVA, restructuring plan, informal deal or sale may all be possible. The lawyer judges which fits the facts.
4. Reading creditor behaviour: the lawyer assesses who will support, block, negotiate, litigate or use the situation for leverage.
5. Protecting value in crisis: good judgment is acting quickly enough to preserve jobs, goodwill, contracts, assets and reputation.

AI Pricing Canvas example

Canvas question	Example answer
What problem is the client solving?	Directors need to know whether the company can be rescued, sold, restructured or must stop trading.
What outcome does the client need?	A fast, realistic plan that protects value and manages director exposure.
What can AI assist with?	Debt schedule, creditor map, chronology, options summary and first-pass risk checklist.
What requires lawyer judgment?	Whether rescue is credible, when duties shift, and whether continuing to trade increases personal risk.
What acumen is required?	Understanding cash flow, creditor behaviour, employee impact, reputational damage and business viability.
What risk does the firm carry?	Advice may affect jobs, assets, creditors, director liability and survival of the business.
What supervision and checking are needed?	Review of financial assumptions, creditor position, security, transactions and AI-generated options.
What value does the client receive?	Decisive guidance when delay may destroy value.
What pricing options could be offered?	Urgent options review / Director protection plan / Full restructuring and creditor strategy package.
AI discount answer	AI can organise the data, but judgment decides whether the business can be saved and what directors must do now.

18. PLANNING LAW

Judgment elements

1. Assessing whether the planning risk is policy, politics, evidence, design, viability or neighbour objection.
2. Judging prospects of permission, appeal or judicial review.
3. Understanding local authority behaviour and committee dynamics.
4. Advising whether to amend, appeal, negotiate or withdraw.
5. Balancing planning gain, timing, cost and commercial viability.
6. Identifying when expert evidence is needed.
7. Forecasting objector strategy.
8. Helping clients avoid winning a permission that cannot practically be implemented.

Five examples of good judgment

1. Knowing whether the problem is legal, political or evidential: AI may summarise policy. The lawyer judges whether the real issue is local opposition, committee risk or weak expert evidence.
2. Advising whether to appeal or amend: the client wants to fight. The lawyer judges whether a revised application would be quicker, cheaper and more likely to succeed.
3. Reading local authority behaviour: good judgment includes understanding officers, members, local politics and timing.
4. Assessing implementation risk: a permission may be granted but practically unusable because of conditions, infrastructure, viability or third-party rights.
5. Knowing when judicial review is worth it: the lawyer judges whether the challenge will produce a useful outcome or merely delay the inevitable.

AI Pricing Canvas example

Canvas question	Example answer
What problem is the client solving?	Developer has a refused application and needs to decide whether to appeal, amend, negotiate or abandon.
What outcome does the client need?	A planning strategy that maximises prospects while protecting timing, viability and cost.
What can AI assist with?	Policy summary, refusal reason analysis, appeal precedent review and evidence checklist.
What requires lawyer judgment?	Whether the problem is legal, political, evidential, design-based or viability-driven.
What acumen is required?	Understanding local authority behaviour, committee dynamics, objectors, funding, timing and development economics.
What risk does the firm carry?	Wrong advice may waste months, damage viability or produce a permission that cannot be implemented.
What supervision and checking are needed?	Review of policy, officer reports, consultation responses, expert evidence and AI-generated analysis.
What value does the client receive?	A route that is more likely to produce a useful permission, not just a legal argument.
What pricing options could be offered?	Prospects review / Appeal-or-amend strategy / Full planning challenge and negotiation package.
AI discount answer	AI can summarise planning policy, but judgment is needed to read the politics, evidence and commercial reality.

19. ENVIRONMENTAL LAW

Judgment elements

1. Assessing operational, civil, criminal, regulatory and reputational exposure.
2. Judging whether contamination risk is tolerable, insurable or deal-breaking.
3. Forecasting regulator behaviour.
4. Advising on remediation strategy.
5. Balancing disclosure, privilege and cooperation.
6. Understanding the supply chain and ESG consequences.
7. Identifying personal liability risk for directors or officers.
8. Translating technical reports into legal and commercial choices.

Five examples of good judgment

1. Judging whether contamination is tolerable: AI can summarise a report. The lawyer assesses whether the issue affects value, funding, insurance, development and future liability.
2. Understanding regulator expectations: good judgment is knowing whether to cooperate, challenge, remediate or disclose.
3. Seeing director and officer risk: environmental problems can become personal exposure. The lawyer spots this early.
4. Balancing legal and reputational risk: the client may be legally defensible but publicly vulnerable.
5. Advising on transaction risk: the lawyer judges whether environmental risk should lead to indemnity, price reduction, insurance, escrow or walking away.

AI Pricing Canvas example

Canvas question	Example answer
What problem is the client solving?	Buyer needs to know whether environmental risk makes the site acceptable, negotiable or deal-breaking.
What outcome does the client need?	A transaction position that manages contamination, liability, funding, insurance and future development risk.
What can AI assist with?	Technical report summary, issue list, regulatory background and due diligence checklist.
What requires lawyer judgment?	Whether contamination risk should lead to indemnity, price reduction, escrow, insurance or walking away.
What acumen is required?	Understanding site value, development plans, lender concerns, remediation cost, ESG and reputational exposure.
What risk does the firm carry?	Poor advice may leave the client with expensive liabilities and unusable land.

What supervision and checking are needed?	Review of reports, warranties, indemnities, environmental searches and AI-generated summaries.
What value does the client receive?	A clear commercial decision about environmental risk before completion.
What pricing options could be offered?	Environmental red flag review / Transaction risk report / Full negotiation and remediation strategy package.
AI discount answer	AI can summarise the report, but the value lies in judging whether the risk is tolerable, insurable or fatal.

20. EDUCATION LAW

Judgment elements

1. Assessing the child, parent, school, local authority and safeguarding dimensions.
2. Judging whether the dispute is legal, educational, medical or relational.
3. Forecasting tribunal or panel reaction.
4. Advising whether to escalate, negotiate or gather more expert evidence.
5. Understanding the emotional pressure on families.
6. Balancing speed against the need for a stronger evidential record.
7. Spotting disability discrimination, SEND, exclusion or admissions issues.
8. Helping parents make decisions in the child's long-term interests.

Five examples of good judgment

1. Seeing the child behind the paperwork: AI can summarise the SEND framework. The lawyer judges what the child actually needs to function and learn.
2. Knowing when more evidence is needed: good judgment is delaying action until the right educational psychologist, medical or specialist evidence is available.
3. Judging the forum and route: complaint, appeal, tribunal, negotiation or judicial review may be possible. The lawyer chooses the route most likely to help the child.
4. Managing parental emotion: parents may be exhausted and frightened. The lawyer must be legally clear and emotionally steady.
5. Spotting discrimination issues: what looks like behaviour or absence may really be disability, failure to accommodate or unmet need.

AI Pricing Canvas example

Canvas question	Example answer
What problem is the client solving?	Parent needs the right educational provision for a child whose needs are not being met.
What outcome does the client need?	A properly evidenced route to secure support, placement or provision in the child's best interests.
What can AI assist with?	Document bundle summary, chronology, SEND framework overview, evidence checklist and draft appeal structure.
What requires lawyer judgment?	Whether to appeal, negotiate, gather further evidence or pursue a different route.
What acumen is required?	Understanding the child, parental pressure, school dynamics, local authority behaviour and expert evidence.
What risk does the firm carry?	Advice affects a child's education, wellbeing and long-term development.
What supervision and checking are needed?	Review of reports, EHCP wording, evidence gaps, appeal grounds and AI-generated summaries.
What value does the client receive?	A focused plan that sees the child behind the paperwork.
What pricing options could be offered?	Initial SEND review / Appeal preparation / Full tribunal and negotiation support package.
AI discount answer	AI can summarise the framework, but judgment is needed to decide what the child actually needs and how to secure it.

21. PUBLIC LAW AND JUDICIAL REVIEW

Judgment elements

1. Assessing whether a decision is unlawful, merely unfair, or politically unattractive but legally defensible.
2. Judging urgency and interim relief risk.
3. Forecasting permission prospects.
4. Identifying the best ground: illegality, irrationality, procedural unfairness, legitimate expectation, proportionality or human rights.
5. Advising whether pre-action correspondence may resolve the issue.
6. Balancing cost, delay, publicity and remedy.
7. Understanding institutional behaviour by public bodies.
8. Helping clients decide whether challenge will produce practical benefit.

Five examples of good judgment

1. Knowing the difference between unfair and unlawful: the client may have been treated badly. The lawyer judges whether there is actually a public law ground.

2. Assessing whether the remedy is useful: winning judicial review may simply send the decision back to be made again. Good judgment asks whether that helps.
3. Acting quickly enough: public law delay can be fatal. The lawyer judges urgency and timing immediately.
4. Choosing the strongest ground: the lawyer avoids throwing in every possible argument and focuses on the point most likely to win permission.
5. Using pre-action correspondence strategically: good judgment is knowing when a strong letter can solve the problem without proceedings.

AI Pricing Canvas example

Canvas question	Example answer
What problem is the client solving?	Client wants to challenge a public body decision and needs to know whether it is unlawful, urgent and worth pursuing.
What outcome does the client need?	A realistic challenge strategy that identifies grounds, timing, remedy and practical benefit.
What can AI assist with?	Decision chronology, public law ground summary, case law research and draft pre-action letter.
What requires lawyer judgment?	Whether the issue is actually unlawful, whether interim relief is needed and whether the remedy helps.
What acumen is required?	Understanding institutional behaviour, publicity, political context, cost, delay and practical consequences.
What risk does the firm carry?	Delay, weak grounds or poor remedy analysis may destroy the claim or produce a hollow victory.
What supervision and checking are needed?	Review of AI case law summaries, limitation, grounds, evidence and pre-action correspondence.
What value does the client receive?	A fast answer to whether this is a legal challenge worth making.
What pricing options could be offered?	Urgent prospects review / Pre-action strategy / Full judicial review package.
AI discount answer	AI can find authorities, but judgment is needed to decide whether there is a public law case and whether winning would matter.

22. CHARITY AND NOT-FOR-PROFIT LAW

Judgment elements

1. Assessing trustee duties, mission, governance and reputational risk.
2. Judging whether a decision is legally permitted and mission-consistent.
3. Managing conflicts of interest.
4. Advising on regulator engagement.

5. Balancing donor expectations, beneficiary interests and public perception.
6. Identifying governance weaknesses before they become scandals.
7. Helping boards make difficult decisions transparently.
8. Translating charity law into practical trustee behaviour.

Five examples of good judgment

1. Helping trustees make defensible decisions: the answer is not just 'is this allowed?' It is 'can the trustees show they acted properly?'
2. Spotting conflicts of interest: good judgment is identifying when personal loyalty, founder influence, family connection or donor pressure is distorting decision-making.
3. Balancing mission and money: a funding opportunity may be attractive but inconsistent with the charity's purpose or values.
4. Knowing when to engage the regulator: the lawyer judges whether silence, delayed disclosure or informal handling will create a bigger problem.
5. Protecting reputation and beneficiary trust: charities depend on public confidence. Good judgment includes legal, ethical and reputational consequences.

AI Pricing Canvas example

Canvas question	Example answer
What problem is the client solving?	Trustees need to make a difficult decision involving money, mission, conflicts, donor pressure or regulator risk.
What outcome does the client need?	A defensible trustee decision that is lawful, mission-consistent and properly documented.
What can AI assist with?	Governance document summary, trustee duty checklist, draft board paper and regulatory guidance summary.
What requires lawyer judgment?	Whether the decision is permitted, properly made, conflict-free and reputationally safe.
What acumen is required?	Understanding mission, beneficiaries, donor expectations, public confidence, board dynamics and regulator behaviour.
What risk does the firm carry?	Poor advice may create trustee liability, regulatory scrutiny, reputational damage and loss of public trust.
What supervision and checking are needed?	Review of AI-generated guidance summaries, conflicts, governing document powers, board minutes and regulator correspondence.
What value does the client receive?	Confidence that the trustees can explain not only what they decided, but why they were entitled to decide it.
What pricing options could be offered?	Trustee decision review / Governance and conflict report / Full board support and regulator engagement package.

AI discount answer	AI can summarise the rules, but judgment is needed to help trustees make a decision they can defend.

APPENDIX 2: MANAGING PARTNER CHECKLIST

In *Ditch The Billable Hour!*, I included a detailed RACI template to help firms think through who should be Responsible, Accountable, Consulted and Informed during a value-based pricing implementation project. I did consider doing something similar for *Stop The Clock*, but the more I thought about it, the more I felt it risked becoming too complicated for what many firms need at this stage.

AI, pricing, value and change management are already enough to make even the hardiest managing partner reach for the biscuits. So, instead of creating a long RACI template, I have created a practical Implementation Checklist, which appears below. It is not intended to be perfect, exhaustive or carved into a stone tablet carried down from Mount Penguin. It is intended to be useful. I hope it gives you a good starting point for working out what needs to be done, who needs to be involved, where the risks sit and how your firm can start moving from discussion to action.

MANAGING PARTNER CHECKLIST

Implementation risks and how to manage them

Before launching value-based pricing, ask these questions honestly.

This is not a test designed to make the firm feel clever. It is a practical checklist to stop the project falling over because everyone assumed someone else had thought about the awkward bits.

1. Leadership

☐ Have we clearly explained why value-based pricing matters now?

☐ Have we connected the pricing issue to AI, margin, client value and firm strategy?

☐ Does the leadership team understand that this is not just a billing project?

☐ Have we agreed who owns the implementation?

☐ Have we given the project owner enough authority, time and support?

☐ Are we prepared to keep talking about this after the launch excitement has faded?

2. Partner buy-in

☐ Have we identified the partners most likely to support the change?

☐ Have we identified the partners most likely to resist it?

☐ Have we listened to the genuine concerns rather than dismissing them as negativity?

☐ Have we shown partners how better pricing can protect margin?

☐ Have we addressed the fear that value-based pricing simply means charging less?

☐ Have we created a safe space for partners to test new pricing approaches without being punished for every imperfect attempt?

3. Scope discipline

☐ Do we have clear scoping templates?

☐ Do our proposals set out assumptions?

☐ Do our proposals set out exclusions?

☐ Do our proposals explain what happens if the client changes the brief?

☐ Do lawyers know how to have a scope-change conversation?

☐ Are we tracking where scope creep occurs?

☐ Are we learning from matters where the scope was wrong?

4. Pricing confidence

☐ Do lawyers have examples of properly priced matters?

☐ Do they know how to explain price by reference to value rather than time?

☐ Do they know how to offer pricing options?

☐ Do they understand the difference between value-based pricing and discounting?

☐ Do they have permission to move away from hourly billing where appropriate?

☐ Do they know when to ask for help?

☐ Are we reviewing early pricing decisions and feeding the learning back into the firm?

5. Client communication

☐ Can we explain value-based pricing in plain English?

☐ Can we explain why certainty, clarity and outcome focus benefit the client?

☐ Can we explain where AI may assist the work?

☐ Can we explain why AI does not remove lawyer judgment, supervision, accountability and risk?

☐ Can we explain what the client is paying for beyond production time?

☐ Have we prepared answers to likely client questions?

☐ Have we stopped apologising for price?

6. AI costs and economics

☐ Do we know what our AI tools cost?

☐ Do we understand subscriptions, token usage, implementation, training, supervision and governance costs?

☐ Do we know whether AI is reducing billable time, non-billable cost, or both?

☐ Are the CFO, CIO, risk team and practice leaders involved?

☐ Are we tracking the cost of AI-enabled delivery by matter type?

☐ Are we avoiding crude "AI surcharge" thinking?

☐ Are we pricing the value created, not simply the tool used?

7. Management information

☐ Do we know which types of work are genuinely profitable?

☐ Do we know where write-offs occur?

☐ Do we know which matters regularly overrun?

☐ Do we know which clients create repeated scope creep?

☐ Do we compare estimated cost, actual cost, price and margin?

☐ Do we capture lessons from completed matters?

☐ Are we building the Big Book of Usefulness as we go?

8. Incentives and behaviour

☐ Are we still rewarding lawyers mainly for recorded hours?

☐ Are our targets consistent with value-based pricing?

☐ Are we measuring margin, client satisfaction, pricing discipline and scope control?

☐ Are we recognising lawyers who price well?

☐ Are we celebrating quick wins?

☐ Are we removing barriers that push people back to the billable hour?

☐ Are we making the desired behaviour easier than the old behaviour?

9. Training and support

☐ Have lawyers been trained in value conversations?

☐ Have they been trained in scoping?

☐ Have they been trained in pricing options?

☐ Have they been trained in handling objections?

☐ Have they been trained in AI-related client conversations?

☐ Have junior lawyers been given new ways to develop judgment and commercial acumen?

☐ Have support teams, finance, BD and operations been included?

10. Governance and consistency

☐ Do we have a common pricing language across the firm?

☐ Do we have templates and guidance people can actually use?

☐ Do we know who approves unusual pricing arrangements?

☐ Do we have a process for reviewing failed or difficult pricing decisions?

☐ Are departments sharing examples with each other?

☐ Are we avoiding each partner inventing their own system?

☐ Are we building consistency without crushing sensible flexibility?

11. Pilot projects

☐ Have we chosen sensible pilot areas?

☐ Have we avoided starting with the most complex work in the firm?

☐ Have we selected matters where scope can be understood and managed?

☐ Have we agreed what success looks like?

☐ Have we agreed what data we will collect?

☐ Have we agreed when we will review the pilot?

☐ Have we told people that imperfect progress is still progress?

12. Staying power

- ☐ Is value-based pricing on the management agenda regularly?
- ☐ Are departments reporting progress?
- ☐ Are we sharing stories of what is working?
- ☐ Are we being honest about what is not working?
- ☐ Are we updating our tools, templates and guidance?
- ☐ Are we still talking about client value, not just internal process?
- ☐ Are we prepared to persevere when the novelty wears off?

If most of the boxes above remain unticked, do not kid yourself that the firm is implementing value-based pricing.

It is having a meeting about value-based pricing.

There is a difference.

APPENDIX 3: PEOPLE TO FOLLOW

Below, I have set out a list of people I suggest you follow if you want to understand where legal services, pricing, AI and legal technology are heading. It is not meant to be a definitive list. It is simply a useful starting point. Many of those in the list featured in *Ditch The Billable Hour!* These are people whose thinking, writing, experiments and challenges may help you see what is coming before it arrives on your desk disguised as a client demand, a competitor move or a management headache.

Jonno White has also helpfully created a curated list of "50 Essential Thought Leaders in Legal Technology Globally" (https://www.consultclarity.org/post/thought-leaders-legal-technology-globally), bringing together people who are writing, building, challenging, explaining and testing what is happening in this space.

Between the two lists, you will find plenty of wise people to follow. Read the sceptics as well as the enthusiasts. Notice who is asking good questions, not just who is shouting loudest about the next shiny thing. In an AI world, part of the job of a modern lawyer is not to become a technologist, but to become intelligently curious about technology and its impact on clients, pricing, risk, service delivery and the future of the profession.

Name	LinkedIn profile URL	Business website URL
Andrew Allen	uk.linkedin.com/in/andrewallen1	www.pkf-francisclark.co.uk/
David C. Baker	www.linkedin.com/in/dcb	punctuation.com/david-c-baker/
Ron Baker	www.linkedin.com/in/ronbaker1/	www.verasage.com/
Mark Barrett	https://www.linkedin.com/in/markbarrettautomationoutcomes/	https://www.automationoutcomes.co.uk/ai-for-legal-resource-library/
George Beaton	https://www.linkedin.com/in/georgerbeaton/	beatonglobal.com/dt_team/dr-george-beaton/

Name	LinkedIn profile URL	Business website URL
Virginia Briggs	au.linkedin.com/in/virginia-briggs-307a6155	www.minterellison.com/people/virginia-briggs
John Chisholm	www.linkedin.com/in/chisholmjohn/	https://www.chisconsult.com.au/
Jordan Furlong	www.linkedin.com/in/jordanfurlong/	www.law21.ca/
Joanna Gaudoin	https://www.linkedin.com/in/joannagaudoin/	https://client-wise.co.uk/
Roch Glowacki	uk.linkedin.com/in/roch-glowacki	www.lewissilkin.com/en/experts/roch-glowacki
Adam Grant	www.linkedin.com/in/adammgrant	adamgrant.net/
Robert Hanna	uk.linkedin.com/in/roberthanna	www.kcpartners.co.uk/rob/
Alex Herrity	www.linkedin.com/in/legalopshezzle/	https://lawwhatsnext.substack.com
Kerry Jack	https://www.linkedin.com/in/kerryjack/	https://blacklettercommunications.co.uk/team
Shaun Jardine	uk.linkedin.com/in/shaunjardine	www.bigyellowpenguin.co.uk/
Wendy Jephson	https://www.linkedin.com/in/wendyjephson/	https://letsthink.com/
Noo Jones	www.linkedin.com/in/nicolajoneslearningexpert/	athenaprofessional.co.uk/
Mathew Kerbis	www.linkedin.com/in/kerbisverse	mathewkerbis.com/
Lorna Khemraz	www.linkedin.com/in/lorna-khemraz-0328bb5b/	https://substack.com/@lornakhemraz

Name	LinkedIn profile URL	Business website URL
Professor John Kotter	www.linkedin.com/in/johnkotter	www.kotterinc.com/
Mitch Kowalski	www.linkedin.com/in/mitchkowalski/	kowalski.ca/
Josh Kubicki	www.linkedin.com/in/jpkubicki	joshkubicki.com/
Greg Kyte	https://www.linkedin.com/in/gregkyte /	https://ohmyfraud.com/people / greg-kyte-cpa
Renae Lattey	au.linkedin.com/in/renae-lattey	www.mallesons.com/au/en/people/renae-lattey.html
Colin S. Levy	www.linkedin.com/in/colinslevy	www.colinslevy.com/
Ryan McClead	www.linkedin.com/in/rmcclead/	https://www.geeklawblog.com/author/ryanmcclead
Jonah E. Perlin	www.linkedin.com/in/jonah-perlin-7554025	www.law.georgetown.edu/faculty/ jonah-e-perlin/
Nicola Shaver	www.linkedin.com/in/nicola-shaver/	www.legaltechnologyhub.com/
Karolina Šilingienė	https://www.linkedin.com/in/ksilingiene/	https://crespect.com/
Quentin Solt	https://www.linkedin.com/in/quentin-solt/	https://factsarefriends.substack.com/
Aku Sorainen	https://www.linkedin.com/in/aku-sorainen/	https://www.sorainen.com/
Sam Stamp	https://www.linkedin.com/in/sam-stamp/	https://legalengine.co.uk/about.html
Heather Suttie	ca.linkedin.com/in/heathersuttie	heathersuttie.ca/

Name	LinkedIn profile URL	Business website URL
Simon Tupman	www.linkedin.com/in/simontupman/	simontupman.com/
Ben Weinberger	uk.linkedin.com/in/benweinberger	benjaminweinberger.com/
Tim Williams	www.linkedin.com/in/timwilliamsicg/	www.ignitiongroup.com/
Jon Whittle	uk.linkedin.com/in/jonwhittle	jonwhittleconsulting.co.uk/
Abby Winkworth	https://www.linkedin.com/in/abbywinkworth/	https://www.linkedin.com/company/ambire-advisory-limited/about/

ENDNOTES

[1] *AI & Client Value* by Colin Levy. https://www.colinslevy.com/post/ai-client-value

[2] *Does AI signal the end of the billable hour?* by Ken Crutchfield. https://abovethelaw.com/legal-innovation-center/2024/01/23/does-ai-signal-the-end-of-the-billable-hour/

[3] *The State of AI Keynote 2026* by Nikki Shaver. https://www.lawdroidmanifesto.com/p/the-state-of-ai-keynote-2026

[4] *Money Spent, Earned, and Prompted.* Brainyacts Special Briefing. https://thebrainyacts.beehiiv.com/products/money-spent-earned-and-prompted-a-brainyacts-special-briefing

[5] *Build what only you can build. Don't be the OS* by Christian Brown. https://www.linkedin.com/pulse/build-what-only-you-can-dont-os-christian-brown-oiatc/

[6] *Bride of the Token Cost Panic* by Ryan McClead. https://www.geeklawblog.com/2026/06/bride-of-the-token-cost-panic.html

[7] *Out of Tokens: Insert Coin(s) to Continue* by Alex Herrity. https://lawwhatsnext.substack.com/p/out-of-tokens-insert-coins-to-continue

[8] *The Gap Is Closing: Why AI Is Breaking The Billable Hour Model* by Ken Callander. https://xira.com/p/2026/04/28/the-gap-is-closing-why-ai-is-breaking-the-billable-hour-model/

[9] *Zscaler Outside Counsel Billing Guidelines.* https://www.zscaler.com/legal/outside-counsel-billing-guidelines

[10] *The end of the billable hour* by Lorna Khemraz. https://substack.com/home/post/p-195723643

[11] *Australian law firms are taking a lead on navigating best use of AI.* Financial Times. https://www.ft.com/content/63e1f03f-9b98-4c02-a268-08e6713bd561?syn-25a6b1a6=1

[12] *Pricing trends: When clients are willing to pay more* by Beaton Research. https://beatonglobal.com/when-clients-are-prepared-to-pay-more?utm_source=Linkedinpost

[13] *How The Billable Hour Can Survive* AI by Jonah Perlin. https://scholarship.law.georgetown.edu/facpub/2694/

[14] *Tell us the rules for using AI in court, say solicitors.* Law Society Gazette. https://www.lawgazette.co.uk/news/tell-us-the-rules-for-using-ai-in-court-say-solicitors/5126757.article

[15] *Texas Bar Association Opinion 705.* https://www.legalethicstexas.com/resources/opinions/opinion-705/

[16] *Why the era of the professional services pyramid has passed* by George Beaton. https://www.linkedin.com/posts/georgerbeaton_ugcPost-7434011362445443074-JU6M

[17] *Fighting the Hypothetical: Why Law Firms Should Rethink the Billable Hour in the Generative AI Era* by Nancy B. Rapoport and Joseph R. Tiano Jr. https://papers.ssrn.com/sol3/papers.cfm?abstract_id=5080449

[18] *Legally Speaking Podcast.* https://legallyspeakingpodcast.com/

[19] *Law In The Era of AI* by Bjarne Tellmann.

[20] *If I Started A Brand New Firm* by David C Baker. https://www.linkedin.com/pulse/i-started-brand-new-firm-david-c-baker-qmmle/

[21] *The Role Of Inhouse Counsel Is Changing.* KPMG Global General Counsel Report_2026. https://kpmg.com/xx/en/our-insights/transformation/global-general-counsel-outlook.html

[22] *Law In The Era of AI* by Bjarne Tellmann.

[23] *How To Create Change* by Simon Sinek. https://youtu.be/fDILpuiLuAI?si=UlGLgWllBLAQv1JR

[24] *The Creative Power of Misfits* by Adam Grant. https://www.ted.com/talks/worklife_with_adam_grant_the_creative_power_of_misfits?utm_campaign=tedspread&utm_medium=referral&utm_source=tedcomshare

[25] *Angry People Make Change* by Tom Peters. https://youtu.be/A2EdCl-CX4Q?si=3zmK7f2vZnDIdi2H

[26] *Beyond the Chatbot: Meet the Agentic Law Firm* by Damien Riehl. https://mnbars.org/?pg=BenchBarofMinnesota&pubAction=viewIssue&pubIssueID=69276&pubIssueItemID=459569

[27] *Ditch & Switch!* by Shaun Jardine.

[28] *Barney – The End of Lawyers* by Douwe Groenevelt. https://youtu.be/c_OMFSCUyZA?si=q3p_U4_SQjZeCt6I

[29] *The Last of Them* by Douwe Groenevelt. https://youtu.be/ndGaqdYYX30?si=uz1JCl5OhqTvUcF6

[30] *Rewired: The McKinsey Guide to Outcompeting in the Age of Digital and AI* by Eric Lamarre & Kate Smaje.

[31] McKinsey is rethinking its pay structure because clients are no longer paying for hours. The Times Of India. http://timesofindia.indiatimes.com/articleshow/131131220.cms?utm_source=contentofinterest&utm_medium=text&utm_campaign=cppst

[32] *The Billable Hour Is Dead. AI Just Signed the Death Certificate* by Armando Hernandez. https://www.linkedin.com/pulse/billable-hour-dead-ai-just-signed-death-certificate-armando-hernandez-gzozf/

[33] *Navigating The Million Dollar Problem.* BigHand. https://www.bighand.com/en-us/resources/whitepapers/navigating-the-million-dollar-problem/

[34] *The Riddle of Perception* by LexisNexis. https://www.lexisnexis.co.uk/bellwether/assets/pdfs/Lexis-nexis-report-2016_interactive%20version03.pdf

[35] *The KPMG Global General Counsel Report 2026.* https://kpmg.com/xx/en/our-insights/transformation/global-general-counsel-outlook.html

[36] *Juro State of In-House 2026.* https://www.linkedin.com/posts/juro_the-state-of-in-house-2026-report-is-now-activity-7425562153954349056-vdpq/

[37] *I Said It Would Escalate. It Has* by Josh Kubicki. https://thebrainyacts.beehiiv.com/p/282-i-said-it-would-escalate-it-has

[38] *Celebrate Good Times.* Kool & The Gang/Ziggy Mack. https://youtu.be/3GwjfUFyY6M?si=dZEXEuvI8Ga9Qwym

[39] *Junior solicitor used AI to draft misleading letters to court* by Neil Rose. Legal Futures. https://www.legalfutures.co.uk/latest-news/junior-solicitor-used-ai-to-draft-misleading-letters-to-court

[40] *How to Start a Cultural Change?* by Simon Sinek. https://youtu.be/zClAdLw4yRI?si=OFwq7eTiv43gKwpz

See all our titles for law professionals, including both of Shaun's previous books – *Ditch The Billable Hour! Implementing Value-Based Pricing in a Law Firm* and *Ditch & Switch: 50 Value-Based Pricing Examples for Law Professionals* at:

www.ingramcontent.com/pod-product-compliance
Lightning Source LLC
LaVergne TN
LVHW070907210926
848482LV00017B/1016
9781915855503